Society as Text

Society as Text

Essays on Rhetoric, Reason, and Reality

Richard Harvey Brown

The University of Chicago Press
Chicago and London

THE UNIVERSITY OF CHICAGO PRESS, CHICAGO 60637
THE UNIVERSITY OF CHICAGO PRESS, LTD., LONDON

Library of Congress Cataloging-in-Publication Data

Brown, Richard Harvey.
  Society as text.

  Bibliography: p.
  Includes index.
  1. Sociolinguistics. 2. Rhetoric. 3. Literature and society.
4. Discourse analysis. I. Title.
P40.B76 1987   401'.9   86-30893
ISBN 0- 226-07616-4
ISBN 0- 226-07617-2 (pbk.)

∞ The paper used in this publication meets the minimum
requirements of the American National Standard for
Information Sciences—Permanence of Paper for Printed
Library Materials, ANSI Z39.48—1984

For my parents, Samuel Robert Brown and Sylvia Brown

My theory and practice are nourished by
the generosity of his spirit and
the courage of her moral will.

Contents

Acknowledgments

MANY PEOPLE have helped in the formation of this book. Its governing spirit owes much to Norman Birnbaum, Aaron Cicourel, John Pierce Clark, Remi Clignet, George Coelho, Randall Collins, Sigmund Diamond, Jack Douglas, Barbara Finkelstein, Serge Gavronsky, Joseph Gusfield, Stanford Lyman, the late Herbert Marcuse, Michael Overington, George Ritzer, Manfred Stanley, Arthur Vidich and Trutz von Trotha. Kenneth Burke, through example and correspondence, also has inspired my thought. My wife, Nathalie Babel, and my son, Ramiro, provided much encouragement over many years, as have Geraldine Todd and other staff who typed many drafts of the manuscript for me at the University of Maryland. My students there also have been a source of support and critical feedback.

I sincerely thank Fred Dallmayr, Michael Overington, and Manfred Stanley for their close criticisms and advice.

I am also grateful to those who read and criticized specific chapters of the volume. An earlier version of chapter 1 on sociolinguistics was written jointly with Trutz von Trotha, and appeared in *Acta Sociologica* 25: 4 (August 1982): 373–88. Chapter 2, on personal identity, drew on suggestions from Remi Clignet, George Coelho, and Barbara Finkelstein. Different parts of it appeared in George Coelho and Paul I. Ahmed, eds., *Uprooting and Development: Dilemmas of Coping with Modernization* (New York: Plenum, 1980): 41–66, and in *Current Perspectives in Social Theory* 8 (1987). Chapter 3 on reason as rhetorical was prepared for the Iowa University Symposium on the Rhetoric of the Human Sciences, March 1984, and was improved through criticism by other symposiasts, especially Clifford Geertz, Paul Hernadi, John Nelson, and Herbert Simons. Michael Overington and Arthur Vidich were good enough to criticize an earlier version of chapter 4 on theories of rhetoric, which appeared in *Social Research* 50:1 (Spring 1983): 126–57. My understanding of rhetoric generally, and especially its relation to historical science as discussed in chapter 5, owes much to John Angus Campbell, Walter Fisher, Michael Overington, and Herbert Simons. An earlier version appeared in the *Quarterly Journal of Speech:* 72: 2 (May 1986): 148–61. Chapter 6 on society as narrative text benefited from remarks by Walter Fisher and Scott McNall, and was published in an earlier form in *Current Perspectives in Social Theory* 6 (1985): 17–37. Chapter 7, on narrative fiction as social text, draws on work published in *New Literary History* 17:2 (Winter 1986): 223–28, and 11: 3 (Spring 1980): 545–50, and in *Poetics Today* 6: 4 (1985): 573–90. It is inspired by the guidance and critical advice of Ralph Cohen, Serge Gavronsky, and Kingsley Widmer. Chapter 8 draws on the work of Douglas Colin Muecke and Edmond Wright, and was published in a different version in a special number of *Poetics Today* on irony, 4: 3 (1985): 543–64.

Society as Text

How MIGHT social theory be linked with political praxis in a humanizing, nontechnicist way? How may we join knowledge of society with public moral action? My belief is that for this to occur we must restore judgment to its former privileged status in intellectual and public life. One resource for this project is the critical theory of rhetoric, since rhetoric on the one hand shows that all knowledge is achieved through the persuasive use of language, and on the other hand provides canons of reasoned judgment in political discourse.

Political discourse presupposes some conception of "polity," some community in which knowledge for the sake of action can be communicated across groups, classes, and statuses. Ideally in a democracy, such a community is composed of citizens acting as whole persons in the collective sphere of life. In chapter 1, however, using work done with Trutz von Trotha, I show how such community and communication today are not possible. As revealed by a sociolinguistic and ethnographic understanding of class-limited speech codes, each group's world appears as an impenetrable mystery to members of other groups, even to people of good will who are seeking to help or to form alliances.

This theme is developed in chapter 2, in which I argue that personal identity is shaped through a "language of the self" that is embedded in contemporary political economy. Though this modern Western self is an ideal type and is incarnated differently in different classes, genders, and other groups, its constant characteristic is the loss of positive linkage between person and polity, a bifurcation between a public self defined as a functionary guided by positive, instrumental reason, and a private, affective self that is the locus of arational feelings, values, and emotions. By limiting moral action to the purely private sphere, and by restricting the public sphere to purely instrumental behavior, this bifurcation has engendered a crisis of citizenship, legitimation, and political obligation.

The construction of polity and persons through language has its counterpart in the rhetorical constitution of reason itself. Thus chapter 3 suggests that epistemology, reason, and politics are all bound together through different forms of discourse. For example, the aesthetico-dialogal conception of reason in the ancient Athenian *polis* accorded with the leisured existence of the dominant aristocracy. Similarly, the theological rationality of the Middle Ages served the cognitive and political requirements of a transnational clerisy that largely monopolized literacy and revelation. In the present era, a positivistic, instrumental conception of rationality serves the needs of a techno-administrative corporate or statist elite in a world of privatized individuals, universalized legal and technical norms, and commodity consciousness. By relativizing our conceptions of reason, this analysis returns us to the same question posed by chapters 1 and 2: What form of rationality, polity, and self would invite a discourse of societal self-direction founded on and serving the dignity of agents?

To encourage such a discourse one must begin within some tradition. The tradition of rhetoric suggests itself, since rhetoric, both as analysis and as practice, has been precisely a place of the integration of knowledge about society with political efforts at social transformation. Emile Durkheim's career and writings exemplify such an effort to use rhetoric to construct theories of society, and to use such well-crafted theories for moral-political interventions. In chapter 4 I examine Durkheim's work rhetorically in order to illuminate both theories of rhetoric and the rhetoric of theories, and to show how both involve authorial intentions, audience perceptions, and political praxes. In this light, the tensions within Durkheim's discursive practice stand as an emblem for contradictions between the theoretical and political discourses in our culture as a whole.

The rhetorical construction of theories is further illustrated in chapter 5, in which I deconstruct the debate between functional evolutionism and experimental empiricism as a conflict between two different but unacknowledged root metaphors. Seen rhetorically, evolutionism is an elaboration of the metaphor of organism; and empiricism, of mechanism. Thinkers from both these schools tend to be literalists, who deny the origins of their truth forms in language. For evolutionists there really is a total history or society that evolves in homogeneous time and that is described by evolutionary theories. Conversely, for empiricists there really are discrete historical events that are knowable according to various mechanisms and causes. Each group claims a literalness for its own position, and empiricists especially scathe evolutionists for using metaphorical models. A metaphorical-metalogical analysis, however, construes this debate to be founded in error or bad faith, in that each side is unaware of its own linguistic processes as well as those of its opponent. Hence, all parties tend to be insensitive to the possible moral-political implications of their own rhetorical practice.

If we took rhetoric seriously as a context-giving tradition, how would that affect our making of theories? For one thing, as I suggest in chapter 6, we would become more aware that there are alternative ways of truth telling, and that we are therefore responsible for the forms we use to tell our truths. In this way the relativity of reason accords with the responsibilities of communication. Furthermore, the tradition of rhetoric suggests the metaphor of society as narrative text. This metaphor explicitly pays homage to the rhetorical nature of both theoretical and political praxes and also invites an intelligible "plot" that reconciles hostile theoretical-ideological positions. These positions include, among others, structuralism versus hermeneutics, grammatics versus pragmatics, and determinism versus intentionality. The image of society as narrative text might help overcome such fissures within social-science discourse itself, as well as the dual alienation of positivists and romantics within the larger political culture.

Yet, as I suggest in chapter 7, contemporary society is eviscerated of narrative form. The notion of moral agency in protagonists, or of meaningful plots in social events, has become harder to find in fiction, social science, and life. This is because factual or fictional narratives presuppose a social order of meaning in which public action by moral agents is possible, and in which lived connections between personal character and public conduct prevail. Because such a presupposition is no longer valid in advanced industrial societies, the narrative social text has become an extinct or endangered species. Despite this, however, narrative remains vitally needed in contemporary civic discourse.

In such a situation, I argue in chapter 8 we may turn to the rhetorical trope and the logical method of dialectical irony as a potential discourse for humanizing political practice. Irony is a metaphor of opposites, a point of view that distances and derealizes what is taken as real in order to permit the realization of new meanings and forms. Irony is thus the uniquely dialectical trope, in that the resolution of its opposites is left to its public. To be ironic, irony thus demands participation and completion by its auditors. Such participation *is* enlightenment and freedom.

A rhetorical understanding of knowledge and of politics (that is, an understanding using such concepts as metaphor, point of view, narrative, or irony) can help align what scientists and politicians do and what all of us do in our workaday lives. We all inherit and create worlds. True, the world of the theorist requires greater concern for formal properties of cogency and fit, whereas the world of the citizen, activist, or leader focuses more on audience reception and reader response. Yet, seen rhetorically, both are processes of reality construction through linguistic action, both are ways in which we author and are authorized by our worlds.

One

Discourse and Polity

Sociolinguistics, Language Communities, and the Mobilization of Low-Income Groups

Ishmael says, "We were trying to create anger—organized anger that would lead to revolution." Weather missionaries tried to convert the blue collar young but, Ishmael concedes, "it didn't work out so hot. We talked about racism and imperialism and the greasers talked about motorcycles and girls."

Newsweek (1982)

STUDENT: I know you have been deprived and are impatient with the power structure . . .
GANG MEMBER: Let me tell you something. I have never been denied 'cause I go out and steal what I want, man, take what I want, man, and I get it, boy! Anything I want in life, I'm going to get. And I'm not going to let no fool tell me, well, look here, Jack, you can't do this here because it's against the law, and that kind of bullshit.

Krisberg (1972:69)

INTELLIGIBLE COMMUNICATION between groups and classes in a society is a precondition for the existence of a public in the classical, political sense of that term. The importance of such communication for a democratic polity was highlighted in the sixties when both reformers and revolutionaries generally failed in their efforts to educate or politicize low-income groups.

One of the more frustrating experiences of both American and European students was the lack of communication between them and their "clients." Slum dwellers, and especially gang youths, were attractive to rebels because they were oppressed and ready for direct action. Yet in the end they seemed to be politically ignorant and disinterested, oblivious to larger social issues. Spergel (1969), for example, reported that civil rights and black militant organizations sought to mobilize gang youths politically, but came to realize that gang members were more motivated to enter the system than to subvert it. This was highlighted during riots in American cities, where gang participation was not a major factor except to mollify protests (Short 1976). There seemed to be no bridges between educated radicals and gang members. Each appeared to be living in a different society and speaking a different language.[1]

Cases of greater political development that were exceptions—the Blackstone Nation, the Black Panthers, or instances of community power—were brought about by forces external to the gang (Short 1976). Political development occurred, when it did, not as a consequence of a beginning dialogue between poor gang members and nonpoor radical organizers, but as a response to structural factors that were not intended as such to radicalize the poor. These factors include economic changes in the communities to which gangs belong, federal governmental policies, particularly those concerned with municipalities and local communities, and police interference with gang activities. Thus, though certain structural changes have affected the political role of poor youths, the problem of communication and political solidarity between groups of different strata remains.

This problem is theoretical and moral as well as strategic and tactical. It involves the relation of language to politics and the relation of the intellectual to the polity, whether this person be the expert involved in conservative technical reforms or the activist engaged in radical institutional change. Any person who claims a right to alter societal processes on behalf of others thereby presupposes some talent or knowledge superior to that of the persons he presumes to help.[2] But this very assumption of greater foresight would seem to turn clients into objects upon which the expert exercises his technique or the activist his moral mission. In this context it becomes vital not only to imagine alternative social orders, but also to invent alternative means for achieving them. The problem is both to define the purposes of social policy and to identify the means of social intervention. It is in part the problem of creating an emancipatory method.

Central to any such method are speech acts, not only the speech acts of clients but also those of the agents of social change.[3] Sociolinguistics thus has moral as well as scientific import. By investigating the linguistic capacities of persons, sociolinguistics presumes their agency as creators of language and culture. In so doing it offers hope for developing practical definitions of morally and politically competent communication, and of equal access to the resources for such competence. In this sense, sociolinguistics is central to what Habermas and Stanley regard as the next stage in the moral evolution of reason: the development of an ethic of civic communication (Habermas 1970; Stanley 1978). Such an ethic and practice is most needed by those who would engage in instrumental social change.

Analyses of language may illuminate this question, especially if we can relate them to broader social structural and political issues. In this chapter we discuss theories that apply the methods of linguistics to microsociological studies of speech behavior. Our task is to relate this work to the rich ethnographic literature on culture of low-income groups, and then to place this amalgam in a larger political-economic context. Finally, we hope to make explicit some moral and political implications of this project.

The Social-Structural Foundations of Language

It is a curious fact that both the right and the left tend to perceive differences between middle-class and lower-class speech in terms of the linguistic inadequacy of the latter. The intellectual armament of conservatives and liberals includes social-science notions of the "culture of poverty," "cultural disadvantage," "cognitive retardation," "articulation defects," and "linguistic deprivation." Similarly, among left-wing writers and students in America and Europe, lack of understanding between organizers and low-income youths is often attributed to the false consciousness or the verbal and political backwardness of the poor (e.g., Mueller 1973).[+]

Though widely held by educational psychologists (e.g., Bereiter and Engelmann 1966; Deutsch et al. 1967), the theory of verbal deprivation has been challenged on various grounds (Bernstein 1972a; 1972b; Labov 1972a, 1972b; Lawton 1972; Leacock 1972; McCormick-Piestrup 1973). Basil Bernstein's work in particular provides a privileged site for entering this debate, because of its ambivalence concerning verbal deprivation. On the one hand Bernstein's work is used to support the deprivation theory; on the other hand his findings can be recast to show that this use is an abuse and that the verbal deprivation theory is misleading.

Arguing from the disproportionate failure of black children in school and from extensive experimental data, theorists of verbal deprivation maintain that the speech of low-income groups is an inherently inferior vehicle of thought and communication. In this view, for example, the language of ghetto children entering preschool is regarded as a "series of emotional cries . . . not merely an underdeveloped version of standard English, but basically a nonlogical mode of expressive behavior" (Bereiter and Engelmann, 1966). Though this might be an extreme position, it is supported by others and often defended by reference to the theoretical concepts of Bernstein (McCormick-Piestrup 1973:11). With some modifications, we agree with Bernstein's objection that his work does not support theories of verbal deprivation (Bernstein 1972).

A fuller understanding of Bernstein's concepts of linguistic codes and speech variants is important for ideas we wish to develop concerning the relationships between language and politics. Bernstein (1964) describes two main codes of speech—the *restricted* and the *elaborated*. The former orients the speaker toward particularistic orders of meaning; the latter orients him toward universalistic ones. While using a restricted code, the speaker does not make explicit the general principles and operations that govern relationships between objects and persons. Instead, the speaker assumes an order of meaning that is more bound to specific contexts. Conversely, by using an elaborated code, the speaker can make explicit (or at least more explicit) the principles and operations governing his world of meanings.[5]

The main point, says Bernstein (1972a), is that the differing speech accomplishments of children differentially located in the class structure must be understood in terms of the socialization setting of their families. In the case of a working-class child, the dominant relationships in the family are "communalized roles," that is, roles in which consensus between the actors is the most important property. There is consensus in the sense that the actors share the same cultural history, stress the similarity of their experiences, and hold many common assumptions. Conversely, the social relationships of a middle-class child in his family setting are characterized by "individualized roles," that is, roles which stress the difference between the actors, their experiences, their assumptions, and their points of view. Restricted speech variants have their basis in communalized roles, whereas elaborated speech variants are rooted in individualized roles.

By relating different speech variants to different social orders, Bernstein created a framework for analyzing the speech of persons acting in different forms of social relations. Bernstein argued that the class structure, and particularly working-class socialization, limits access to the universalistic order of meaning that is realized in individualized role relations. Though this leads to difficulties for the working-class child in handling individualized roles, Bernstein (1972a) emphasized that, on the level of grammatical and linguistic choices, the working-class person has access to a rich vocabulary, a highly differentiated noun phrase, and a wide range of syntactical choices that involve the use of logical operators such as "because," "but," "either," "or," and "only." He also noted that there is an elaborated variant even in the predominant restricted code of lower- and working-class persons. Nonetheless, said Bernstein, "If you cannot manage the role, you cannot produce the appropriate speech" (1972a:166). In other words, "because the code is restricted it does not mean that speakers at no time will use elaborated speech variants. Only that the use of such variants will be infrequent in the socialization of the child in his family" (Bernstein 1972a:173). The children are not linguistically deprived. Rather, they are restricted as to contexts in which elaborated speech variants might be properly expressed—that is, contexts of individualized roles. Theorists of the verbal deprivation of lower-class children have claimed Bernstein's work as part of their argument. But this is made possible only by ignoring his key concept of different orders of meaning encoded through different social-structural and contextual relationships. This is a distortion and abuse of Bernstein's writings.

The Myth of the Nonverbal Child

The theory of linguistic deprivation is also criticized in studies by William Labov (1972a, 1972b). Through linguistic analysis of the speech mainly of black gang members, Labov showed that nonstandard English dialects are not radically different from standard English, but on the contrary are closely related to it and have alternative versions of the same basic rules. Despite differences in the phonological, grammatical, and lexical aspects of lower-class language, argued Labov, there is no indication of a logical or semantic difference between it and standard English, or in Bernstein's terms between a restricted and an elaborated code. In addressing this problem Labov resolved ambiguities that remained in Bernstein's formulation.

One decisive advantage of Labov's studies is that he consciously varied the setting in which the experimental interactions took place. Labov was aware that the speech behavior of his subjects might vary from one social situation to another, and that failure to note this could lead to the thesis of the nonverbal lower-class child. Let us give two examples (Labov 1972a:184ff). The first is an interview of a black child in a New York City school. The interviewer, who is white, places before the boy a block or a fire engine, saying, "Tell me everything you can about this." What follows is mainly silence on the part of the boy. Though such reticent, monosyllabic speech is normally taken as a proof for the thesis of lack of verbal capacity of lower-class children, Labov interpreted it as the child's effort to defend himself in a hostile setting, as such a test might be described. Suspecting that when a child is interviewed in a sympathetic situation things might turn out differently, Labov changed the interview situation. This time a skilled black interviewer brought along a supply of potato chips, invited the child's best friend to come too, sat on the floor with the boys, and introduced taboo words and topics. What followed was a highly vivid conversation in which the "nonverbal" lower-class child disappeared entirely. Instead, we had two verbally animated boys who had much to say and had no difficulty in using the English language to say it.

We do not wish to overemphasize the similarities in the theoretical approaches of Bernstein and Labov, especially as Labov did not develop a social-structural concept of linguistic codes, but on the contrary stressed the situational aspect of verbal behavior. Both authors deny any difference in the linguistic competence of different social groups. Instead, they explain differences in overt verbal behavior in terms of differences in the cultural or situational organization of various speech events. As Labov put it, "The social situation is the most powerful determinant of verbal behavior" (Labov 1972a:191). If the situation that the child confronts is asymmetrical or hostile, and thereby provokes a defensive reaction, then we will not find a verbally active child. The main speech problem for low-income people is not that they cannot express themselves effectively, but that others too often control the situations in which they are expected to speak.

The Problem of Logic and Abstraction

Though Bernstein's and Labov's work can be used against the theory of verbal deprivation, there still remains an important problem: Even allowing that language differences between different socioeconomic groups reflect different cultural settings, it could still be argued that these are also differences in logic and abstraction.

Bernstein stated that the grammatical structure of the restricted code supports a nonlogical way of thinking: reason and conclusion are often confounded to produce a categoric statement. Restricted speech is of low generalization, lacks differentiation, is inconsistent, limits interest in general relationships that transcent the immediate situation, and thereby makes discursive thinking difficult. For example, Bernstein (1972a) wrote that persons speaking an elaborated code realize an order of meaning that is "less context bound," whereas speakers of a restricted code realize an order that is "more context bound." In the case of elaborated codes, the speech is freed from the social structure that evokes it and takes on an autonomy. Realizing a "universalistic order of meaning" implies that "individuals have access to the grounds of their experience and can change the grounds." Conversely, restricted codes are "more tied to a local social structure" and therefore have a "reduced potential for change in principles." Speakers of a restricted code have great difficulties in entering into "a reflexive relationship to the social order" that they have interiorized (Bernstein, 1972a:164). "Restricted codes draw upon metaphor whereas elaborated codes draw upon rationality" (Bernstein 1972a:161). Don't these formulations suggest a lack of abstraction and logic in the restricted code? Though Bernstein tries to highlight an important feature of the cultural and social order of low-income groups, he remains ambiguous concerning abstraction, logic, reflexiveness, and the potential for "change in principles."

To clarify this problem, we turn to yet another sociolinguist, Eleanor Leacock. Leacock (1972) called the sympodium of abstract and concrete speech a "false dichotomy."[6] Reviewing the historical and ideological roots of this dichotomy, she saw it as an oversimplified version of the Whorfian hypothesis, an expression of ethnocentrism, and a consequence of the establishment of standard English as a status criterion. "Strictly speaking," said Leacock, "there is no such thing as concrete speech or language" (1972:126). Every language by its very nature is abstract because it is essentially a system of rules. Every time we use a word we abstract relational properties from the totality of "concrete" given entities. As Lenneberg (1969:641), cited by Leacock, put it: "In all languages of the world, words label a set of rational principles instead of being labels of specific objects. Knowing a word is never a simple association between an object and an acoustic pattern, but the successful operation of those principles, or application of those rules, that lead to using the word 'table' or 'house.' ""

If there is a difference in styles of speech of different groups, it does not lie in the abstractness of their language, "but in differences in the areas wherein conceptualization is more consciously developed, and in the ways in which concepts are expressed or elaborated upon" (Leacock 1972:127). As an example Leacock discussed the use of metaphors noted to be a common characteristic of black speech communities, and of black-lower-class speech in particular. For instance, there is a wide range of metaphorical expressions concerning the difficulties of black people in the world of employment: "They clip your wings and tell you to fly," "You take the starch out of a shirt and it don't iron too good," "You have to learn to step between the raindrops," and so on (1972:129). Far from being merely concrete or nonrational, however, metaphors are forms of symbolization that abstract qualities perceived as similar from dissimilar phenomena. In the metaphor, the relevant features of a situation are stated as an analogy. Metaphors are logically economical, eliminating the need for an overload of qualifying terms (Brown 1977). Referring to Kenneth Burke, Leacock noted that the features of metaphoric symbolization are inseparably part of any scientific inquiry, which itself proceeds metaphorically "through the processes of oversimplification, abstraction, and analogical extension" (1972:129). In short, the analytic value of the dichotomy between "abstract" and "concrete" speech codes is doubtful; it solves no problems and conceals more than it reveals.

If we cannot characterize the vernacular of low-income groups as less abstract than the elaborated code, what then distinguishes their restricted code? To answer this question we turn to a provocative analysis by Labov of two interviews focusing on matters of belief (Labov 1972a:193–96). One interview, about witchcraft, was conducted with an adult, upper-middle-class, college-educated black. The other, about God and life after death, took place with Larry, who at fifteen years old was one of the roughest members of a black gang and had troubles in school.

Comparing the two interviews, Labov (1972a:194) noted different kinds of speech regarding their lexical and grammatical properties. The middle-class speaker used forms of language close to the elaborated code described by Bernstein. He used longer sentences, more subordinate clauses, more evaluative statements, and a more learned vocabulary, and he took a rather "individualized" role. Conversely, the gang member used speech that was almost paradigmatic of nonstandard black English. There was the characteristic negative inversion, negative concord, invariant "be," "it" instead of "there," and a lack of evaluative statements such as those used by the middle-class adult.

Given these different forms of language, was there any indication of a difference in their logic, such that one of them implied a superior use of reason? Labov analyzed the logical structure of both answers to show explicitly that Larry, the gang member, presented a complex set of interdependent propositions organized within the rules of logic. Even if some of his propositions were unstated or implicit, indicating the use of a restricted code, when challenged by the interviewer Larry gave an account of the underlying relationships that showed a thoroughly logical reasoning.

Turning to the account of the middle-class speaker, Labov did not find a superior use of logic. Indeed, by reducing the arguments of the speaker to their basic content, Labov discovered one not very exciting statement: I believe in witchcraft. By bracketing the redundant or contradictory information, Labov showed that this middle-class form of speech was not more rational, more logical, or more intelligent. It was merely verbose and "educated."

In short, standard and nonstandard English, or restricted and elaborated codes and speech variants, are all abstract. There is no reason to presuppose a deep logical difference (if any at all) between different speech codes and their variants. There might be some aspects of the elaborated code or formal middle-class speech that facilitate the acquisition of knowledge and verbal problem solving, but this question remains open. And even to address it we would have to distinguish that aspect of speech which is functional for learning from that which is functional for acquiring and demonstrating middle-class status or relating easily to middle-class teachers. For the time being, educational practice, and especially theories of verbal deprivation, confound both aspects.

A Sociological Reconsideration of Bernstein's Concepts

In light of the foregoing it seems appropriate to reconsider Bernstein's formulations. If there is no deep difference in the logical or abstract character of different speech codes, Bernstein's notions become problematic. This can be shown by extending his assumptions even further; by reaffirming his Durkheimian perspective on language we can reveal its limits. Central to Bernstein's view of middle- and lower-class cultures are Durkheim's concepts of organic and mechanical solidarity (Durkheim 1933).[7] These concepts lie behind Bernstein's models of elaborated and restricted codes, explicitness and implicitness, and universalistic and particularistic orders of meaning (see Lawton, 1972). In accepting these Durkheimian concepts, Bernstein weakens his own formulations: the concepts are too imprecise for Bernstein's task, and he confronts the same problems that led Durkheim to abandon the dichotomy in his later writings.

Before suggesting an alternative sociological model, we should note the empirical features to which Bernstein refers. We will confine our discussion to problems of lower-class culture. The most prominent feature of this culture is suggested by Bernstein's notion of "context-bound" and "implicit," or what in early studies William F. Whyte called the "hierarchy of personal relations" or "systems of particularistic loyalties" (Whyte 1955). These terms describe three distinct features of life in low-income or slum areas. The first feature is the emphasis on primary group relations. Living in settings that expose them to unpredictable changes, and faced with poor public services, and crowded apartments, slum inhabitants rely primarily on groups whose members they know and can trust—the family and the gang (Cohen 1955; Firth 1956; Miller 1958; Parker 1974; Silberstein 1969; Thrasher 1963). Second, such primary relationships are based on the principle of reciprocal assistance. This principle consists on one hand in accepting and using the resources of friends without feeling guilty or ashamed, and on the other hand in feeling committed to help one's friends and to give them back some version of what one has received (Cohen 1955; Silberstein 1969; Whyte 1955). A third feature of lower-class life might be called the personalization of social relations. Being dependent on the help of particular others, the lower-class person tries to establish very personal and intimate relationships between himself and the persons he needs (Silberstein 1969; Spinley 1953). "Open criticism seldom is based on general mores but measures each individual according to the premises and commitments laid down in history. What might be praiseworthy behavior for one individual can be shameful to another" (Suttles 1968:79).

Now, instead of conceptualizing these features of lower-class life solely in terms of vague ninteenth-century notions, we can draw upon the large corpus of empirical studies of such lower-class attributes as particularistic loyalties (and betrayals), affectivity, and so on. In other words, we must supply the empirical analysis of lower-class behavior that both Durkheim and Bernstein omit. Such an analysis must draw on the close study of ongoing situations and be formulated precisely, so that its propositions are falsifiable by further empirical observation. One approach that might meet these criteria is the theory of norm and sanction as developed by Geiger (1964), Popitz (1961, 1967, 1968) and his former students Blankenburg (1969, 1970), Spittler (1967, 1970), Treiber (1973a, 1973b), and Trotha (1974).

According to Popitz, the concept norm refers to regularities of behavior (*Verhaltensregelmässigkeiten*) that are compulsory for an actor. One can recognize norms by the reaction that follows when an actor regularly violates them. Deviance is followed by sanctions, that is, by reactions that express disapproval of the conduct in question. Like every social construct, norms are abstractions of realities. Norms idealize relationships between actors in specific ways; that is, they standardize definitions of situations, the behavior appropriate to these situations, and the actors to whom they are addressed. Similarly, sanctions standardize reactions toward norm violations, that is, toward deviant behavior.

Using the concepts of norm and sanction in a study on the conditions of sociation (*Vergesellschaftungsbedingungen*) in slum areas, Trotha (1974) reformulated much of the literature on lower-class neighborhoods. His main finding was that the concepts of "particularistic loyalties," "systems of personal relationships," or the greater amount of "spontaneity" in lower-class social relations, can be understood as analytical descriptions of a specific kind of normative order. That is, studies of lower-class areas, and in particular the world of gangs, in effect describe settings in which

1. The kind and degree of standardization of behavior called normative is not much found in the ordering of social relations between members, and
2. To the extent that it is found, its enforcement through sanctions is highly inconsistent.

Typically in lower-class settings great scope is left to the individual to interpret the situation. Instead of finding fixed intersubjective standards to guide them, lower-class persons must incessantly focus on the cues and clues of specific situations to discover, or to invent ad hoc, the meanings and actions that might be appropriate. The procrustean bed of the kind of idealization of reality we call norms is often not given—at least not to the degree as in higher-class settings. In short, though the discretionary power of the lower-class actor is reduced with reference to the larger political economy, it is increased and even required with reference to his specific situations. Much more than the upper- or middle-class actor, members of the lower class must decide what game is being played and how they are to play it.

The first consequence of this clarification is that we can understand more precisely what Bernstein may intend by his concept of "communalized roles." These are roles for which the standardization of behavior has not been consolidated (*verfestigt*) into norms. And this phenomenon is strikingly inconsistent with a picture of lower-class social relationships as "mechanical solidarity," with its corresponding sociolinguistic models. This reformulation of communalized roles also enables us to redefine the problems of abstraction, and to reinterpret Bernstein's propositions from the point of view of both linguistics and social structure.

A Redefinition of Abstraction

We have shown that on the cognitive level there is no difference in the degree of abstraction between standard English and a vernacular. The same can be said for all forms of social relationships and for all forms of socialization. As Simmel argued in his "Exkurs ueber das Problem: Wie ist Gesellschaft moeglich?" (1968b), society has to be understood as a relation between socially generalized persons. At no time and in no place do we see the other in his total individuality, as an individual as such. We always see the other as something more general, as a man or child, as a worker or a professional, as a lover or a spouse. We abstract from the singularity of individual existence and standardize its features by creating intersubjectively recognizable categories. We typify; and our typifying the acting, feeling, thinking, and the very nature of individuals is a precondition of the possibility of society. The abstract property of social relations is a basic principle of the construction of social reality, a daily accomplishment by all members out of their intersubjective existence.

Viewed in terms of this phenomenological insight, the concept of abstraction becomes ambiguous as a means of discriminating between different kinds of social relations. Rather than using this notion to describe the social structure of the lower classes, we look for different ways, or forms as Simmel would say, through which social relations are established. In this perspective the dichotomy between individualized and communalized roles appears to describe a form, differentiated by class, for standardizing conduct. Does this formulation not reintroduce the concept of abstraction? Certainly it does. But it does so in a way that redefines the problem. Instead of using the word "abstraction" we can say more precisely that the actors take into account a different set of circumstances in constituting their situations. In this formulation the properties of communalized and individualized roles do not appear as ordered in a hierarchy of abstraction. Instead they are different modes of responding to the universal challenge to establish the typifications basic to our social existence. All humans share the burden of living their social beings through abstract realities, but they can use different forms to construct these abstractions. Generally speaking, in abstracting or constructing her immediate reality, the lower-class person must consider a wider range of imponderables and take less for granted than does the middle class person. Thus Bernstein's original notion of abstraction is completely transvalued.

The Problem of Flexibility and Social Change

In one of the articles we discussed, Labov asked the question: "Is the elaborated code of Bernstein really so 'flexible' . . . as some psychologists believe?" (Labov 1972a:192) According to Bernstein, the answer seems to be yes. For example, we cited Bernstein saying that "in the case of elaborated codes, speech . . . takes on an autonomy" in that the individuals using an elaborated code "have access to the ground of their experience and can change the grounds." On the other hand, speakers of a restricted code have a "reduced potential for change in principles." Yet in discussing the problem of abstraction and the logic of different speech codes, we saw no linguistic evidence that verifies these propositions. At the same time, we had to reformulate Bernstein's Durkheimian concept of social structure in order to resolve problems on the linguistic level. In short, the notion of the inflexibility of a restricted code is grounded in the assumption of an inflexible lower-class social order. We now want to extend the concepts of norm and sanction to argue that the idea of the inflexibility of lower-class persons is incorrect.

There are two aspects of the "culture of poverty" that are likely to produce what appears on the surface as restricted or inflexible speech and conduct. These aspects are the reduction of the normative standardization of behavior and the reduction of sanctioning. For example, one dominant feature of lower-class groups is that the relation between wife and husband may easily be revoked. The breach of the conjugal bond in such settings is not a last resort but an ordinary experience. Instead of making it a normative obligation to stay together, the wife's attitude to men might be described by the expression "I'll let him love me (and I'll love him) until he don't act right. Then I'll kick him out." The attitude of the man is 'Love 'em and leave 'em." The man is a guest, often only a tolerated guest, especially when he is broke (Drake and Cayton 1962; Bartels 1975). In other words the reduced normative standardization of conjugal behavior is expressed in the ease by which that relationship may be broken.[8]

A second feature of lower-class life is that children are often without adult supervision; the mother is overburdened with the tasks of the household or out of the house entirely, working in a factory or an affluent home. Thus when deviant acts are committed by lower-class children no one is there to impose sanctions. Violations of parental norms are less recognized and the child has, so to speak, a temporary immunity from punishment.

These examples (and others in Trotha 1974) suggest that lower-class orders are ones in which people have great flexibility in defining their immediate relationships and actions. Though they have scant influence on official definitions of deviance, they do have ample existential possibilities for violating such definitions. Moreover, such flexibility appears to be a rational coping device for individuals who have little control over actions by members of other classes that directly affect their lives. For example, for those who are "last hired, first fired," unemployment is an everyday possibility, integral to the expectations of slum dwellers and especially of the young. Moreover, to find a job does not mean that one will be able to keep it, or even go to work tomorrow. One imponderable is health. White-collar employees can work despite a broken leg. But a warehouseman cannot. And the warehouseman is more likely to be exposed to unsafe and unsanitary conditions of work, transportation, and domestic life. Thus going to work and being in good health do not become taken-for-granted conditions for low-income people. Instead, they are problematic and uncertain.

There thus seems to be an inverse relationship between the degree of control over one's conditions of existence and the degree of control over one's existential actions. The middle- or upper-class person has more control over the conditions or is less affected by changes in them. But he buys this security by acting in accordance with normatively standardized and routinely sanctioned patterns of behavior. The lower-class person, in contrast, is more vulnerable to changes in his conditions, but just because of this he displays those existential qualities of spontaneity, daring, physical courage, loyalty to peers, resistance to authority, and fatalism that Miller, Whyte, and many others have noted as characteristic of low-income people, and especially of urban, delinquent groups.[9]

Seen in this perspective, flexibility becomes almost a functional prerequisite of a social order in which the individual in his daily life is exposed to changes that affect the essential conditions of his well-being, but over which he has little or no control. It is the lower-class person who is struck most by economic crises, illness, and war. And it is he or she who has to adapt. Thus the Durkheimian concept of a tightly knit social structure, in which the individual is completely enclosed, misunderstands the nature of lower-class neighborhoods and particularly of gangs, and grossly underestimates the effects of more general social changes on the lives of members of the lower class. Sociologists holding this view have been preoccupied with observing interactions within peer groups, for example, without noting the ease by which gangs dissolve (Kobrin 1951, 1961; Yablonsky 1967) and without considering the forces and factors external to gangs. If one looks at such structural pressures the whole picture changes, and we see why in some situations we encounter an almost monosyllabic speaker, whereas in others we find a speaker who is a very effective narrator, reasoner, and debater (Labov 1972b:193).

Language as Ideology

If language is the principal medium of thought for a society—its forms of consciousness exteriorized—it follows that repressive restrictions on the use of language, what Habermas calls distortions of communication, are of their nature ideological. It also follows that linguistics can be used as a highly refined instrument for analyzing this consciousness and its ideological constraints. As Hannah Arendt said, "The impact of factual reality, like all other human experiences, needs speech if it is to survive the moment of experience, needs talk and communication with others to remain sure of itself" (1958:25). Distortions of communication reduce the range of experiences taken by people as real and the scope of interests perceived as legitimate. This in turn contracts the parameters of the political community, "since a political system depends on communication and since political interests have to be articulated before they can be acted upon or expressed in policy" (Mueller 1973:192). "It is not only capital, in the strict economic sense, which is subject to appropriation, but also *cultural capital* in the form of the symbolic systems through which man may extend and change the boundaries of his experience" (Bernstein, 1972b:172, see Bourdieu and Passeron 1964).

In making visible and audible the microrealities of class structures, Bernstein and others have contributed crucially to a larger theoretical enterprise—the integration of micro and macro approaches to understanding social reality. Using newly available observational apparatus such as audio and video recording, sociolinguists have rendered available for close inspection the methods by which class structure is reproduced in everyday interactions. The focus on childhood socialization and schooling, especially, gives precise empirical grounding to the concept of cultural capital. Sociolinguistic methods also make it possible to test in situ the adequacy of such concepts as false consciousness, authoritarian personality, and so on, with a degree of empirical precision far beyond that achievable by conventional interviewing techniques (see Collins 1981:161–182; Knorr-Cetina and Cicourel 1981).

In spite of these important advances, however, sociolinguistics has not adequately related microlinguistic studies to the broader political economy. Let us again turn to Bernstein's work as a starting point for articulating this relation. Despite occasional disclaimers, Bernstein describes working-class speech codes as having "poor syntactic construction," "rigid and limited use of adjectives and adverbs" (1964:1:42), and "descriptive concepts of a low order of causality" (1964:1:52). Contrary to Bernstein, however, sociological observation reveals working-class persons to have a very practical understanding of causality in society, as expressed in such sayings as "money talks," "it's not what you know but who you know," or "if you're white, you're all right; if you're black, get back." Furthermore, the impression of greater abstraction of middle-class speech comes largely from its greater use of nominalizations. That is, middle-class speakers delete contexts and participants to create a reified world in which qualities can be actors. The objectivity characteristic of such speech is produced rhetorically, by desubjectivizing language through agentless actions and use of the passive voice. An example of this is the difference between two newspaper accounts of the June 1975 shootings in Harare, Salisbury:

RIOTING BLACKS SHOT DEAD AS ANC LEADERS MEET (*London Times*)
POLICE SHOOT 11 DEAD IN SALISBURY RIOT (*The Guardian*)

The first version weakens the link between the police and their act of killing, and also provides an excuse for it (the blacks were rioting). The second is less elaborated, more direct and concrete.[10]

Perhaps a personal anecdote will be excused, which will further illustrate these points. In 1968 when I was a Commissioner of New York City's antipoverty program, part of my job was to act as liaison between the upper world of banks, foundations, and think tanks, and the lower world of welfare-mothers' day-care centers, youth employment programs, and the like. It struck me that my manner with these two constituencies met with opposite responses. On the eighty-sixth floor at One Chase Manhattan Plaza, the rule seemed to be, "The less you say the better." Here one displayed membership by asking no direct questions and taking all the ground rules as given. In contrast, in low-income communities everything had to be made explicit, for the failure to tell all was seen as an attempt at a swindle, and "bankerly discretion" was considered sly.

The facts that the big banks spent more on advertising ghetto loan programs than on ghetto loans and that city hall usually did ignore or exploit poor communities obviously had something to do with these attitudes and linguistic practices. What struck me, however, was that the discourse of the bankers and the welfare mothers had almost exactly the opposite properties from what much sociolinguistic theory would have us believe. The poor people I knew were sensitive to the structural constraints on their own actions, they had clear ideas about causality, they were highly verbal, and they made explicit and sought to transform the principles governing their situations (sometimes through collaborative action, but more often through manipulating the representatives of the system). The bankers, by contrast, were practically nonverbal, used stereotyped expressions and concepts, were rigid in their apparent incapacity to shift from technical to political levels of discourse, and resisted reflecting on the principles governing their own practice.[11]

The very elaborateness of elaborate speech may or may not enhance its communicativeness, but it does enhance its functions as ideology. This can be seen, for example, with legal language, which is perhaps a paradigmatic instance of the elaborated code, and which is notoriously less communicative the more it is elaborated. Through punctilious attention to legalistic rationality, said Douglas Hays in his study of judicial conduct in eighteenth-century England, "the law thereby became something more than the creature of a ruling class—it became a power with its own claims, higher than those of prosecutor, lawyers, and even the scarlet robed assize judge himself. To them, too, of course, the law was The Law. The fact that they reified it, that they shut their eyes to its daily enactment in Parliament by men of their own class, heightened the illusion. When the ruling class acquitted men on technicalities they helped instil a belief in the disembodied justice of the law in the minds of those who watched. In short, its very inefficiency, its absurd formalism, was part of its strength as ideology" (Hays 1970:33).[12]

A similar example of language as ideology is Bernstein's interpretation of hesitation phenomena as a reflection of the greater range of cognitive alternatives available to middle-class children, which, he said, cause them to reflect more frequently before forming their sentences. But this explanation is gratuitous and ethnocentric, that is, ideological, for it interprets the inferior communication of middle-class children as a sign of their cognitive superiority, whereas the direct and vivid language used by lower-class children is described as "rhymes and catchphrases [that] are stark and revolting to the adult." Verbal clumsiness is turned into cognitive grace in middle-class children: verbal economy and directness are defined as revolting in lower-class children.

These points have implications for broader theories of ideology, culture, class consciousness, and the possibilities of political community. Hegel argued that the slave, because he was engaged in the practical activities of production, had a better understanding of historical realities than the master. Lukács and other neo-Marxists took up this theme, arguing that the *habitus mentalis* of dominant groups operates with reifications, that is, with abstractions that mask relations of domination. This in fact seems to be supported by Bernstein's findings, once they are recast in this critical framework. The working-class speech code, said Bernstein, allows the child to use "savage and unfeeling terms quite freely, without a sense of guilt or shame. . . . Respectable figures or institutions may be caricatured, denigrated and slandered quite happily with joyous unconcern" (1964:1:73).

Reinterpreting Bernstein's own data, we could say that middle-class children tend to obfuscate political reality through hesitations and equivocations, abstract and complex verbiage, subordinate clauses and other qualifications, ample use of the passive voice, and appeals to reasonableness, conscience, and guilt. This does not mean, of course, that the usual speech modes of lower- and working-class persons are without limitations. Indeed, their very directness, expressing communal or personalistic roles, may pull attention away from longer-term and more complex relations through which class power is mobilized. The cynical realism of working-class people on the micro level may become naive cynicism regarding macro societal phenomena.

This certainly should not be surprising, given that the working and lower classes take orders. They experience hierarchy and power quite directly by being told explicitly and regularly what to do, but they are simultaneously excluded from those peak positions from which broad interorganizational connections become more visible.

By contrast, the middle and upper classes give orders, establish the conditions for other people's work, direct organizations, and keep the greater part of what is produced for themselves. They are thus engaged not in physical labor but in ideological labor. Operating habitually within a system of rules that largely serves their interests, middle-class people tend to take the background assumptions for granted and to become expert in mystifying and reifying power. Caught outside of these rules, however, they may appear as linguistic and social dopes.

"Middle-class occupations deal more with the manipulation of ideas and symbols, while working-class occupations deal more with the manipulation of things. . . . Getting ahead in middle-class occupations is more dependent upon one's own actions, while in working-class occupations it is more dependent upon collective action" (Collins 1981). Middle-class jobs have longer reporting periods and require greater self-direction; working-class jobs have shorter reporting periods and require that one follow explicit rules set down by someone else. Such rules, of course, are subverted, so much so that one could say that innovative subversion, and not obedient conformism, is the central property of the system for lower-level workers. In the terminology of game theory, though the rules of superordinates require obedience and conformity, the moves of subordinates within these rules are innovative and nonconforming. Something similar appears to operate in lower-class family settings. Though directives by parents are ostensively non-negotiable, in practice the lower-class child has ample scope for personal choice and, indeed, given the often precarious circumstances of his or her life, is situationally required to exercise such choice. In contrast, middle-class parents may be less authoritarian in "laying down the law," but their capacity to enforce their wishes is much more pervasive. The same seems to be true for middle-level organizational professionals. They are officially given much greater scope for initiative than blue-collar workers, but they also are expected informally to reconstitute their entire selves as "company men" (Harrington 1959).

Extending our structural analysis still further, it might be possible to explain the differences between lower- and middle-class life-worlds without much resort to ideas of cultural transmission, socialization, or language codes. As Liebow stated, "Many similarities between the lower-class Negro father and son (or mother and daughter) do not result from 'cultural-transmission' but from the fact that the son goes out and independently experiences the same failures, in the same areas, and for much the same reasons as his father" (1967:222–30). Similarly, the findings of Kohn and Schooler, "emphasizing as they do the structural imperatives of the job and de-emphasizing the importance of interpersonal relatedness, support the argument of the structuralists. A man's job affects his perceptions, values, and thinking processes primarily because it confronts him with demands he must try to meet. These demands, in turn, are to a great extent determined by the job's location in the larger structures of the economy and the society" (1973:117). In this perspective, the essence of language differences is not the functional inferiority of the lower-status code for the effective performance of higher-status positions, but rather the functional efficiency of the higher-status code as ideology that legitimates higher-class domination. As we have seen, sociolinguistic theories and data have been used to justify both of these interpretations.

Let us summarize: Arguing from a linguistic point of view, we saw that there is no indication of a lack of logic and abstraction as such in lower-class speech or in black vernacular. Further, having rendered problematic some of Bernstein's notions, we took his Durkheimian concepts seriously and looked for the conditions of social structure that produce different kinds of speech. We saw that the ambiguities in Bernstein's ideas arise from his misconceptions about the social structure of lower-class social relationships. We also suggested how language may function ideologically to justify or mystify class domination. Let us now return to our original question: What have these considerations to do with the difficulties that middle-class organizers have in communicating with lower-class persons in general and with gang members in particular?

The Problem of Communication

Reasoning from our observations of lower-class speech, we can imagine various situations in which middle-class persons cannot produce the right sentence in the right way because they cannot accomplish the appropriate role. This in fact is precisely what happens when intellectuals try to talk with poor people. Middle-class persons—conservative, liberal, and radical alike—have systematically failed to discover the kinds of role relations necessary for communicating with adults or children who realize different orders of meaning. Only through such roles could middle-class persons become able to produce the adequate speech. But rather than confronting this difficulty and establishing new role relationships with the poor, middle-class experts or organizers have tended to rationalize their inability by constructing theories of linguistic deficiency and programs of compensatory education, or by simply giving up on the poor as backward or authoritarian.

But the problem of communication is much more challenging than such concepts as lower-class authoritarianism, lack of education, or even false consciousness suggest. What is at issue here is not the limitations inherent in lower-class culture as such, but rather a profound conflict between members of different cultural and social structural orders, a conflict between lower-class persons and upper- and middle-class persons who presume to help them. One problem concerning the role of the intellectual in reformist or revolutionary practice is not that the intellectual is an intellectual, but that she is middle class. Such a person is confronted with an alien system of meaning, realized in alien ways of ordering social relations, and expressed in alien forms of speech.

In terms of these considerations, the questions, What is education? and Who is to be educated? become crucial. If language deprivation is a myth, if there is no indication of a lack of logic encoded in lower-class speech, if low-income persons are not inflexible conformists, then the following questions arise. Were concepts of education or politicization grounded in what might be called cultural imperialism? Have we regarded middle-class styles of life and speech as the criteria for being accepted as an educated or politically aware person? Did Bernstein avoid the radical consequences of his concept of different orders of meaning? Did we label the "passivity" of street-corner groups in politics incorrectly as either working-class authoritarianism or false consciousness? And did this simply misconstrue what was going on, by misunderstanding either the interests of the street-corner groups or the significance of these interests for their daily lives? For instance, when an organizer talks about the deprivation of the gang member, he gets a very straightforward answer (see epigraph). But this answer, contrary to any simple concept of lower-class conservatism, shows a profound disrespect for the present system of power, even while it reflects its materialist values. In Merton's terms (1957), such persons are innovators, not conformists.

Concepts of verbal deprivation or false consciousness are correct; but they are correct mainly when applied to middle-class experts or activists seeking to help the poor. Applied to low-income people as they relate to each other in their own words and worlds, these ideas become misconceptions. Of course, we are not saying there is no lower-class authoritarianism. There is authoritarianism and even more there is deprivation. But we want to emphasize the following: As we develop concepts or programs to educate or to politicize members of the lower class, we should realize that we are involved in a conflict between different social orders. And in accepting this we must recognize that the problem of communication can be resolved only if we become in a very radical sense participants in the ongoing communication process. That is, we ourselves have to be as much educated and politicized as the members of the lower class to whom we address our speech acts and our programs. We must train ourselves to take the viewpoint of the other, and to establish a communication process that by its very nature is dialogal and dialectical. We must be ready to take psychic and cultural risks, just as we demand risks of the persons we presume to help. We have to represent our truths as witnesses and not merely represent them as bureaucratic or radical technicians. This is not only a moral requirement for an emancipatory method of politicization. It also is a technical requirement for any democratic political intervention, a requirement that is logically implied by our theoretical analysis. To meet these requirements would be to make our theories practical and our speech acts acts of political and moral courage. It would liberate us from unreflective theorizing even while engaging us in emancipating practice.

Two

Personal Identity and Political Economy

Western Grammars of the Self in Historical Perspective

Monday: Cloudy today, wind in the east, think we shall have
rain . . . We? Where did I get that word? . . . I remember now—the
new creature uses it.

Mark Twain (1904:3)

We felt that the right to say "we" required so much more than the
simple "revolution" that was to resolve everything.

Richard Zorza (1970:2)

IDENTITY IS GIVEN neither institutionally nor biologically. It evolves as
one orders continuities in one's conception of oneself. This immanent
self-image emerges and is shaped through meanings that are derived
from interactions and infused with affect. To the extent that the polity
is expressed through the everyday contexts of such meanings, that
polity may be said ideally to embody not only the formal organization
of public interactions but also the personal participation and collective celebration of moral community. In this sense, the self-conception
of persons as agents is dialectically interdependent with a societal image of self-renewing institutions designed for and through citizens'
collaboration.[1]

The wholeness and integrity of the person depends on his possess-
ing a coherent vision of his own essential continuity through life
stages, social roles, crises, and bereavements (Turnbull 1983). Affective relations between persons of different generations and social positions are critical to such a vision of self, for it is through these
relations that an integral significance can be conferred on otherwise
separate stages in the life cycle and places in the social system. Personal integrity is thus logically and pragmatically bound to the wholeness and integrity of the polity. The essence of citizenship is the
participation of the individual in the polity as a whole person. But

when the self is fragmented into its various personae and roles, and when the citizen is replaced by the functionary or consumer, there is a concomitant fragmentation of that society's notion of moral agency and political obligation.

I want to show the relationship between the political economy and personal identity, particularly the identity of a citizen in a democratic polity. My vehicle for this is a "semiotics of selfhood." That is, I deploy a textual analysis of culture and society to reveal self and polity to be emblems of each other. Such an analysis derives from contemporary language-oriented modes of interpretation—usually applied to scriptive rather than social texts. But it also draws heavily on classical sociological theory—for example, Marx's theses on political economy, Weber's conception of rationalization, Durkheim's theories of a collective symbolic order, Mead's social psychology, Simmel's phenomenology of the emergence of social forms, and the critique of modernism by both conservatives and critical theorists. In the nineteenth century all these theorists took for granted some relation between personal identity and political economy. In contrast, most contemporary thinkers embody in their very theories the radical separation between "individual" and "society" which they should instead describe and explain. The bifurcations in our general culture are reflected (more than critically analyzed) in social theory itself. Conflicts such as those between micro and macro, subjective and objective, or humanistic and positivistic sociologies, for example, are high-toned versions of the debates between the contemporary followers of Rimbaud and the admirers of Saint-Simon. Only by uniting and transcending these two bifurcated aspects of our culture can we achieve a fuller understanding of ourselves and enact a polity in which moral agency by whole persons in public life is fundamental.

The most embracing medium of such relations between personal identity and political economy is language, especially those vocabularies of motives, protocols of intentions, and images of selfhood that are expressed in the philosophic anthropologies and popular psychologies that dominate in any given culture. I begin by sketching two major "grammars of selfhood" in terms of positivist and romantic responses to the process of modernization. The modernization of Western societies has involved transformations not only in our social structures, but also in our experience and conception of ourselves as human. Some examples that I treat are the ways that bureaucracies redefine what it means to be an ethical person and how changes in the modern family have led to the psychic narrowing and emotional specialization of its members. I note that the oppression of workers in early industrial states and the trivialization and serialization of productive labor in advanced societies have lowered persons' self-esteem as producers and heightened their anomic narcissism as consumers. In another section I discuss how the splitting of the modern self into positivist and romantic aspects has led to a kind of collective political schizophrenia. I conclude with some observations of the relation of self to language, to those paradigmatic grammars through which possible selves may be realized.

My discussion of contemporary alienation, identity confusion, and political schizophrenia, however, is not meant to suggest that former ages were mentally healthy. My references to the preindustrial past intend not to exalt previous epochs but to imply a future humanization. True, my analysis shares much with that of reactionaries such as Solzhenitsyn, Ortega y Gasset, and Robert Nisbet, who have lamented secularization, the revolt of the masses, and the democratization of culture. But it also draws on critical theorists such as Lukács, Adorno, Benjamin, and Marcuse. All of these writers are antistatist. Yet I categorically reject the pseudonostalgia of reactionaries for the past, as well as the despair of disenchanted Marxists for the future. Critical descriptive analysis that implies a normative utopia does not have to justify itself by showing that the past was better than the present. Nor does it have to specify a plan for the future. Both are unnecessary and would probably be unconvincing. Most ages, with their privations and lack of freedom, were not particularly happy. And Communist regimes have turned the Marxist dream into a totalitarian nightmare. Awareness of this is reason enough for retreat or despair, but I yield to neither. The normative utopia implied in this essay is not an homage to the past nor a blueprint for the future. Instead it is a moral use of reason that attempts to provide standards for assessing our inheritance, conditions, and possible futures.

Romantic and Positivist Grammars of Selfhood

As a framework for my analysis of contemporary positivist and romantic grammars of self, I invoke the traditional Western conception of the person as an enduring ego that is an active, integral agent. This renders my critical comments nonarbitrary in that they derive logically from a core value of our civilization: that the irreducible essence of personal identity is moral agency—the capacity to intend and to act. Without agency we do not act, we merely behave. As agents, however, we become responsible for everything. We become social, historical, public, and political beings. Agency is therefore a precondition of moral being.

Just as personal identity presupposes moral agency, so the democratic political community presupposes citizenship. This is because the polity is the arena for the public expression of freedom. Without citizenship the polity is no more than a beehive. With it, the polity becomes the *agora*, the public space for the enactment of moral choices, for the expression of duties or evasions, of reciprocity and betrayal, of justice or oppression. Human societies require persons and democratic polities require citizens. Citizens are persons who act publicly as moral agents. They may act selfishly, they may be wrongheaded or evil. Still, when they act as citizens they act as persons whose public conduct reflects their choices, intentions, and commitments.

In this view, moral agency is understood as the capacity to create culture. This capacity is central to being human, and as linguists and philosophers have shown us, every person has acquired it by the time she has learned to speak (Vygotsky 1972). Indeed, to be a person as opposed to an object means to be able to symbolically construct reality. And if reality is accessible to us only through such mediations, it follows that choices of or within reality require a mastery of our symbol systems. In this sense personal autonomy is not a matter of happiness or adjustment. Instead, it means potency in creating meaning and form.

Within this historically Western conception of the person are two grammars of selfhood that are essentially modern: one that finds its essence in *peak experiences* and another that centers on *casual encounters*. As Vytautas Kavolis noted, the first of these

> conceives of the true self as a submerged luminosity (or a
> hidden savagery) that gives a hint of its presence only in
> moments of the most vivid, or purest peak experiences which
> are overwhelmingly complete in each case, but not
> necessarily consistent with each other over a period of time or

with any order external to the individual. . . . This logic is
evident in Rousseau's *Confessions* and has attained perhaps
the most extreme modern expression in Arthur Rimbaud's
'immense and calculated disordering of all his senses'. . . .
Peak experience logics tend to appeal most strongly to the
subjectively 'underprivileged' and 'emotionally deprived,'
. . . to people on the boundary between two or more socio-
cultural structures or statuses, . . . or in times of consciously
experienced civilizational crisis. (1980:45; see Bays
1964:251–52; Dumont 1965)

As Walter Pater urged, and as Oscar Wilde's Dorian Gray embodied,
the goal of life for such persons is to "burn always with this hard
gemlike flame." This grammar of selfhood is romantic.

The second grammar conceives of the true (or untrue) self as an
inventory of masks or performances that are displayed in a series of
casual encounters, either passively or manipulatively. The self is seen
"as an image pieced together from the expressive implications of the
full flow of events in an undertaking; and as a . . . player in a ritual
game who copes honourably or dishonorably, diplomatically or un-
diplomatically, with the judgemental contingencies of the situation"
(Goffman 1967:31; see Goffman 1959; Kavolis 1980:47). Any more
substantive description of the self, in terms of this grammar, is only a
deceptive performance staged before an audience. Tocqueville's
(1945:2:3–55) description of the experience of the self in democracies—as a constant reshaping through small, distressing motions—
accords with this grammar, but its fuller appearance had to await the
twentieth-century dissolution of the "symbolic foundations (the particular conception of the 'destiny of man' and the obligations imposed
by it) on which democratic institutions are based. Individuals adhering to this logic are likely to be 'game-players' or 'technicians' not
committed to anything beyond the methodology (whether of action or
of observation) of the enterprise in which they currently find themselves. The interpreters of this logic [that is, social psychologists] tend
to be 'observers of techniques'" (Kavolis 1980:48; see Ruitenbeek
1964). Because of its instrumental and technical orientation and its
nominalist or pragmatic conception of being, this modern grammar of
selfhood may be called positivist.

These two grammars together form a dialectic of mutual transformation. As opposites, the romantic and positivist grammars dialec-

tically interpenetrate, change, and engender each other. Each when carried to its extreme becomes its other. The casual encounters of bureaucratic life anesthetize the emotions and thence invoke escapes into peak experiences. Peak experiences in their nature are unstable, however, and their repeated pursuit can trivialize sensibility—the peak experiences become routinized and calculated performances in a series of casual encounters. We vacillate, as Gabriel Marcel said, between "the termite colony and the Mystical Body" (1962:138).

Moreover, since the romantic grammar of self is in principle opposed to institutionalization, its behavioral realizations presuppose a more instrumentally oriented social order. The romantic self thus depends on the very bureaucratic system that it hates. Romantics who would shock the bourgeoisie require the bourgeoisie as their public. The reverse dependency also obtains. The positive control of conduct through large organizations yields efficiencies which then carry both forces and relations of production to a higher level that has its own psychological features. Tertiary production—the technical, administrative, and service sector—replaces secondary and primary production and thereby requires new forms of control and new levels of skill. Labor discipline in the new settings cannot be achieved through coercion or mere wage incentives; instead psychic rewards emerge in response to new needs (or old needs that the system can now afford to satisfy and that workers are now secure enough to demand). Thus at the same time that the system becomes more totalistic and productive, it also generates new organizational forms and rewards and new psychic needs and possibilities. Many of these needs can be partially fulfilled through peak experiences, or what I have called "ritual" or "safety valve" irony—symbolic protests against or escapes from the system that are in fact controlled by and serve to maintain the system. In bourgeois circles this is precisely the function of peak experiences such as EST, orgies, and the packaged romanticism of the Club Mediterranée.

Both the romantic and the positivistic grammars invoke a modern, fluid, and alienated identity. By contrast, traditional grammars are appropriate to societies in which persons experience themselves as inherent parts of their social universe and hence in which alienation in the modern sense can hardly occur. In the Western tradition, for example, the Hebrew and Germanic tribes, the Greek polis, and the medieval communes all had clear conceptions of the human personality, but none conceived of it as separate and distinct from the larger social order. Instead the Jew was what he was because his people had been chosen by God; the Greek's identity as a free person meant that he was head of a household and member of a polis; "Medieval men thought of one another . . . not as personalities with deep inner drives and tensions, but as moral characters whose virtues and vices were apparent in their speech and actions" (Robertson 1968:5).

Changes in this pattern can be seen in the early modern period. Martin Luther was one of the first in Western civilization to conceive of the person as a subjectivity independent of his objective social setting and to confine man's freedom and authenticity to purely inner experiences, outside of the roles and institutions of society. This conception is the deepest root of German pietism, which later issued into secular romanticism. Sincerity—the matching of the self to its social expressions—was benighted. Authenticity—the assertion of a self against social conventions—was ennobled. For Luther, of course, the peak experience was an encounter with God. For Everyman today, an encounter group suffices.

If Luther is a precurser of the peak-experience self, Machiavelli heralds the casual-encounter identity, for Machiavelli was the first to articulate the view of life as a game of impression management. Indeed, if one substitutes "Everyman" for the "Prince," Machiavelli's texts come close to those of Goffman. The reverse is also true. By replacing Goffman's "individuals" with Machiavelli's "Prince," Goffman's microsociology of impression management is transformed into a macrosociology of power. Machiavelli, like Goffman after him, formulated a vocabulary of winning for its own sake, demoting all the professed ends of power to mere tactical instruments: "*Qua* performers, individuals [rulers] are concerned not with the moral issue of . . . living up to the many standards by which they and their products are judged, . . . but with the amoral issue of engineering a convincing impression that these standards are being realized. Our activity, then, is largely concerned with moral matters, but as performers [rulers] we do not have a moral concern with them" (Goffman 1959:251).[2]

The intimate interpenetrations of the romantic and positivist grammars of self were understood by such analysts of culture as

Kierkegaard and Weber. Kierkegaard, for example, described an erotic-aesthetic mode of being in which "Your life resolves itself . . . into interesting particulars . . . everything is possible for you . . . enjoyment is the chief thing in life. . . . Life is a masquerade. . . . In fact you are nothing; you are merely a relation to others and what you are, you are by virtue of this relation" (1959:2:15, 25, 163). Kierkegaard juxtaposed this sensualism to the existential, religious mode of being. In the contemporary era, however, sensualists without spirit have divorced existentialism from religion and have made the erotic itself into a religious quest. Similarly, Max Weber, in his essay, "Religious Rejections of the World and Their Directions," suggested that what had come to be called the "erotic" was a last refuge of intellectuals from the forces of rationalization and demystification. Since the death of God, the more we seek ultimate redemption in secular peak experiences, the more our encounters become tenuous and shallow. With weakening ties to God, kin, community, or any other enriching symbolic structures larger than himself and given a priori rather than solipsistically created, the modern person moves from one casual encounter to the next, playing out a moral identity without quite believing in it, a specialist in doubt, a master of cameos, the virtuoso of a smaller and smaller self.[3]

Bureaucratization and Selfhood

In democratic polities the symbolic construction of self and society is done ideally through the role of citizen. Yet in the contemporary world citizenship is difficult. With the decline of intermediary associations such as neighborhoods, union halls, and town meetings, public action has increasingly come to mean action taken as a worker or a professional, as an expert or as someone who is "just following orders." Marx was correct in saying that capitalism turns things into commodities. But Marx did not go far enough, for, as Max Weber showed, it is not merely capitalist societies but all modern social formations that redefine their worlds in terms of utilities. Weber's great insight was not only that bureaucracies are the quintessential expression of modern rationality, but also that they are the quintessential vehicle of modern power. Such bureaucracies use their instrumental, rationalistic ideology to control both their members and their clients. Moreover, because this ideology discourages substantive criticism, bureaucratic power is by definition incapable of ethical self-reflection. Those who direct bureaus may be moral or immoral in their private lives. But this need not—in fact it must not—have anything to do with their actions in their bureaucratic roles. The application of rational calculation to social relations not only affects the external environment. It also creates transformations of consciousness. To be made an object of technical manipulation is not just to feel manipulated; it is to be manipulated. The human result is not merely a personal opinion or attitude but an objective existential state with its concomitant political correlates.

If charisma and tradition provided the ideology for preindustrial domination, elites of the modern world have found a new vocabulary for objectifying things as they are. This new vocabulary is scientific rationality, and particularly cybernetic systems theory (Stanley 1978). A cybernetic state governed by bureaucratic functionaries is the collective counterpart of an atomized individuality estranged from authentic intersubjective communication (Belohradsky 1981). Instead of citizens interacting in a polity, functionaries act out their bureaucratic roles, roles defined not in terms of moral intentions but in terms of self-maintaining organizational ends. "Except in the highest leading positions" of bureaucratized societies, said Simmel, "the individual life and the tone of the total personality is removed from social action. Individuals are merely engaged in an exchange of performance and counter-performance that takes place according to objective norms" (1965:347). Fascism and communism are extreme forms of personal atomization and collective statism, but they are neither isolated nor aberrant. Instead such forms of total domination express a central logic of modern culture, the logic of value-neutral, instrumental efficiency, the constructing of people through the language of things. Even in the relatively free and prosperous capitalist democracies, there is a tendency toward "friendly fascism," a totalism in which efficiency becomes the guiding principle for all domains of social praxis (Gross 1980; see Simmel 1978).[+]

Such extreme rationalization produces absurdity. The more social practice is dominated by the instrumental calculation of experts and managers, the less scope is left for average people to exercies practical

insight and moral judgment. As Seeman put it, "the structural conditions of mass society (e.g., high mobility, rationalization of industrial
processes, bureaucratization) encourage a sense of powerlessness
which leads the individual to be insensitive to, and uninformed about,
an environment over which he believes he has little influence"
(1967:106; see Gerth and Mills 1964:470). Unable to participate in
formulating the purposes of their institutions, or even to know what
such purposes are, many persons are alienated. The common clerk,
factory worker, or technician, for example, can carry out an endless
series of actions that, while rationally functional to command objec-
tives, are meaningless to him.[5]

Just when bureaucratic armies nullified the volition of the individual, the Nuremberg Tribunal proclaimed that each soldier is morally accountable. Having army recruits dig trenches and fill them up
again, for example, serves precisely as training in the unquestioning
amoral performance of organizational tasks. Similarly, the Maharishi
insists that all participants in his group-think have their "personalized" mantra, much as the clothing salesman insists that his mass-
produced garment is "made for you."

Liberal capitalist societies have also invented a number of formal
organizations to bureaucratically regulate conduct that was previously managed personalistically through village, guild, and kinship
systems. Social agencies such as the juvenile court, the mental hospital, and the welfare agency all supervise conduct in the interests of the
state, but without requiring its direct intervention. As medicine became more scientific, licensed, and allied with the state, for example,
official intervention was extended to hygiene, mental and physical,
public and private. Private therapies for privileged groups and therapeutic incarceration for the lower classes have also emerged as forms
of social control authorized by the dominant scientistic ideology
(Warren 1982). Public charities and philanthropic foundations deal
with the pauperism generated by the capitalist economy, and thereby
mask its causes.

The persons who ambulate in large bureaucracies are redefined as
functionaries. Everyone is there to perform a function, a function that
is designed to serve the interests of the organization. And whose interests does the organization serve? This question is rarely asked and
often subversive. Instead, the system or the revolution or some other

reified concept of collectivity is seen as generating its own self-maintaining ends. A century ago the public good or "socialist humanity" could still be understood as substantively rational goals that instrumentally rational bureaucracies might serve. In America, for example, Hamiltonian means could be justified as serving Jeffersonian ends. But as industrial capitalism has eroded the bases of a shared moral order, such justifications have become anachronistic, and "rationality" has become the ideological catchword for the mystification of political domination.

Modern culture began with the separation of the public from the private and may end with the absorption of even this residual private sphere of life into the technocratic structure. The private sphere—or what is left of it—becomes the sphere of romanticism, of intentions, feelings, and sentiments, of the irrational and subjective. In contrast, the public sphere becomes the sphere of instrumental calculation, scientific objectivity, causes and effects. Our collective life comes to be construed through the language of cost-benefit analysis, input-output equations, and social engineering. Thus it becomes possible to say of ethical considerations, "That's your personal feeling, but let's look at the problem objectively." The language of objectivity is well suited to such questions as how to raise the body temperature or the body count, but it is unsuited for considering *why* or *for whom* we engage in the imperious maintenance of brain-dead patients or the imperialist destruction of recalcitrant nations. And when moral agency is relegated wholly to the private realm—when it is atomized into purely subjective consciousness—then it is bereft of social consequence and hence of moral meaning.

In such a society the individual experiences pervasive public control, which he calls "alienation," as well as extensive private autonomy, which he calls "freedom" (Benn and Gaus 1983; Luckmann 1967; van Gunsteren 1979; Zijderveld 1970:128). Institutions are experienced as distant, phantomlike structures, much as in Kafka's *Kastel.* Freedom, removed from this alienated public sphere, comes to lack institutional and hence political consequence. Adrift from its institutional moorings, freedom cannot be reinforced by its expression in conventional roles, particularly those institutional roles where we spend the greater part of our lives—as students, soldiers, workers, and members of various formal groups. Without public space for its enactment, "freedom" becomes apolitical, thereby signaling the death of citizenship.

We have lost many of those "little republics" that Jefferson said would be a bulwark against tyranny and a guarantee of liberty. Modern societies have become mass societies in the sense defined by C. Wright Mills (Mills 1974; see Brenkman 1979; Geiger 1969). Mills distinguished the "mass" from the "public." The latter is the citizenry of a democratic polity that forms its opinions through discourse emerging from personal and collective experience. In contrast, members of a mass do not participate as moral agents in the larger common life. For the mass, this life has been absorbed up into the state, the corporation, or the party, and is experienced only through reified and segmented images conveyed by media of information and propaganda. "The grandchildren of men and women who once stayed late into the night at the Grange hall or the union hall, talking intensely with each other about what kind of society they wanted to build, now stay home watching TV" (Harrington 1985:18). For the mass, opinion is really merely subjective opinion; by contrast, for a public, opinions are informed judgments achieved through political discussion. Having neither a stable core nor consistent institutional support, the opinions, sentiments, and feelings of modern persons become more and more susceptible to manipulation, including, at the extreme, communism or fascism. These are indeed the modern diseases, for they combine positivistic rationality of organization with romantic irrationality of the emotions.

Integration of identity, in the sense of integrity as well as unity, presupposes the capacity to integrate diffuse role identities on the one hand and to prevent total absorption into excessively harmonious roles on the other. But the diffusion of roles has become so acute in advanced societies that to maintain integrity within them the ego must operate at ever more abstract levels, finally losing connection with any social experience whatever and becoming a purely inner self. Such disassociation may be a means of moral survival in situations of domination, what Goffman called "being away" (Goffman 1961; see Arendt 1951; Solzhenitsyn 1973/75). But today such diffusion of identity is not confined to total institutions. It is revealed whenever the clerk says "I can't help you with that, I only work here." It shows when the chemist says, "I make solvents for industrial use. It's not my fault if they dump wastes into the river." It was revealed when the Smithsonian researcher for biological warfare said "The Pacific program was one of the most successful modern day field studies ever done. . . . What they [the Department of Defense] did with it was their business" (Gup 1985:9–12). It showed in the advice of a prospective CIA employee that "You can compartmentalize. . . . If I'm an analyst with them, they may knock off a Chilean leader, but I didn't do it. I'm an analyst" (Rothschild 1984:18). It appeared in the statement of the pilot in Viet Nam, "I don't think about what the targets are. We just fly the missions" (Kann 1973).

This type of thinking and being is highly functional for the efficiency of large organizations, as well as for the day-to-day performance of the people who inhabit them. But it also has profound consequences for humane and democratic values. For when such a way of being becomes dominant in a society, then machines and bureaucracies are seen as having a life of their own. The human purposes that they were designed to serve are forgotten, and the mechanistic organizations come to generate ends and purposes of their own. The institutional space in which we could act as moral agents is thereby diminished. And since public moral action precisely defines the role of the citizen—the person who acts civically as a whole person—the loss of space for such action represents a crisis for citizenship as well as for the humane democratic values of which citizenship is the practical expression.

Identity and the Modern Family

A central locus of the patterning of the emotions is the family, and it is through transformations in the family that one can see correlate transformations in the boundaries between public and private. Everyday interactions within the family help construct the reality of self and social structure. For example, when I tell my son "Be a good boy," I am not only seeking to make him obey; I also am seeking to make him become a certain type of person—one that will fit into and reenact American culture and society. "The Yanomano Indians of Brazil encourage childish temper and physical attacks against parents," for this is taken to indicate fierceness of temperament, which is highly valued (Chagnon 1968). But I don't encourage temper tantrums and attacks because, as a middle-class American, I suspect that such displays "may signal serious difficulty in children's attempts at self-mastery" and eventual ability to function in, and thereby reproduce, American society (Kohn 1969; see Di Renzo 1977; Gordon 1981:587).

In traditional societies, the family was the fundamental unit not only of child bearing and rearing, but also of production, of political decision making, and of legal responsibility. The clan in China, the tribe in Africa, the caste group in India, the gens and phratry in ancient Greece, and the estate in medieval Europe were all extended kinship networks, whether through biological descent or through rituals that bound members mythically as by blood (see Bohannan 1952; Peters 1960, 1967). The modern distinction between private and public spheres—with the family relegated to the private realm—did not exist, since the family was the source of early socialization and affective closeness as well as a central political and economic institution.

All this was changed by the rise of capitalism, especially industrialization and the factory system. One of the greatest transformations brought about by the new forms of production was the separation of the household from the productive economy, resulting in the privatization of the family. The family ceased to make things for its own use; it became separated from both the new commodity production and the realms of day-to-day civic interaction. This development heightened the division of labor between social institutions, narrowed and specialized the functions of the family still further, and encouraged the ideology of individualism and of individual rights and duties guaranteed by the state (Aires, 1970; Engels 1884; Laslett 1960; Sennett 1978; Zaretsky 1976).

Public bureaucracies on the one hand and the privatized family on the other took over the activities that formerly were conducted through kin and community relations. Legislation against child labor or wife beating for example, though clearly humane, also reflected a depersonalization of the family, not only because such legislation was necessary (it may always have been necessary), but because it assumed a new role for the state as a defender of persons against their own kin. New roles for the state have also emerged in areas such as education and sexuality. Today, for example, the state is officially concerned about what were formerly private abilities to read and write. The real literacy of some and the illiteracy of many, characteristic of former times, has been replaced through official actions by the functional literacy of almost all, with "functional" being defined by the state and for the state (Freire 1970; Stanley 1978). "With the control of education by the state, authority over children has been transferred from fathers to governments, from private families to public agencies" (Finkelstein and Vandell 1984:75).[6]

Similarly, sexual conduct that once was regulated by families is today processed in batches. Advertisers have turned the erotic imagination into a storage bin for mass-produced icons. Family planners have made sexuality a question of state policy even while advancing under the banner of Women's Liberation. Market researchers and statistical demographers now provide a scientific basis for designing sexy product images and national fertility goals. Either through media titillations or statist puritanism, sexual life is depersonalized. As sex is transformed from pleasure into work, sexual acts are performed as if to be evaluated by time-motion engineers. "Women achieve masturbation by the end of the treatment," says one report on efforts at more efficient sexual production. "They are good girls; they do their homework" (Mittenthal 1979; see Clignet and DiTomaso 1981; Foucault 1978; Hudson 1972; *Newsweek* 1979:77).

In recent times, however, even the private, affective, sphere of the family is no longer a "utopian retreat from the city" (Jeffrey 1972), a haven into which males could withdraw from the dominant system. Instead, this rationalistic system absorbs affective family relations into itself. The psychological sciences, for example, are consciously applied to tasks that formerly were thought to be merely conventional or instinctual. This has made motherhood a kind of science, especially in upper-middle-class families where women, freed from immediate material responsibilities, direct more of their activities to social reproduction and the maintenance of the symbolic order. As socialization within the family has become a preparation for functioning in the serialized and disconnected worlds of civil society, affection from parents is transformed into a scarce commodity that is used to stimulate individual achievement and rivalry between siblings. Such competition is a requirement not only for success in capitalist societies but also, and more importantly, for the attribution of the causes of failure to oneself.

These observations suggest a need to reformulate the functionalist notion that the family is predominantly the domain of affective relations. As many analysts have pointed out (e.g., Bernstein 1971; Engels [1884] 1970; Sears, Maccoby, and Levin 1957), one of the principal means of child socialization in the bourgeois family is rationality.

> Although academic research stresses the *affective nature of family life, the same body of theory and research [also] stresses the importance of affective control by subordination to rationality.* Indeed, the parental use of reason, explanations of the consequences of behavior, frequency of verbal exchange, etc., typical of the bourgeois family, is highly associated with "empirical" measures of self control, moral development, identification, and guilt over transgression. Parsons' concept of the family as a mini-gemeinschaft in which ascriptive, particularistic, affective, diffuse relationships prevail must be qualified. Rather, the [middle class] family, as a microcosm of the rational political economy which shapes it, transmits domination by rationality. (Langman and Kaplan 1979:27)

The family did not create these circumstances; it is their victim. And, like most victims, the family is blamed for what it suffers. The modern family exists at the intersection of the positivist and romantic dimensions of society and personality, between the rationalized power of official institutions and the irrational emotions of anomic individuals. By exploiting parental ambition with the promise of social advancement, modern society reconstituted the family as a site for civilizing "primitive" emotions (Elias 1978). Just when its autonomy as a social institution is curtailed, the demand that it make persons whole has been redoubled. Saturated as they are with injunctions from educators, psychiatrists, and other representatives of official norms, parents no longer have the right, as they did in the old days, to let their children fail (Hessel 1969). The family is thereby doubly bound. If it is successful in nourishing autonomous and self-directing personalities, it may be shaping failures—that is, persons who are unfit for modern bureaucratic life—because personal authenticity is coming to equal social maladjustment. Conversely, when the family is successful in socializing children with the appropriate personalities for bureaucratic society, it produces neurotics who, like the family itself, receive high demands for performance but little practical autonomy and support.

Whichever way the stream of socialization flows, it heaps up victims on either of its shores: social misfits with strong emotions or conformists who are well adjusted but personally empty. The first type has deep personal experiences but little social connection. The second type is socially connected but has little emotional engagement. Instead of being society's original hope, the family has become the individual's first disappointment (Donzelot 1979:227–228).

From Production to Consumption as a Source of Identity

Major social thinkers of the nineteenth century noted the simultaneous integration of people through the capitalist economy and the national state and disintegration of identity through the collapse of traditional family and community relations. As work was removed from the home and farm to the factory or office, people had not only fewer embracing contacts with each other, but also less and less direct contact with nature or even with their own bodies as these might be known through agricultural, manual, or craft production. The growth of tertiary-sector employment in advanced capitalist societies has contributed to a further abstraction of relationships of production. The increase of personnel in service or coordinating roles reduces the proportion of people who can touch, feel, see, smell, or hear—and hence evaluate—the end products of their individual or collective labor. Even at managerial and executive levels there has been a decline in the immediacy and visibility of results by which excellence in job performance can be assessed (Clignet and DiTomaso 1981; Collins 1979). And at the lower levels of organizational life, Tocqueville's warning was prophetic:

> When a workman is unceasingly and exclusively engaged in the fabrication of one thing, he loses the general faculty of applying his mind to the direction of the work. He becomes every day more adroit and less industrious; so that . . . in proportion as the workman improves, the man is degraded. . . .
> As the principle of the division of labor is more extensively applied, the workman becomes more weak, more narrow-minded, and more dependent. The art advances, the artisan recedes. . . . Thus, at the very time at which the science of manufactures lowers the class of workmen, it raises the class of masters. (1957:2:168–69)

Specialization not only brings abstraction of productive processes and relations. It also makes jobs uniform. Mass manufacturing technologies with interchangeable parts also bring interchangeable workers. Labor becomes less specific and primary social bonds that might be established at the workplace loosen further. Carried too far, the division of labor becomes an alienation of labor. On the one hand, specialization has elevated a technomanagerial elite whose function it is to guide the productive process; on the other hand, it has so reduced each role within this process that the role becomes meaningless to its incumbent. For most people the work site is not the place to try to become a master of what one does; instead, the goal of excellence is relegated to the private worlds of hobbies, sports, and purchasing, as opposed to the more public worlds of work, political participation, and formal organizations. Labor thus loses its value as a source of positive identity for an agent, because the organization of work reduces most workers to factors of production (Braverman 1974).

The anomie generated by the modern division of labor was not merely transient, as Durkheim had predicted, nor was the alienation of factory workers accompanied by greater class solidarity, heightened consciousness, and ultimate revolution, as Marx had expected. Instead, privatization and serialization of social life, along with the material success of the dominant system, forestalled both the development of class solidarity and the emergence of a broadly based counterideology (Langman and Kaplan 1979:11). As advanced capitalism discovered an internal market in the proletariat, the consciousness industry emerged to redefine Americans as consumers instead of workers or citizens. Identity came to be derived not from production so much as from consumption. This began among upper-class women around the turn of the century and today extends to the masses (Veblen 1899; Atlas 1984). Prestige based on marginal differences in modes of consumption gradually took the place of esteem based on quality of performance. Former captains of industry became captains of consciousness (Ewen 1976).[7]

Contemporary capitalism is not the capitalism of Marx nor even of Lenin. The problem of the absorption of surplus is managed in the advanced capitalist states through mass consumerism. State-regulated oligopolies divide major economic sectors according to different product lines that are marketed through the mass advertising of subtle image distinctions. The triumph of the system, however, has been its integration of the new ideology of mass consumerism with the older, religiously tinged bourgeois ideologies of individual self-development. By marketing products that are designed to sell on the basis of a continuous substitution of attractive images of the self, production of things is transformed into production of signs (Barnett and Silverman 1979:33; Baudrillard 1972, 1975). As one ad for a television brand put it, "The movie may be lousy but the picture is great!" In this spirit, as the consumption of products becomes equivalent to the purchase of personae, there is a shift in the icons of identity (Clignet and DiTomaso 1981; see Hirsch, 1976b).[8]

Media-guided choices by consumers have come to be equated with the personal autonomy of citizens. This is an ironic realization of the neoclassical economic theory of freedom. Instead of people choosing things, things now choose people, in the sense of defining their identities. When people buy designer clothes, for example, they are paying for the look and label, and in so doing they acquire an identity as that sort of person. Similarly, smoking a certain cigarette is associated with cowboys or canoeing; using a certain menstrual napkin is presented as liberating one for skydiving or gymnastics. Even those displeased with advanced capitalism display their protest against it by shifting to alternative purchases, thereby reaffirming the assumption that self and value are defined by consumption. Daily life becomes a kind of manic propitiation to the products/gods that determine our identities/destinies (Goffman 1967:95). Yet these products, though they have a magical power to suggest an image of the self, do not in fact convey an integral identity. And how could they, since the items to be purchased are substitutable according to stylistic affinities and imminent obsolescence? As with cars, modes of leisure, dress, and pleasure, so the distinction between alternative modes of being is always within a limited and exterior universe of meaning—that of alternative "life-styles."[9]

The shift from production to consumption is nowhere more seen than in contemporary approaches to the problem of identity itself. As the Protestant ethic is replaced by the spirit of consumerism, we hear not of building one's character, but of acquiring a better personality. Adult education, which was conceived as a movement to bring higher learning to the masses, or at least the middle classes, often becomes a place where one "acquires a more positive self-image"—that is, a place for consumption of new personae. The adult-education branch of the New School for Social Research, for example, which once sponsored the first courses on race and on psychoanalysis, taught respectively by W. E. B. Du Bois and Sandor Ferenczi, today offers classes on "How to Educate Your Dreams to Work for You," "Body Awareness," and "Personal Growth." Hofstra University, a relative newcomer to the identity market, will teach us about "Masculinity," as well as "Pitfalls and Possibilities: A Couples Workshop." If we are to believe the announcements in the catalogs, these courses have essentially no content. Instead, their topic is "life" and how to deal with it. But dealing, if it has any humanistic sense, involves practical competence in jointly shaping one's world. But like much of the human development movement in general, what such courses provide is an "experience of participation" and a "sharing of insights."

Politics too becomes a matter more of stance than substance, more the consumption of signs than the production of community (Lefebvre 1968). With oligopolies in industry and a duopoly in politics, marketing directors and campaign managers become interchangeable. Each stresses "image differentiation" for consumption rather than labor and use values of production. The political candidate is no longer the charismatic or traditional leader of former societies, or even the efficient technocrat. In the advanced modern period he or she may literally be an actor. Like Machiavelli's Prince or Goffman's Everyman, today's politician studies the demographics and packages his personae for consumption by various market sectors.

Privatization and the Emergence of Political Schizophrenia

In the early modern period, Protestantism stressed an inner definition of each person, and the Enlightenment beliefs in universalistic science and reason encouraged the evaluation of each person by unbiased strangers such as judges, doctors, or teachers. The self was at once imploded into the discrete spiritual monad and exploded onto a broader field of impersonal public interactions. With this conquest of new social territory, however, the self became overextended and isolated. The larger the empire of the self, the less stable was its center. Finally this center became a stranger within its own frontiers. Public appearances became more problematic with the increased range and

diversity of our publics, so that today we are less sure which aspect of
the self, or which self, we should present. The anxious attention that is
required to modulate our marginality is paralleled by a withering
away of those primary social bonds that nourish a core identity. As
authentic individuality loses its practical base in clan and community
life, the person depends less on his own agency and more on market
forces or bureaucratic norms.

This process began in England about two centuries ago, then
spread to Europe and America, and is now pervading the entire globe.
The quotation below resonates with the experiences of Latins or
Asians today, but it was written 150 years ago by Thomas Carlyle in
England.

> Not the external and physical alone is now managed by
> machinery, but the internal and spiritual also. . . . The same
> habit regulates not our modes of action alone, but our modes
> of thought and feelings. Men are grown mechanical in head
> and in heart, as well as in hand. . . . Mechanism has struck
> its roots down into man's most intimate, primary sources of
> convictions; and is thence sending up, over his whole life and
> activity, innumerable stems—fruit-bearing and poison-
> bearing. (1896:2:239–40)[10]

The possibility of choosing a career first appeared in nineteenth-
century Europe and even then entailed both the evaluation of various
professions and political regimes as alternative forms of life and value, as well as a dissatisfaction with any choice that one ultimately
might make. What was once available only to such heroes as Eugene
de Rastignac or Julien Sorel is today available to Everyman. When
Balzac and Stendhal were writing, few imagined that society could be
restructured. Yet today most persons can envision alternative futures.
The relativization of time, space, and status through heightened communication and geographic and social mobility has had its counterpart in a psychic mobility, the capacity to imagine oneself into different identities and situations. The view that "Anything is possible,"
held in the nineteenth century by social philosophers and madmen,
today almost universally seems both an article of faith and a cause for
dread. Modern man has a choice of spiritual visions. "The paradox,"
said Herbert Fingarette, "is that although each requires complete
commitment for complete validity, we can today generate a context in

which we see that no one of them is the sole vision" (1963:236). "Man has gradually become less dependent upon absolute standards of conduct, [but] this increase of independence has led to a parallel increase of passivity. Shrewd as man's calculations have become as regards his means, his choice of ends, which was formerly correlated with belief in an objective truth, has become witless" (Horkheimer 1974a:97; see Diesing 1962; MacIntyre 1981). We are rational and efficient in our private instrumental projects but mindless in our public moral pursuits. Retail geniuses, wholesale fools.

In the preindustrial period the reproduction of identity and society was mediated through explicitly collective rituals and ceremonies. The assumption that society was the proper field for the realization of individuality, that the self could be manifested most fully in community, was dominant in the Greek ideal of the polis, the German totemic clan, and the Christian ideal of community that replaced them. But by the eighteenth century this assumption had come into doubt and indeed there emerged a radical opposition between self and society, and between private and public life. These processes continue today. Persons freed from ascriptive roles now find that not only roles but identity itself is something to be achieved. As organizations become more diffused and abstract, so do relations within them, as well as the selves that emerge from such relations. This approach was liberating when individualism itself was a form of social emancipation and a means of broadening the boundaries of human compassion. But today claims to private fulfillment are themselves manufactured through mass media and social agencies (Clignet and DiTomasso 1981; see Adorno 1973). Liberal individualism has become a form of false consciousness, an ideology that legitimates privatization and lack of community.

The struggle to maintain personal integrity in a corrupt society is of course an old one, but writers such as Rousseau deepened this opposition by stressing the difficulty of achieving any personality of one's own in the face of societal demands. Such moral atomism becomes full-fledged, for example, in Diderot's *Le Neveu de Rameau*. The theory of selfish human nature had preoccupied moralists from Hobbes to Kant; now it was the theory of selfish society that became the issue. Meeting the demands of society was no longer a realization of one's higher possibilities over one's baser nature. Instead involvement in the collective life was an abnegation of one's authentic self. Society was no longer a nourishing home, but had become a fate and predicament (Trilling 1971; see Bellah et al. 1985; Foot 1973:23; Zijderveld 1970:130). Such "ideological individualism is a basic method of social control. . . . Convinced that he or she is unique, and mystified to the point where everyday artifacts become surrounded with sacred auras, the isolated person cannot determine his or her social interest. Thus people in hopelessly competitive situations may shun unions; the elderly and not-so-elderly may refuse unemployment and retirement checks, not wishing to accept 'charity'" (Greisman and Mayes 1977:61; see Rosenberg 1953). Though valued in the abstract, individualism is not encouraged in the boardroom or labor union or bureau (Langman and Kaplan 1979:512; Gans 1979).[11]

A modern form of the quest for an authentic self is sensitivity training, combining confession, group therapy, and eroticism between strangers. Similarly, the proliferation of workshops on the techniques of lovemaking and mourning, seminars on divorce or on masturbation, how-to-do-it manuals on childbirth and parenting, psychical and physical disrobing among transient partners in hot tubs, encounter groups, and one-night stands all point to a society in which primal expressions of self have lost their inner meaning (King 1972:176). Such ersatz activities are offered to persons whose needs are very real. But instead of elevating their personal troubles to the level of collective moral issues, these activities privatize discourse and feeling even further.

These quests for authenticity are characteristics of an era in which the social roles that authenticate identity have collapsed. Within the medieval moral community, falling out of role meant falling into sin and was followed by moral regeneration. In contemporary society, where polite Protestantism has merged with humanistic psychology, the socially maladjusted fall into uncertainty, which is followed by a reconstruction of identity (Kavolis n.d.:15, 60). These repackaged identities reflect a consciousness filled with images: the public images of the movies, photonovels, TV, and newspapers; the private images of parents in the home. The all-too-visible public images engender illusions; the private images have an invisible significance that, like a time capsule filled with explosives, brings on later disillusionment. And between the two we find psychiatrists, encounter groups, and growth experiences of all sorts that aim to put everyone back in touch with their true desires, but always within the realities that are the original source of their confusion (Donzelot 1979:229–30).

In these new contexts, the self becomes a project, an "it" to be worked on, a commodity to be reshaped for more effective competition in the job, marriage, or satisfaction markets. Thus when we say something is "good for my ego" we do not necessarily mean that it is good for me. To have a good personality is like having a good car or a good job. Our self or personality is seen as capable of attracting attention and even love. It is like a stock or bond endowed with self-awareness: if demand rises, its value goes up and it feels important; if demand falls, its value shrinks and it feels worthless (Schachtel 1961:122; see Pennock and Chapman 1971; Rubin 1985).

The conception of freedom as resting wholly within the subjective *cogito*—and not something that emerges out of intersubjective practice—implies a denial of the political, as it was denied in ancient Socratic and Stoic beliefs, in Christian and particularly Protestant conceptions of conscience, and in early existentialism as well. Such conceptions attempt to actualize the ideals of wholeness or redemption through a radical inwardness that heroically transcends the objective social context. By defining freedom and authenticity as purely inward matters, however, these views fail to address the deepening dependence of persons in the modern era upon large oligopolistic or statist organizations for their employment, welfare, and ideas.[12] Freedom has come to mean a psychological condition of individuals in their private lives, where it is not functionally relevant to the dominant public system; freedom becomes a dump site for leftover emotions, fleeting sentiments, and floating opinions (Luckmann 1967:97). The "jargon of authenticity," as Adorno (1973) called it, conceals the objective context of unfreedom and, in the name of personal autonomy, joins Madison Avenue in celebrating peak experiences, immediate gratification, and innovative forms of consumption.

If removed from a nourishing political-economic context, individualism does not lead to independence and personal autonomy. Instead it implies social isolation, psychological narcissism, lack of commitment to and support from others, and ultimately a mindless conformism. But if we recognize the political culture as central to both autonomy and cooperation, then these ideas come to have a different relation to each other. It is only through a humane polity that collective goals can be established in a noncoercive, nondogmatic way. Such goals have meaning and efficacy to the extent that individuals become committed to them through personal decisions. By committing oneself to the jointly established goals, one's autonomy is affirmed; but because the goals are collective, such a commitment brings group support. As Joachim Israel said, "whereas extreme individualism in a dialectical way breeds extreme conformism, the existence of collective goals in a similar dialectical way breeds independence and personal responsibility" (1978:21–22). True emancipation is not a liberation of individuals from society but the redemption of society from atomization.

As public institutions are more and more governed by instrumental calculation, the Enlightenment ideal of freedom through reason has been replaced by a romantic conception of liberation against reason. Rationality of public roles and institutions; irrationality of private individuals and emotions. These are the two poles of contemporary identity. The positivist personality type in its anality and conformism, or the romantic personality type in its orality and pop anarchism, confront each other as two symptoms of the same disease. The positivist clings to his sickness with compulsive restriction and the romantic tries to escape it by compulsive immersion in new experiences. But when reason is purely the functional rationality of institutions and when emotionality is purely the subjective feelings of individuals, then reason and sentiment are divorced not only from each other but also from the wider grounds that give to each a more substantial meaning.

The dominant classes in early industrial society sought to get their inferiors to *do* what they wanted them to do. In contemporary societies elites try to make their subordinates *be* what they want them to be (Laing 1969). The first form of domination can be achieved by giving coercive orders. The second is enacted not through orders but through naming. Attributions are powerful directives for constructing identities. Whether a woman is to be depressed and guilty, for example, or angry and assertive, depends on whether she is defined and defines herself as a "traditional" or a "liberated" woman (Scheeman 1979). The courtly expression, "Your word is my command," was realized in early industrial societies by new systems of hierarchy and control. For advanced modern societies, however, a more apt expression might be "Your word is what I am" (Marcuse 1969:74).

The denial by individuals of the practical bases of their own agency has a counterpart in institutional bad faith—the lies organizational elites tell to their members and believe in themselves. On the psychological level, bad faith is an illusion of constraint masking actual choice (or the reverse); on the social level it becomes the appearance of participation covering real exclusion. In the early days of capitalism, antilabor laws explicitly forbade workers to unionize. Church and reform groups did make some efforts at "status acceptance," but there was relatively little ideology and practice aimed at cooling out subordinates and co-opting their means of protest. Today such official propagation of inauthenticity has become part of the normal structure. As power comes to be more concentrated and everyday life is less subject to direction by citizens, more and more investment goes into front activities by official agencies aiming to engineer consent.[13]

The pseudo-Gemeinschaft generated by such manipulation results in political schizophrenia. Studies of schizophrenic children provide striking parallels of surface responsiveness and underlying exclusion between the familial and the political spheres. To illustrate these parallels I note first a conversation that reveals schizophrenic family conditions:

> SON: Well, when my mother sometimes makes me a big meal and I won't eat it if I don't feel like it.
> FATHER: But he wasn't always like that, you know. He's always been a good boy.
> MOTHER: That's his illness, isn't it doctor? He was always most polite and well brought up. We've done our best by him.
> SON: No, I've always been selfish and ungrateful, I've no self-respect.
> FATHER: But you have.
> SON: I could have, if you respected me. I'm the joke of the world. I'm the joker all right.
> FATHER: But, son, I respect you, because I respect a man who respects himself. (Clausen and Kohn 1960:305; see Rosenberg 1984)

Given the father's totally unresponsive response, the son neither receives support nor can he easily blame his father for not supporting him, because the exclusion is presented in a supportive fashion. The son is treated as a feebleminded "gesture-child" who is expected to be gratified by the motion even though nothing has been delivered. Speaking in a similar connection, R. D. Laing wrote that the characteristic schizophrenic situation

> does not so much involve a child [a citizenry] who is subject to outright neglect or even to obvious trauma, but a child [citizenry] whose authenticity has been subjected to subtle, but persistent, mutilation, quite often unwittingly. . . . No matter what meaning he gives his situation, his feelings are denuded of validity, his acts are stripped of their motives, intentions and consequences. The situation is robbed of its meaning for him, so that he is totally mystified and alienated. (1969:91, 135–36)

In modern society the minute tasks in the social division of labor appear trivial in themselves and are linked to broader purposes only through interconnections so complex as to be easily "mystified and alienated." As Marx pointed out, and as Simmel and then Habermas differently elaborated, modern persons are particularly obsessed with one mystical reification par excellence: money (Simmel 1978; Habermas 1984:xxix–xxx). In his studies of false consciousness, Joseph Gabel (1951, 1962) argued that such reification of the phenomena of experience is the social equivalent of psychiatric disorder. Gabel noted parallels between such Marxian categories as ideology, false consciousness, reification, and fetishism (as developed by Lukács and Goldmann), and such psychological categories as melancholia, hysteria, psychosis, and schizophrenia (as developed by Minkowski and others). So analyzed, false consciousness is a kind of collective schizophrenia, whereas schizophrenia is a kind of personalized reification. In reified false consciousness, people construct a false public world and treat it as though it were actually lived by persons; in schizophrenia the person constructs a false private world and treats it as if it were publicly shared. In both, the abstract and logical are taken to be really experienced. The essential trait of both types of mental distortion, on the collective and the individual levels, is their antidialectical nature and their devitalized, atemporal, morbid rationality. Both reification and schizophrenia are semiotic ailments—disorders in the logic of communication. This, by the way, is why we feel so estranged when trying to communicate with either schizophrenics or with bureaucrats; in each case we encounter a world of perfect rationality which is so abstracted and disconnected from shared experiences as to be false and unreal. "Reality is *the fact that* people act meaningfully and that their actions are subjectively and objectively understandable" (Zijderveld 1970:40; Rosenberg 1984). The increasingly abstract, secular, and bureaucratic character of modern society, however, reduces the roles, ceremonies, and public places in which meanings can be realized by individuals. "What characterizes institutions is at the same time what constitutes their similarity with pathological forms. Like the repetition compulsion from within, institutional compulsion from without brings about a relatively rigid reproduction of uniform behavior that is removed from criticism" (Habermas 1971:276). These structural conditions generate sociopathology and psychopathology.[14]

To properly comprehend personal identity and political economy requires a sociohistorical theory of the self that neither reifies the person as a product of deterministic forces nor ontologizes the self as a purely subjective cogito. Most research on political schizophrenia tries to provide a psychological explanation for alienation that is socially engendered. But it is much more important to account sociologically for these existential states.[15] Psychological talk, whatever its adequacy by logical and therapeutic criteria, functions on the ideological level as a mask and symptom of the very problem it discusses. By psychologizing issues that are rooted in political and economic conditions, such discourse atomizes consciousness even further. If we find humanistic psychologies incomplete, through what vocabularies might a future humanization be understood? This question is taken up in the final section of this chapter.

On the Semiotics of Selfhood

Selves are articulated through certain grammars and vocabularies that mediate between political economy and personal identity. In Saussure's terms, the speech through which a particular identity is evinced is an expression of a more durable if less perceptible language, a language of possible selves. The communicative acts and symbolic performances through which we create existential meanings derive their possibility of being meaningful from that larger being that is encoded in the habitus of any given people, time, and culture. Knowledge of the self emerges from historically relative grammars through which possible identities may be articulated. In contemporary Western societies, bourgeois psychologies of individualism provide such grammars of selfhood, and these in turn can be understood with reference to the political economy.

In traditional societies the various situations in which persons play different roles tend to be similar, overlapping, reinforcing, and publicly visible to all. In ancient Greece or classical China, for example, the father's status as a legal member of the larger community depended on his status as a household head, which made the vocabularies of his major public and private roles largely intertranslatable. In such societies ideally a single vocabulary could be used to describe motives and constitute selves in all roles and contexts. And because the same homogeneous vocabulary was used in both civic and domestic settings, as well as when a person was alone, it was less likely to be questioned or even doubted.

Identity confusion can be understood, therefore, not only as a dimension of role conflict, but also as a reflection of semiotic conflict, a conflict and confusion between vocabularies of motive. "Shifting and borderline situations, having no stable vocabularies of motive, may contain several alternative sets of motives originally belonging to different systems of roles" (Gerth and Mills 1964:123). For example, we may feel both cherished and shamed, valued and worthless, if we engage in a love marriage that, as in feudal Japan, is said to express an egoistic self (De Vos 1960; Norbeck and De Vos 1972). Similarly, if we are middle-class bohemians we may feel jealousy at having been jilted, in terms of the bourgeois code, as well as guilt at our jealous feelings, in terms of the bohemian code (Waller 1930:88). Contemporary trends towards women's rights, open marriage, and self-pleasure also are changing not only the meaning of jealousy but also the definition of the jealous person. "Instead of signifying love and commitment, an expression of jealousy may now imply possessiveness or dependency" (Gordon 1981:579; see O'Neill and O'Neill 1972; Clanton and Smith 1977; and Lasch 1976).

Vocabularies of motives provide frames for interpreting the meaning of actions and attributing to them, or creating, "the kind of person" that could do such a thing. Similarly, disavowals, excuses, and other accounts are efforts to constitute the person in a positive image despite apparently negative conduct (Lyman and Scott 1970). One function of ideology is to provide a standardized set of motives that promote or sanction certain acts by placing an official premium on them. In this sense, ideologies may be called "metavocabularies of motive." The end of ideology is not the elimination of such official sanctioning but merely the absence of visible dissent, for the moment, to the regnant vocabulary of motives.

Changes in such metavocabularies in the West include the shift from feudal to competitive capitalist forms of legitimation. The decline of the Church relative to the marketplace involved a decline of religious vocabularies in favor of commercial ones (see Hirshman 1977; Lyman 1978; Nelson 1969; Schott 1984). Conscience was reinterpreted into interests, casuistries were transmuted into ideologies, the cure of souls became a technique of psychological science, and beginning with Machiavelli politics became a secular problem of systems maintenance (Stanley 1978:22). Likewise, the seven deadly sins became lively capitalist virtues: avarice became acumen; sloth, leisure; and pride, ambition; so much so that Samuel Johnson could say, "There are few ways in which a man can be more innocently employed than in getting money." A religious vocabulary of passions had been replaced by a commercial vocabulary of interests.

A similar change of metavocabularies accompanied the transformation from competitive to oligopoly capitalism. Possessive individualism and the profit motive were dominant images of the self and its motivations in a relatively unregulated and open economic era; and the ideological linkage of property to effort, risk, and achievement helped legitimate the new class structure. In the liberal, oligopolistic, multinational phase of capitalism, however, businessmen stress public service and social responsibility and insist that domestic concentration is necessary to meet foreign competition (Gerth and Mills 1964:118). People who act obstreperously or criminally are no longer called "wicked," but "unstable" or "disturbed." The first term constituted selves appropriate for feudal societies that were legitimated through transcendental moral norms. The other terms constitute selves suitable for bureaucratic societies legitimated through legal-rational efficiency.

The above examples suggest what might be called a political semiotics of selfhood. Such an approach would describe the range of identities that are available within a system of ordered procedures for the production, regulation, distribution, and operation of statements, that is, meaningful acts. The self would be seen as revealed in statements that are guaranteed by a cultural grammar of intentions, a vocabulary of motives, and so on. In such a political semiotics it would be possible to conceive the self as neither an atomized monad nor a mere medium for larger social forces. Instead, the self would become an author, at once creating and "authorizing" her own experience, while at the same time emerging from and merging into a pregiven structure of text, context, audience, and interpretation. In this perspective, we would not seek to understand psychologically the actions of particular individuals (including ourselves) as being impelled by drives, motives, or interests, nor by various social forces. Instead we would examine the vocabularies of motives and the grammars of interest that are encoded in and realized through various forms of discourse. In such a semiotics we would bracket not only the categorizations conventionally accepted by ordinary members of a society, but also the categorizations of experts or intellectuals who articulate the self-understanding of such societies. That is, we would make use of neither the popular psychologies nor the philosophic anthropologies of the person. Instead, we would make those psychologies and anthropologies themselves into a topic of dialectical reflection, along with the experiences of being human that such paradigms make available to those who live through them.

The relationship of such a procedure to political economy is exactly the opposite of the traditional and orthodox one. In *Leviathan* and in the *Social Contract*, Hobbes and Rousseau each posited a philosophic anthropology—an image of man—and then elaborated a vision of social order accordingly. Hobbes's philosophic anthropology enabled a theory of the polity and economy as a form of necessary domination; Rousseau's warranted a vision of society as a form of arbitrary oppression. Similarly Locke and after him Rawls posited a self that occupies an "original position" and retains whatever is necessary freely to enter into a "social contract" with similar others. Yet the very abstractions that create such transcendental subjects deprive them of any *principium individuationis*. Such selves are noumenal ghosts thought to exist prior to the very communities of interest and value that in fact create them (Sandel 1982).

If we take a hint from either a structuralist like Foucault or a phenomenologist like Garfinkel, we could reverse this conventional procedure entirely. Instead of focusing on forms of domination as warranted by an image of man, we would look at grammars of selfhood as these are engendered by various forms of subjugation. And we would start with a close investigation of linguistic practices, "at the level of those continuous and uninterrupted processes which subject our bodies, govern our gestures, dictate our behaviors, etc. In other words, rather than ask ourselves how the sovereign appeals to us in his lofty isolation, we should try to discover how it is that subjects are gradually, progressively, really and materially constituted. . . . We should try to grasp subjection in its material instance as a constitution of subjects" (Foucault 1980:97).

The focus of social scientists, then, would be on neither social psychology nor political economy, but on both at once. As C. Wright Mills urged, "The sociological imagination enables us to grasp history and biography and the relations between the two within society, . . . to shift from one perspective to another—from the political to the psychological . . . to range from the most impersonal and remote transformations to the most intimate features of the human self—and to see the relations between the two" (1961:6–7). With such a vision, we would look not only at how constitutions are authored, but also at how authors are constituted. There is no apodictic human nature in such an approach, no prior things or agents that realize their intentions in political action. Instead, both political economy and personal character are seen as constituted through discourse. There are no noumenal selves that can guarantee social contracts or moral orders. Nor are there social contracts or moral orders that determine individual selves in a crude Marxian or Durkheimian sense. Neither democracy nor citizens exist independently of each other; instead both are mutually engendered through public mimesis, through re-presentation of a public in public representation. Both societies and selves are constituted through symbolic interaction. The task of a semiotics of selfhood is to show exactly how, by what, and for whom this gets done.

Such a formulation shatters any ultimate guarantees of what we are or know or do. To the question, What are scientific laws? we answer with Kant that they are symbolic constructions. But to Kant's question, What is Man? we answer with Foucault that he is also a symbolic construction. Whereas Kant had found the conditions of possible experience in the structure of the human mind, Foucault located them within the historical and hence transient conditions of possible discourse (Hocking 1981:34). This is not a pessimistic or nihilistic position. On the contrary, pessimism and nihilism, along with optimism and hope, are all concepts that make sense only within the idea of a transcendental and enduring subject, an idea that is bracketed in our political semiotics.

The understanding that realities are constructed through symbols thus undermines the dual absolutisms of both positivist observation of external facts and romantic intuition of internal phenomena. Introspection, whether Freudian, Buddhist, or Catholic, can never be a direct apprehension of one's interior life, since such apprehension is of necessity mediated by and construed through language. The inner forces that Freud saw as central to his analyses of the psyche, for example, are symbolic artifacts. The fruits of introspection or psychoanalysis are not direct intuitions of psychic facts. Instead they are linguistic representations that are pieced together, ad hoc, with the materials at hand, in terms offered as appropriate for such an account by psychoanalytic, Buddhist, or other paradigms.

If this is true, then "the purported insight achieved by the patient is not the product of a process of veridical *self-discovery*, but rather reflects the patient's conversion to the therapist's interpretation" (Grunbaum 1979). The psychoanalyst of today must "realize that his realm of truth is in fact the word . . . [for] his whole experience must find in the word alone its instrument, its framework, its material, and even the static of its uncertainties" (Jacques Lacan, quoted in DeGeorge and DeGeorge 1972:240). "In other words, the journeys of self-discovery found in Western literature, the self-analysis of Freud, and virtually any sense we have of [apodictic] knowledge of ourselves are all illusions. The self is, in this view, a construct of the social and cultural views of the self. We ascribe processes to our mental life because we have been convinced, by plausible arguments, that they exist" (Rothstein 1980:19; see Kilton 1972; Parfit 1984). Thoughts cannot be reached in themselves without the mediation of language. It is only by our existence in and through language that we can construct our essences and know our minds.

Given all these assertions, what is left of psychological truth?

Much. Freudian theory, for example, does not depend on positivistic observation of perceptual and memorial processes, nor on romantic introspection. Instead it emerges from a reflexive analysis of the external expressions of mental life. Like all hermeneutic interpretations, and including at bottom those of science too, such theory may be verified by the data provisionally, but not ultimately, since these data are themselves constructed in terms of theoretical perspectives (Feyerabend 1978). And in a still further dialectical and moral sense, both knowledge and its objects, and both theory and data, are themselves verified by the kinds of identities and polities they help create.

Changes in the paradigmatic modes of interpretation thus yield transformations in the basic definition of what it means to be and know ourselves. We possess contemporary selves because the deterministic scientism of the eighteenth century has been overthrown by the findings of Schopenhauer, Marx, Freud, and Durkheim, and because the naive hopes of nineteenth-century humanism have been shattered by the ravages of twentieth-century destruction. The Enlightenment equation of reason and freedom has been replaced by a vision of rationally calculated unfreedom. The absolutisms of both positivism and romanticism have been relativized; the twin pillars of objective knowledge and subjective humanism have been broken by cultural anthropology, comparative history, transactional psychology, Godelian limits to mathematical axiomatization, the uncertainty principle in physics, the sociology of scientific knowledge, and the revolutions in modern philosophy.

All of these developments require and enable us to go through scientific determinism and humanistic morality to an understanding of the dialectical processes by means of which determinism and agency are themselves constructed. At one moment in this dialectic, any way of construing the world, including science, intends a human purpose, for even the scientific construction of reality is a human act. The claim of objectivity, for example, can take the form of behaviorism in psychology, formalism in literary criticism, or experimentalism in political science. Whatever form it takes, however, "any such toehold into objectivity makes it possible for some human being to feel he has protected his self against falling into some Other, human or inhuman" (Holland 1975:821). At the other moment of this dialectic, however, any thought, action, or identity is an expression of the larger

political economy, the historical forces at work, and the biosocial requirements of the situation, factors that operate predictably, as
though superintending the intended and determining the chosen. The
principal medium of this dialectic, though not the only one, is discourse, in which language is created in speech and in which speakers
are carriers of language.

Instead of either positivist determinism or a romantic conception of
freedom, each must be understood in terms of the other. Failure to do
so is costly. Among positivists this omission materializes subjectivity
into a pure in-itself of objective facts; among romantics it idealizes
objectivity into the pure for-itself of subjective feelings. In contrast to
these views but embracing both, we may understand subjective
awareness and objective conditions as two moments of the same historical dialectic. So conceived, freedom is not reduced to naturalistic
facts as in positivism, or vaporized into innate mental or spiritual
principles as in absolute idealism. Subjectivity is a product as well as
an agent of historical processes. By reconstructing subjectivity
through a critique of historically embedded grammars of the self, one
can establish a range of possible human experience. And this enables
us to distinguish real historical possibilities of selves and societies
from those utopias that are mere abstract illusions. Such a critique of
the historical and linguistic constitution of the self can show the real
scarcities and structural constraints that provide a framework of necessity for the exercise of human freedom. At the same time, however,
it can also reveal the mythic character of pseudoscarcities and reified
structures, and thereby dissolve the objectivist illusion of causality
and promote an opening of consciousness to formerly utopian freedoms (Schroyer 1973:xii–xiii).

Vico illustrated the working of such a dialectic in his *Scienza
Nuova* of 1744, which laid a foundation for modern human studies.
Vico gave a political interpretation of Solon's famous saying, Know
Thyself. Solon meant to instruct the plebians to reflect upon themselves and to realize that they were of the same human nature as the
nobles and therefore should be made equal with them in civic rights
(Vico [1744] 1972:90–93). Vico then added that Solon might have
been a poeticized historical creation of the Athenian plebes themselves, who used their own history as a means of liberation. Vico thus
transcended the dichotomies between self-knowledge and political

emancipation and between historical determinism and personal agency. Understanding for Vico was neither a positivistic accumulation of
facts nor a romantic rumination. It was rather the mastery of one's
inner life through reflection on its objective expressions and constraints. And this in turn involved a consciousness of one's own historical value and the affirmation of one's political rights and duties
through the collective inheritance of language. Only when we have
trained ourselves to articulate the congruencies between individual
thought and social structures, and between personal values and political conduct, can we say that we are truly human, for only then can we
foresee both the origins and the outcomes of our acts and so be masters of ourselves. The dictum Know Thyself invites neither objective
measurement nor introspective brooding. Instead it is founded on the
belief in the power of ideas and the corollary refusal to permit fear in
any way to restrict our capacity to think (Gramsci 1975:21, 29;
Horkheimer 1974a:162). By understanding ourselves through critical
reflection on our political and economic milieus, we may be able to
create a more democratic polity and a morally deeper conception of
ourselves.

Three

Reason as Rhetorical

On Relations between Epistemology, Discourse, and Practice

> In logic and psychology, signs and language are usually foisted in
> somewhere as an appendix, without any trouble being taken to
> display their necessity and systematic place in the economy of
> intelligence.
>
> Hegel (1971: Sec. 458.213)

> We always mean to say something, for it is through speaking that
> our humanity exists. Speech, that is the original promise of the
> glance, the gesture, and even more, the gaze. Language is solicited
> by the world itself.
>
> Merleau-Ponty 1964:92)

IN SOME TIMES and places persons become aware of their own reasoning activity and so are able to study the workings of reason as an
autonomous process. In such studies in the West, called epistemology,
three basic views appear. The dominant modern view sees reason essentially as calculation, as in Bacon, Descartes, Hobbes, or Popper.
"When a man *reasoneth*, he does nothing else but conceive a sum
total, from *addition* of parcels; or conceive a remainder, from sub-
traction of one sum from another. . . . reason, in this sense, is nothing
but *reckoning*, that is, adding and subtracting" (Hobbes 1957:25). A
second view sees reason as the interpretation of natural laws and their
application to specific instances and actions. Aquinas, Locke, Kant,
and Leo Strauss stand in this tradition. As Kant said, "Everything in
nature works according *to the conception* of laws, that is, according to
principle. . . . The deduction of actions from principles requires *reason*" (1949a:32). In the third view, as in the work of Plato, Hegel,
Whitehead, or Habermas, reason is a transcendental creativity, an
agency or activity that shapes or informs the world but stands above
it.

In this chapter I subordinate the first and second concepts of reason
and de-center and reformulate the third. That is, following Diesing
(1962, 1982), I show how interpretation of natural laws or calcula-

tion are merely two possible forms of reasoning, each appropriate to a different social order. Moreover, I argue that the conception of reason as creative can embrace the two other conceptions if this creativity is seen not as transcendental and idealist, but as a practical and social construction of meaning and order through discourse. In sum, I advance a conception of reason as rhetorical.

The view of reason as rhetorical has two advantages. First, as a heuristic, it facilitates the study of social and political organization as a human product. When one sees reason as purely mathematical, technical, or economic calculation (the first view), one tends to conceive of human reason as an attribute purely of individuals, either the system designer herself, or the persons who seek to optimize benefits within a pregiven set of norms or scarcities. Conversely, when one sees reason purely in terms of natural law and freedom (the second view), one tends to reify social systems into cybernetic processes or transcendental principles. In contrast to both these views, the conception of reason as a creative intersubjective practice encourages us to overcome the dualism of subject versus object and to understand both society and individuals as being emergent from social interactions.

A second advantage of the view of reason as social creativity is that it encourages an appreciation of alternative types of rationality, each with its own social form and telos. Such an appreciation invites a reflective awareness of the interests presupposed in one's own reasoning as well as in that of others. This implies, in turn, the concomitant virtues of tolerance for the limitations in other people's ways of thought, as well as responsibility for the consequences of one's own cognitive choices. In sum, this view of reason is both humanistic and critical, even as it affirms the relative validity of science within its proper domain.

I defend this rhetorical view of reason with four arguments or examples. The first argument is a discussion of Vico's ideas concerning the making of the world and knowledge through language. The second argument starts with a critique of the separation of the sociology of knowledge and the sociology of science, and concludes that scientific method, like other topics within the sociology of knowledge, must forfeit its absolutist privileges and be analyzed empirically as a rhetorical legitimation of belief. Third, I illustrate a sociology of reason as rhetorical by sketching some relations between the forms of reason and the forms of society in ancient Greece, in medieval Europe and, more copiously, in modern industrial states, to show how not only the preconditions for reason but its very essences are rhetorical in nature and function. A fourth argument invokes Garfinkel's analysis of reason as a performance constituted of essentially nonrational or arational elements. I apply this Garfinkelian view to the rational activity of planning in bureaus, firms, and nations, and demonstrate that this form of applied positive reason is rhetorical. I conclude by discussing some implications of this rhetorical view of reason for epistemology, social theory, and practice.

The last great spokesman for the view that knowledge emerges from civic discourse was Vico, who complained in the eighteenth century that prudential wisdom in politics was being replaced by the scientific rationalism of such scholars as Galileo, Descartes, and Hobbes:

> But now to speak of prudence in civic life, as human affairs are governed by chance and choice, . . . those who soley have truth in view only with difficulty understand the paths which these affairs take and, with still greater difficulty, their goals. . . . The impudent *scholars*, who go directly from the universally true to the singular, rupture the interconnection of life. The wise men, however, who attain the eternal truth by the uneven and insecure paths of practice, make a detour, as it is not possible to attain this by a direct road; and the thoughts which *these* conceive promise to remain useful for a long time, at least insofar as nature permits. ([1744]1972:34).

This view of reason as practical and discursive was integral to Vico's theory of language. In Vico's time it was still possible to distinguish three major views of language: nominalism, humanism, and logos mysticism. Nominalists followed Occam in separating language from reality, and cognition from sensation. This view gave rise eventually to the two dominant approaches of positivist theories of science and of language: rationalism and empiricism in the philosophy of science, and syntax and semantics in linguistics. In contrast, the Renaissance humanists stressed pragmatics and rhetoric, the practical wisdom of situated interactions and speech. By locating knowledge in the prudence and common sense of speech, however, the humanists were vulnerable to criticisms based on the theoretical knowledge of mathematics and natural science. To resist the challenge of abstract analysis, humanists derived support from Cicero, who had asserted the natural priority of the "art of discovery" (*ratio inveniendi*), rooted in everyday knowledge, over the procedure of logical-empirical demonstration (*ratio iudicandi*). Moreover the Renaissance rhetoricans also drank from the platonic and biblical springs of logos mysticism. Given the mystical powers of the word, rhetoricians saw language as neither a neutral tool nor casual usage, but instead as the medium of a transcendental act of communication. "Conceived as *kerygma* or disclosure of meaning, language participated in the ongoing and unfinished creation of the world. The alliance between humanism and logos-speculation reached its climactic expression in Vico's conception of a transcendental or universal 'philology,' a theory of the human authorship of the world through language" (Dallmayr 1981:153; see Apel 1963:20, 29, 83, 141).

Vico argued that ordinary language provides the pretheoretical basis and forms that are presupposed in every scientific analysis. But Vico's insights into the practical situational and interactional aspects of language and knowledge were drowned in the rising tide of positivism. The differences in emphasis between Descartes's rationalism and Bacon's empiricism, or between Leibniz's *vérités de raison* and *vérités de fait*, were overcome in the emerging concept of truth as the correlation of logical rigor with empirical content of statements. Instead of persuading the judgment of persons through argument, reason was seen as cognitive coercion through irrefutable logical and empirical proofs. Seen from Vico's rhetorical perspective, however, human language is not a mere conveyor or distorter of knowledge but rather its very medium and constitution. Truth is unavoidably linguistic, since logical rigor is a product of syntactic correctness, and empirical content is a function of semantic propriety.

In addition to syntactics and semantics, there is a third dimension of language—pragmatics. Pragmatics refers to language as performance, as a practical activity much like communal artisanry and crafts. For the ancients, all three of these dimensions of language—syntactics, semantics, and pragmatics—were part of rhetoric. Rhetoric seeks to establish reason as a moral-political practice, a communal speech activity, a pragmatics, even while preserving the syntactics of logical analysis and the semantics of empirical interpretations.

The view that rational discourse creates and is engendered by a social order is of course a principal finding and assumption of the sociology of knowledge. Most sociologists, however, have adhered to the positivists' refusal of self-reflection, with the result that the sociology of science (that is, of positivist science) has been separated from the sociology of knowledge. Sociologists of science study everything social about science except its claims to truth. Sociologists of knowledge treat all nonscientific forms of cognition as ideology. This segregation is perfectly consistent with the positivist distinction between the social processes by which knowledge might be gained and the logical or empirical validity of the results of such processes (e.g., Feigl 1970:4). In this view, discovery may be nonrational—psychological rather than cognitive. Verification (or falsification) of what is discovered, however, is seen as logical and objective, and as the feature that distinguishes science from ideology. In this spirit von Schelting criticized the "nonsense . . . that factual origins and social factors . . . in any way affect the value of ideas and conceptions thus originated, and especially the theoretic achievements" (1953:634). Similarly, Hans Speier said that "the validity of a judgment does not depend upon its genesis" (1953:682). Likewise, in a more sophisticated formulation, Herbert Dreyfus wrote: "The holistic point that *Vorhabe* of pre-cognitive practical know-how is necessary even in the natural sciences does not preclude the possibility of formulating scientific theories in which the interpretive practices of the observer play no internal role" (1980:16).

The positivist position might be called the immaculate conception of theory, in that the profane context of discovery is thought to have nothing to do with the sacred context of justification (for example see Reichenbach 1961:5ff.). But as I argue more fully in chapter 5, this distinction is largely illusory, in that the context of justification is itself theory laden (for examples see Feyerabend 1978; MacCormac 1976; Quine 1960).

The main point, however, which von Schelting and others overlook, is that the acceptability of the canons for such claims to validity do depend on their social context and genesis. Speier's assertions (and others) are consistent within the positivist paradigm, but they provide no basis for understanding the historical origins and social bases of the positivist conception of truth itself. Even if truth claims could be judged absolutely within a given canon of validity, such canons are themselves relative to sociohistorical contexts, and are therefore proper objects for sociohistorical investigation. Canons of validity, and epistemologies generally, are legitimations of belief, and as such they are rhetorical in nature.

Logical criteria of validity are not unitary. There are numerous forms of thought (e.g., teleology and determinism), and numerous criteria of adequacy (e.g., cogency and repeatability), the use and acceptability of which are highly variable in different times and places. The formulation, acceptance, or rejection of the criteria of truth are themselves open to cultural influence and therefore to sociological investigation. In segregating the sociology of knowledge from the sociology of science, however, positivists have declared that whatever validity depends upon, it cannot be examined as rhetorical (Mills 1974a:457–58). Instead of investigating the genesis and legitimation of scientific beliefs empirically and sociologically, therefore, positivist investigators have either reduced them to questions of personal psychology or vaporized them into universal rules and logic.

The relative, rhetorical, and socially constructed character of reason is also highlighted when different forms of rationality are examined in comparative and historical perspective. The leisured civic existence of the dominant class in Greece, for example, accounts in part for their use of socio-aesthetic criteria of truth. For these elites, *episteme* was apodictic knowledge gained through aesthetic-dialogal reflection on the regularities of nature. Such knowledge was not thought possible for practical political affairs, since the latter do not show the consistencies or regularities of occurrence that are the precondition for scientific investigation (Aristotle *Physics*, 2:viii; *Metaphysics*, 11:viii). Instead the cognitive capacity of political thought is *phronesis*, or in Cicero *prudentia*, a prudent judgment of particular cases. This view of political reason as prudence is consistent with the classical conception of the polis as an end in itself, the realization of human nature as a *zoon politikon*. Similarly, politics was meant to cultivate character in the struggle for the good life. Politics was thus an extension of ethics and pedagogy, and unlike modern positivist rationality, had nothing to do with management or technique (see MacIntyre 1981).

By contrast, the theocratic epistemology of the medieval period was influenced by, and helped to maintain, the hierarchically centralized position of the clerical elite, with its transnational political and intellectual power (Mills 1963:455). The high development of moral and theological reasoning was generated by and expressed in a society that conceived itself as a divine and moral order. Prudential judgment was still seen as the proper form of political reason, but the classical focus on civic liberty and justice shifted to civic order and peace. In the Greek polis, order was ideally realized through the direction of law and administration by citizens. For Thomas Aquinas, however, the proper order (*ordo*) was no longer that of the freedom of citizens, but that of *pax*, of tranquillity and peace. As the scope of government expanded, an interest in its quality diminished. The *ordo civitatis* now included labor, the family, and other domains that for Greeks had been outside the sphere of politics. Simultaneously, the emphasis shifted from self-direction by citizens to the power of the state, from polis to police (Habermas 1974).

These concepts of reason and politics continued in various forms until the early modern period when, with Machiavelli, Hobbes, and others, there began to emerge a science of politics (see MacIntyre 1981; Voegelin 1952). In this new science, the technical requirements of survival were divorced from moral obligations in politics. Reason became value neutral and instrumental. As Machiavelli put it, "The sole aim of the Prince must be to secure his life and his power. All means which he employs toward this end will be justified. . . . A Prince . . . [is] often forced, in order to preserve his Princedom, to act in opposition to God, faith, charity, humanity, and religion" (Machiavelli 1954:130). Sir Thomas More, substituting "everyone" for Machiavelli's "Prince," wrote that "everyone knows that however prosperous the republic may be, he will starve of hunger if he does not make some private provision for himself. And so he is forced to believe that he ought to take account of himself rather than the people, that is, others" (More 1965:124). With a similar focus on survival, Thomas Hobbes used Galilean mechanics and Cartesian logic to argue that absolute state power is the only barrier against a life that is nasty, brutish, and short. Seeing citizens' freedoms solely in terms of the monarch's supremacy, Hobbes identified freedom with the private individual, saw reason as instrumental calculation, and reconstituted the public sphere as that of the total power of the state.

Modern science itself came into being as part of such a transformation. As Basil Willey pointed out:

> The spots on the moon's surface might be due, theologically, to the fact that it was God's will they should be there: scientifically [however,] they might be "explained" as the craters of extinct volcanoes. The newer explanation may be said, not so much to contain "more" truth than the older, as to supply the *kind* of truth which was now demanded. An event was "explained" . . . when its history had been traced and described. . . . Interest was now directed to the *how*, the manner of causation. . . . One cannot define "explanation" absolutely: one can only say that it is a statement which satisfies the demands of a particular time or place. (1934:12–14)

As mechanism and determinism replaced organism and teleology, scientific technical rationality was harnessed to serve the amoral raison d'etat, and values, or the natural ends of man, were banished from rational public discourse (MacIntyre 1981). Luther, and later Kant, accepted these terms of discourse by clearly segregating the inward freedom and rationality of the individual from the rational administrative legality that governed his external conduct. The state was no longer seen as the arena for the public enactment of freedom. As freedom was privatized, ethics was thereby made subjective.

This privatized conception of reason and of reason's relation to politics continues today. In modern capitalist and communist states, the calculated rationality of survival dominates in the practice as well as in the theories of such rational practice. In contemporary positivist approaches to planning and governance, for example, scientific calculation is thought to be the only possible form of applied reason. Any method of societal direction that exceeds available scientific knowledge, as Karl Popper said, "simply does not exist: it is impossible" because it violates the principles of scientific method (1969:69).

The application of science to society takes the form of technical-

economic rationality. Technical rationality means the efficient
achievement of a single goal. As such it is a subset of economic rationality, which is the maximum achievement of a plurality of goals.
In technical rationality the end is given and the means may be varied.
In economic rationality there may be trade-offs between the ends and
the means. Most theorists of social planning agree with Popper in
assuming that technical-economic rationality is the whole of applied
rational thought, so they exclude nontechnical and noneconomic processes from reason. Ludwig von Mises for example, asserted that "the
economic principle is the fundamental principle of all rational action,
and not just a particular feature of a certain kind of rational action. . . . All rational action is therefore an act of economizing"
(1960:148).

This is a radically modern formulation. From ancient Greece to the
Renaissance, scientific theory was thought to concern universal or at
least highly regular phenomena, and so was not applied to the vag-
aries of practical affairs. Instead, applied reason was seen as prudential rather than instrumental. It was a process of reflection on the
good life and an interpretation of possible actions in light of this ideal.
But the modern positivist conception of applied rationality is ideological, not only because it denies the legitimacy of other forms of thought
and action, but also because it mystifies the political, economic, and
cultural preconditions for its own existence. That is, positivist rationality assumes, but does not account for, the cultural division of
means from ends, the definition of things as commodities, and the
social world of markets, all of which are required for technical-economic calculus.

None of this is to say, of course, that economizing is inappropriate
for a given range of problems—chiefly those involving scarcities between
comparable utilities. Such problems are properly called economic. What
is more interesting for an analysis of reason as rhetorical, however,
is the process by which circumstances come to be represented as
economic problems in the first place. One of the preconditions for
considering things as economic is that different ends can be seen as
comparable alternatives. The universalization of economic calculation therefore requires in practice the elimination of cultural barriers
to the comparability of ends. Americans, for example, may experience
a choice between sending their parents to a nursing home or keeping

them at home. In such a choice, some cost-benefit calculation certainly would play a role. For traditional Hindus, however, there are cultural barriers to the occurrence of a parallel situation, and if one somehow did arise it would not be experienced as one of choice, much less an economic choice. Similarly, it is not culturally permitted for an American male to calculate the value of sexual pleasure with his wife in comparison to his pleasure from their wedding presents, but such an economic calculation is possible for Trobrianders. These cultural limits are not experienced as cultural by members of the culture, of course, but are apprehended as absolute canons of decency, unquestionable duties, and the like.

Such cultural definitions and practices limit the application of instrumental rationality; yet the universalization of economizing presupposes an abolition of such boundaries. This is made clear by Swift's economic solution to the problems of famine and overpopulation: Eat the babies. Positivist reason cannot explain why this is not an adequate solution. It can calculate the efficiency of means toward comparable ends, but cannot assess the rationality of the ends themselves or the cultural acceptability of the means. Jeremy Bentham, writing with neither the irony of the eighteenth century nor the cybernetic mystification of the twentieth, expressed matter-of-factly the attitude satirized by Swift. "Money," said Bentham, "is . . . the measure of . . . pleasure. It is the same between pain and pain; as also between pain and pleasure. . . . If we would understand one another, we must make use of some common measure. The only common measure [that] the nature of things affords is money. . . . Those who are not satisfied with the accuracy of this instrument must find out some other that shall be more accurate, or bid adieu to politics and morals" (quoted by Mitchell 1918).

Bentham reduced morals and politics to economic comparability and commodity exchange. In the century since he wrote, this philosophic vision has been realized in a world in which virtually all things, including people, can be used as means and subjected to calculations of efficiency. This is a world of commodities. Commodities are not things as such, but things understood as comparable items and as means for getting something else. They are for exchange rather than for use. Commodities therefore presuppose a cash market or some functional equivalent, since without a market goods would remain incomparable, like apples and oranges, with no price to express their exchange value. Without commodity consciousness and a market mechanism, there is no rational and objective basis for comparing and choosing.

Economizing assumes both comparability of ends and commonality of means; that is, it requires that the use of particular means be culturally permitted for a plurality of ends. Work rules imposed by unions in factories are often irrational in just this sense, since they impose limits on the use of the means (human labor) for alternative ends. For example, if hod carriers are not permitted to lay bricks or bricklayers are not permitted to hang drywall, this will likely inhibit the most economical use of manpower through the most profit-efficient assignment of tasks.

Since commodities are neutral, the more that labor or anything else is turned into a commodity, the more it can be used purely as a means. The definition of things as commodities increases with the development of a market economy, and with the market economy more and more means become available to people in their daily lives. Actions formerly taken on the basis of tradition become allocation decisions in which means are allocated to alternative ends. Hence people come to think of decisions in terms of means and ends; they come to take as common sense what for Weber was only a heuristic model: that all practical rationality is a calculation of means and ends (Diesing 1962:36; see Parsons 1937:xiii).

The applied rationality of positivism is not only rhetorical but also ideological. It unreflectively denies other forms of rationality, and it universalizes and therefore mystifies the historically specific conditions for its possible operation—the cash nexus, commodity consciousness, and marketlike exchange. All of these preconditions are the interest of such applied reason, an interest that this form of rationality does not itself acknowledge.

In addition to comparative historical analyses, another step toward a sociology of reason as rhetorical has been taken by ethnomethodologists such as Harold Garfinkel and Aaron Cicourel, who have revealed what might be called the nonrational nature of rational conduct. By looking beyond the question-begging assumptions of functionalists (and beneath the analytic heuristics of Weberians), ethnomethodologists have shown that reason itself is composed of what ordinary folk would call nonrational activities. By unmasking rationality as itself a social, rhetorical construction, Garfinkel and others demystify the positivist mystique.

In theoretical as well as detailed observational studies, ethnomethodologists have demonstrated how social actors employ rationality retrospectively to account for actions that, from a rationalistic point of view, were chaotic and stumbling when performed. For example, in "Some Rules of Correct Decision that Jurors Respect" (1967:104–55), Garfinkel described in detail the talk, bargaining, and muddling that go on in jury discussions, and how rules emerge from this process, rather than guide it. At first the jurors do not quite know what they are doing, but as their sentiments take shape through the contesting of various viewpoints, they begin to invoke rules of evidence and rationality to justify positions they have taken or are in the process of forming. The rational justification of their decisions crystallizes at about the time the decisions do, or in many cases even afterwards, when a summary is being prepared for presentation to the court. Thus Garfinkel showed how rationality does not instruct us as to what action to take, nor is it a property inherent in conduct or in the social system. Instead rationality emerges in discursive interaction, and is then used retrospectively or reflexively to legitimize what has already taken place or is being enacted.

Ironically, our interpretation of Garfinkel's studies reveals their affinity with the neo-Marxist critique of instrumental reason. Horkheimer (1974a) and Adorno (1973), to name but two such theorists, have argued that means-ends rationality serves as an instrument as well as a rationale for technocratic domination. For example, just as rationality can provide a rhetoric for legitimizing past conduct (a la Garfinkel's microsociology), so it can be employed as a prospective rhetoric for closing off unwanted alternatives and advancing one's own agenda. Moreover, by focusing discourse on the efficiency of alternative means, instrumental reason displaces attention from the inappropriateness of pregiven ends and the class interests that they serve.

A principal use of rationality as a prospective rhetoric is the planning done by firms, agencies, and nations. The organizational plan, for example, can be seen not as a set of instructions for what will actually take place, but rather as a rhetorical intervention to build constituency, to define the limits of responsible opinion, and in general to impose the planners' or managers' definition of reality upon discourse and conduct within and around the organization. Just as statements made by jurors must be susceptible to rationalization in terms of the emergent rules of evidence, so public talk about what goes on within organizations must be couched in terms of how it rationally serves (the directorate's statement of) the organization's nature, purpose, and goals.

This rhetorical function of rationality appears inevitable. For example, even if the organizational plan is taken seriously as a set of instructions for future action, it is readily reinterpretable as a vocabulary for covering the difficulties that will unfold as attempts are made to follow it. That is, in actual practice the plan of action produces problems, the responses to which are reconceptualized as the solution or achievement of the organization's goals. According to Garfinkel, this upside-down process is in fact what rationality is all about. A good example of this is the work of coroners, who must classify bodies as dead by "accident," "criminal intent," "suicide," or "natural causes." According to coroners' instructions, the number of definitions they may use for dead bodies is limited. However, corpses do not come already labeled. The coroners' instructions are thus in effect instructions on how to generate a set of difficulties in naming, the solution of which will constitute the production of the instruction's goals. In doing their duty, coroners find convenient but nonrational mechanisms for solving the problem of fitting recalcitrant cadavers into the limited categories of an organizational agenda. Such postmortem efforts to restate an ad hoc process in terms of some formal structure is that of which rational action is constituted (Garfinkel 1967:18; Douglas 1967:186–88).

The ethnomethodologists have also performed this sort of analysis on the activities of reasoning engaged in by scientists. And they have found scientific discourse to be just as pieced together as the production of nonscientific realities. Even more embarrassing, they have found that this historically specific, patched-together aspect of formal explanations is not merely a flaw or an embellishment on scientific rationality. Instead, it is the means by which that rationality is itself created. It is not a knowledge of the formal rules themselves so much as tacit knowledge and skill in applying these rules to specific settings that defines a person as a member of a given scientific community (Polanyi 1958). And in this process of applying the rules, the formal protocols of reason and decision making function largely as covering accounts for purposive reality constructions that were put together in response to local economic requirements, carrer pressures, and other nonrational contingencies. All of us—scientists included—are continually engaged as on-the-street or at-the-lab-bench rhetoricians.

Thus rather than being a guiding rule of individual, organizational, or scientific life, rationality turns out to be a rhetorical achievement— a symbolic product that is constructed through speech and actions which in themselves are nonrational. We could even say that this dichotomy between rationality and nonrationality is itself ultimately unfounded, since it emerges in our culture mainly from the legitimacy of "rational" conduct and the illegitimacy of "nonrational" conduct. Precisely because this high evaluation of rationality prevails in the modern West, Westerners tend to legitimize their activities by accounting for them with rationalistic vocabularies of motive. At the level of microprocesses, however, the dichotomy between rational and nonrational conduct breaks down completely, suggesting that both these forms of activity have the same basic components.

Such a radical critique also suggests a means of radically reformulating our sociological understanding of reason. Rather than seeing reason solely as a conscious calculus of individuals or an unconscious casuistry of systems, we may now focus on persons and groups as engaged in continuing processes of constructing rationality.

All these observations support a view of reason as a civic rhetorical practice, for all of them illuminate the ongoing creativity of members within social and linguistic systems. Reason is not something that belongs only to experts. Instead it exists through public discourse. For Marxists as well as for ethnomethodologists, reason is a practical human activity, a dialectic of form and performance. Social structures canalize rational thought; reasoning creates and recreates social structures. Economic reasoning creates a market system, legal reasoning creates a world of law, and moral discourse creates a moral order. The reverse, of course, is also true. Reason is the child of the order it creates (Diesing 1962:243). It is not a matter of transcendent reason working upon the world, but of persons creating ordered worlds through rational processes, worlds that embody reason in their structured properties and thus serve as guides and contexts for further creative human reason. For example, modern economies are orders that embody millions of decisions of marginal utility, a form of reasoning that is possible because markets exist which enable the comparability of various raw materials and end products. Similarly, a legal order embodies the multifarious decisions of judges past, thereby providing algorithms of tradition as well as contexts of creativity for judges present. A legal order can develop only through the continuous, historical application of jurisprudential reasoning to cases. Jurisprudence is a public practice, a collective civic reasoning about the law (Diesing 1962). As Garfinkel noted, participants in particular cases or transactions may focus only on validating a privilege or making a deal. But the rules of evidence or calculations of efficiency that they invoke to justify their claims are those of the legal or commercial or scientific orders, just as these orders exist in and are continually reconstituted through such invocations and usages.

In such a conception of reason as rhetorical, abstract individual reasoning and concrete social order are both seen as emergent from practical intersubjective symbolic action, two moments in the same dialectic, each engendering the other.

If reason for humans is a rhetorical construction, if facts like fictions are things made, then the absolutist pretensions of positivist science are shattered, and new paths are opened between literature and science, between subjective and objective ways of knowing, between interpretation and explanation, and between public action and personal praxis. Just as rhetorical analysis reveals the relative objectivity of fiction in literature, so it also destroys the fiction of absolute objectivity in science. The writer and the reader, the scientist and her public, are now seen as joined in a sociohistorical world, and our focus becomes one of exploring the life interests that inform the rhetor and her audiences. While following the canons of her craft—while achieving the aesthetic distance or scientific objectivity that is available through her methods—the rhetor still constructs her report in the context of an imagined future and an historical past, a frame of time and experience that she presumes to share with her audience, if not her subjects. The representations of the sociologist, like any writer/rhetor, can exist only within the boundary of her sociohistorical situation (Wellmer 1971:33). Consequently, her findings "remain suggestions, which have to be proven not only in regard to the material already available, but also in regard to the future historical practice of human beings," a practice that will create its own historical context and its own vision of the future.

Four

Theories of Rhetoric and the Rhetoric of Theories

Emile Durkheim and the Political Symbology of Sociological Truth

> Since the world expressed by the entire system of concepts is the
> world as society represents it to itself, society alone can furnish the
> generalized notions according to which such a world must be
> represented. . . . Since the universe does not exist except insofar as
> it is thought, and since it can be thought totally only by society
> itself, it takes its place within society, becomes a part of society's
> interior life, while society may thus be seen as that totality outside
> of which nothing else exists. . . . The world is inside of society.
> It is not at all true that concepts, even when constructed according
> to the rules of science, get their authority uniquely from their
> objective value. . . . In the last resort, the value which we attribute
> to science depends upon the idea which we collectively form of its
> nature and role in life; that is as much as to say that it expresses a
> state of public opinion. In all social life, in fact, science rests upon
> opinion. . . . Science continues to be dependent upon opinion at the
> very moment when it seems to be making its laws; for it is from
> opinion that it holds the force necessary to act upon opinion.
> Durkheim (1965a:490, 486–87)

ALL SPEECH IS POLITICAL. Explicitly political speech, such as that used in
election campaigns, employs virtually all other forms of discourse;
similarly, relations of power and authority are aspects of even ostensibly nonpolitical speech. The political properties of both everyday talk
and scientific speech may be illuminated by a political analysis of
language or by a social phenomenology of discourse; that is, by
rhetoric.[1]

That social realities are created through symbolic and especially
linguistic interaction is a commonplace. In accepting this view many
social scientists, like abandoned children, have refused the foster care
of traditional positivism and have instead sought to return to their
philosophic home, to find in their natural parents a legitimation of
their social-theoretical existence.[2] Several candidate genitors have
been uncovered. For example, it has been noted that such theories of
knowledge as pragmatism, ordinary-language philosophy, hermeneu-

tics, existential phenomenology, and Kuhnian history of science over-
lap not only in their rejection of Cartesian and Baconian assumptions,
but also in their conception of knowledge as embedded in a shared
historical and social world. In this conception, scientific theories, like
fictional narratives or political speeches, are necessarily based on
group practices and commonsense understandings. The articulations
of reality constituted by science are seen in these views as intersubjective constructions, symbolic public realities whose truth is not independent of the political and linguistic processes and purposes by
which they are engendered.

Given this awareness, it is surprising that social scientists have
made little use of theories of rhetoric to justify a new, more sophisticated research practice, because rhetoric is precisely the study of the
persuasive use of language.[3] The purpose of this chapter is therefore
to propose critical rhetoric as a mode of self-understanding for social
scientists. In this project, my own rhetorical strategy is as follows:
First, I outline the history of rhetoric and some contemporary theories. Second, I focus this rhetorical perspective on social-science theory as a form of political speech; I do this by comparing everyday
speech with texts written by Emile Durkheim, showing that both are
rhetorical constructions through and through. I argue that, though we
use different symbol systems as scientists than as ordinary people, in
both capacities we are engaged in the creation and advocacy of realities through the invention, elaboration, or imposition of discourse.

Rhetoric as Epistemic, Epistemology as Rhetorical

The political interpretation of the inner meaning of speech was not
invented by Marxists or ethnomethodologists or political sociologists.
Over two thousand years ago theories of discourse developed in legal,
military, religious, and other public settings. The name of this theory
was rhetoric (Eagleton 1981:101; see Corcoran 1979; McGee 1977;
Ong 1971:61). Its goals were to explain relationships between the
practice of language and the exercise of power and to train elites to
use speech effectively for political purposes. Stylistic analysis was
therefore a tool for political hegemony, because the correct use of
stylistic devices enabled one to establish ideological dominance in the
arenas that counted—in the tribunals, the public forums, and the

military counsels. Because an aesthetic error could result in a political disaster, literary criticism was not the scholastic pursuit it became in the Middle Ages, nor was it the largely academic exercise that it is today. Instead the criticism of speech and texts was entirely integrated with the public social relations of the ancient state.

As the Greek polis and the Roman republic declined, however, so did the practice of political discourse in public assemblies. Rhetorical analysis became the analysis of texts, more a scholastic than a civic pursuit. Yet rhetoric and the connection between public symbolism and the collective life continued to be honored throughout the Renaissance. The symbolism of Christianity was exoteric and didactic; allegorical pageantry pervaded public life; seals, emblems and coats of arms expressed the identities of persons, dynasties, guilds, and cities; and the gardens and buildings of the time, like the front pages of Renaissance books, were rich in symbolic associations that invited textual analysis. Even Bacon, often an enemy of symbols, thought enough of them to provide his New Atlanteans with an elaborate iconography. The mastery of symbols continued to be symbolic of power (Yates 1972:89–127; Kerrigan 1980:265).

During the seventeenth century, however, Protestants revived religious scripture and thereby loosened the hold of Latin oral and aesthetic precedents in the educational system; at the same time, rationalists and empiricists scorned classical authorities (Debus 1970; Webster 1976). Reformers such as Jan Comenius devalued literary and humanistic education, calling for a return to "things." Thomas Sprat, historian of the Royal Society, argued that eloquence distorts our capacity to think (Rossi 1970). Gradually thought became disassociated from speech, rhetorical theories of language were narrowed to apply only to stylistic adornments or purely literary works, semantics was separated from pragmatics, and romantic ideas of inspiration, natural diction, and self-expression severed originality from its root connection with origins in a historical community (Kerrigan 1980:275).

By the mid-nineteenth century, when positivist science claimed regnancy over all forms of knowing, rhetoric was relegated to the psychology of crowds or was regarded as a conveyor or ornament for truths elsewhere discovered. The positivists' unlimited faith in deductive logic and direct observation, their separation of cognitive from affective awareness, their refusal to grant intersubjectivity or audience agreement as criteria for knowledge, and their lack of interest in the way that the contact of minds alters the shape of truth—all these militated against conceiving rhetoric as having epistemic status (Leff 1978:77; see Nelson 1983).

Rhetoric became separated from the general theory of knowledge and communication; it referred to methods of persuasion rather than to methods of truth. Symbols, the instruments of persuasive discourse, were seen as interfering with the objective perception of reality. The Enlightenment faith in reason was replaced by a new faith in science. Science was thought to have bypassed rhetoric with such procedures as operationalization, pointer-reader indicators, and other techniques for locating concepts directly in observable facts. Evidence had replaced persuasion: the personal evidence of Protestantism, the rational evidence of Cartesianism, or the sensible evidence of empiricism (Perelman 1982:7). And rhetoric was considered to be either absorbed into logic or to reside in entirely different and alien domains—the domains of fiction or politics, domains where the credence of the audience mattered and the truth of the statement did not. In France, for example, just as Durkheimian sociology was being instituted as part of its national curriculum, the French Ministry of Education ended the teaching of rhetoric as the general study of discourse and consigned it instead to the *classe de littérature*, where it provided an emblem of a classical education and a veneer of cultivation to the upwardly mobile children of the bourgeoisie. This too militated against the conception of rhetoric as epistemic.

Most rhetoricians accepted this subordination. But there was also a countermovement that sought to elevate the disciplinary problems of literary criticism to the level of general philosophic theory. The countermovement was begun in Germany by Schiller, Schlegel, and Novalis.[4] Schiller defined modern or romantic art as being characteristically self-conscious, reflective, and critical, in contrast to the naive and immediate naturalism of classical art. Schlegel extended this distinction into a criterion for all art, and for criticism as well. "Great works of art criticize themselves," he said in his introduction of the book reviews of the *Athenaeum* in 1798. "The work of criticism is therefore superfluous unless it is itself a work of art as independent of the work it criticizes as that work is independent of the material that went into it."

A contemporary exemplar of this approach is Walter Benjamin. In the "Epistemo-Critical Prologue" to his essay on German baroque drama, Benjamin sketched a theory of criticism as an element of a general epistemology. Unlike either deterministic or purely formalistic critics before him, Benjamin treated the political, moral, and social aspects of the drama as formal elements of the work itself, examining them exactly as he did the figures of speech, the verse forms, and the grammatical structure of the style. In this way Benjamin eschewed the usual historical approach that simplifies and reduces the work to signifying something outside itself, and also avoided the usual formalist approach that blinds itself to the larger social-contextual aspects of art (Rosen 1977:37). Instead, Benjamin engaged in a social analysis of the text and a textual analysis of its sociohistorical context.

Until recently, rhetoric as an intellectual discipline had been cut off from these developments in literary theory. Rhetoricians tended to accept the positivists' claims that only science yields *episteme*—truth—and that all else is *doxa*, mere opinion. And having abandoned the criticism of science to logicians, rhetoricians found themselves restricted to stylistic analyses, in which style was defined as an embellishment instead of a constituent of the truth or reality that was conveyed.

This paradigm of rhetoric has been changing, however, and a new critical theory of rhetoric has emerged. In this view, Plato and Aristotle were wrong, and Gorgias of Leontine was right.[5] Gorgias held that rhetoric is not merely a sophistical way of persuading innocents that illogical arguments are valid. Instead, for Gorgias rhetoric was basic to the constitution of logical discourse. Gorgias denied the possibility of absolute and immutable knowledge and instead advanced a dialectical and consensualist theory of truth. Truth is a matter of collective opinion gained through persuasive argumentation. We know what we know on the basis of encounters with actual situations as they are defined by the perceptual screen of language. As its antithetical structure suggests, language operates through conflict and is therefore fundamentally persuasive in character. Language creates the conviction of reality and truth by framing our responses in terms of simple oppositions, models and antimodels that allow us to make sense of the world. "Consequently, the rhetor commands the whole field of epistemology" (Leff 1978:84).

Gorgias's perspective is being revived. There is "a heightened interest in the relationship between rhetoric and epistemology," says Leff (1978:73). "At any given moment," says Wander, "what we know to exist in the world is a product of an evolving set of human agreements" (1976:226). "It seems safe to conclude," asserts Cherwitz, "that there is a new rhetoric," grounded not in the quest to make truth effective, but rather in the quest to evoke truth via rhetoric (1977:219). "Rhetoric can no longer be seen simply as a means of persuasion," adds Ognibene. "It becomes instead the medium in which selves grow" (1976:84). "While rhetoric may be defined in many ways and on many levels," says Brummett, "it is in the deepest and most fundamental sense the *advocacy of realities*" (1976:31). "In many circumstances," notes Weimer, "one can 'know' only through engagement in rhetorical activity" (1977:19). We may view "rhetoric," concludes Scott, "as epistemic" (1967).

Indeed, today an even stronger claim is made: not only that rhetoric is epistemic, but also that epistemology and ontology are themselves rhetorical. In this view, reality is regarded as fundamentally symbolic, action is seen as embodied language, and language therefore becomes the primary unit of empirical knowledge. This perspective has been elaborated by Kenneth Burke, who established a "total distinction between the realms of (symbolic) action and (nonsymbolic) motion." Burke then argued that, whereas "action is not reducible to motion," symbolic action does encompass brute motion. Though the modes of analysis of natural science cannot explain the nature of literature, for example, the methods of symbolic interpretation can help us understand the "literature" of nature. "I began to see," said Burke, "how my defining literary form in terms of 'expectations' could be extended to the empirical notion of 'reality' itself as a structure of expectations" (1976:65). To this way of thinking, words are not mere copies of things. Instead, things are signs for words. In the beginning was the logos. "Things" already are "words"; that is, things are symbolic constructions that we invest with a noumenal or objective reality. Burke's view is not merely the reverse of the behavioristic dictum that words are signs for things; it also transvalues that dictum and becomes interchangeable with it. In Burke's linguistic realism, both words and things are signs. They reciprocally form and inform each other. Each is a symptom of a larger reality. Each is constructed through collective experience in the inter-subjective life worlds of those persons who share a given paradigm, who operate within the same range of rules and practices. Words and things are made, as Burke would say, by persons who "entitle" their worlds similarly (Burke 1966:368).

The view of rhetoric as central in the constitution of truth holds that all social reality is symbolic, and that there is no reality that is not experienced through a social matrix of discourse. In this critical rhetorical view, rather than there being a single reality of which nonscientific accounts are erroneous representations, there are multiple ways of construing realities, each of which is privileged for the reality so construed. For example, empirical science provides special access to reality defined as a naturalistic fact world. Art theory affords superior entry to the world defined as an object for aesthetic contemplation. Yet these particular utilities of various symbol systems do not warrant an absolute and universal priority for any one over the others. Each is more or less appropriate for certain purposes with reference to certain domains. Each symbol system constitutes a reality according to its aims and resources. This is equally true of the world of common sense and the specialized worlds of scientific truth.

Yet the question remains as to what particular rhetoric is involved in the construction of realities, or the statements about reality, that are to be taken as true. Here our understanding is incomplete, but I would suggest that the authorization of perceptions as veracious requires representations of reality that are vivacious. That is, the representation—the theory, explanation, description, or interpretation—must provide an economical and perspicuous mimesis. To elicit credence, such representations not only must have an internal consistency, but in addition must be consistent with the rules and assumptions that govern that domain of discourse. For example, the everyday statement, "The baby cried so the mother picked it up," is much more credible than "The baby cried so the leopard picked it up," because "mother" is more consistent with the domain of babydom than is "leopard." Similarly, if the first statement were put, "I heard the baby cry, and then I saw its mother pick it up," this would be still more credible than "The voices of my ancestors told me in a dream that when the baby cried the leopard picked it up," because the former version assumes a fact world and employs accepted observational techniques for knowing this world.

Such rules and assumptions are not merely abstract universal norms, as they might appear to be if formulated in purely logical, rather than rhetorical, language. Such rules and assumptions involve interactive social processes, communitarian conventions, historically inherited protocols, and political power. For example, imagine our community of discourse to be a traditional African village instead of (as we might have supposed) a modern Western group. In such a context the sentence, "My ancestors appeared in a dream" might be taken as self-evidently veracious. The point in both cases, however, is that the claims of each are authorized by their respective rules of perception and interpretation. It is according to the vivacity of a representation in terms of the communitarian assumptions of its usual domain that the alternative explanations or descriptions advanced within their auspices are judged to be believable, adequate, true, or compelling. These criteria of truth are aesthetic and political—that is, rhetorical.

The principal though not the exclusive vehicle through which such mediations occur is language. This is no less true of scientific as it is of fictional or political symbolizations. As Chaim Perelman pointed out, sociological practice is governed by rules of method that provide for its objectivity and validity. But such rules of discourse for any public emerge socially and historically, and cannot themselves have apodictic warrant. Thus to choose social science as one's preferred domain or mode of discourse, or to choose a tradition within sociology itself, cannot be an objective or scientific decision, since it is a choice between the traditions by which objectivity and science themselves are defined (Perelman and Olbrechts-Tyteca 1969; Overington 1982).

Feyerabend said something similar in his discussion of "observational theories," where he held that a fact is a fact only in terms of some theory of what constitutes valid observations. The theories are themselves peculiar to given historical settings. Direct perception in this view, always has ideational elements. There can be no innocent eye, because what counts as observational has a historical character and depends on theories that may be outdated or not held consciously at all. In criticizing observational theories, moreover, one invokes other observations that are themselves equally theoretical (Feyerabend 1978; Ferguson 1973).[7] As Nietzsche showed us, there is no escape from this. There is no such thing as a natural, unrhetorical, politically neutral language that articulates the world without some point of view. "Language is itself the result of rhetorical tricks and devices. Tropes are not something that can be added or subtracted from language at will: they are its truest nature" (Nietzsche 1960; de Man 1974:35).

The use of scientific methodology does not permit the social scientist to avoid rhetorical discourse. Instead the scientist's lack of self-consciousness about the assumptions and limits of such a method of logic results in his using a naive and immoral rhetoric. This is the rhetoric of antirhetoric, a pretence that truth claims can have an absolute foundation. As Weigert put it, the sociologist engages in "a naive rhetoric of possible identity deceptions" whenever he "adopts the epistemological position that insists that a group of concepts and propositions is unbiased and value-free simply because it is labeled a 'theory,'" or whenever he presents a reconstructed logic of research as the way in which the research actually took place (Weigert 1970:112; see Burke 1965:24; Kaplan 1964). The scientist also misleads himself and his public if he presumes to have found a routine method for insuring that the reality he intends to measure is actually the one he is measuring and, further, that this reality is identical to the concept in which he is interested; or if he asserts that choices of problems in applied research are intellectual and never economic; or if he holds that the practice and results of sociology, unlike any other social practice or knowledge, are guaranteed by an ultimately privileged epistemology.

These political dimensions of sociological texts become clearer when we remember that any communication is also a commitment. Any formalized language is a political phenomenon in the sense that it constitutes a structure of authority (Pocock 1973:15). The communication, and especially a highly formalized scientific or literary communication, not only conveys information but also defines a relationship between author and audience, between rhetor and public, and between the persons in the communicative act. The content of the text may be factual or fictional, correct or invalid. The commitment implied by the text refers to what sort of a message it is to be taken as, and in so doing it defines the relationship between the communicants. Extending the point, we could say that communication imposes comportment, in that the definition of the relationship as conveyed through language involves roles to be performed, tasks and duties, and rules about prescribed or necessary conduct. In the prison house of language, a sentence is also a "sentence," as Kafka showed in his tale, "In the Penal Colony," where the printing press is an instrument of torture.[8]

Normally the denotative, explicit aspects of a text convey the informational content, whereas the commitment or relationship aspect is conveyed implicitly or even nontextually by the manner or context of the text. An inauthentic communication is one in which these two dimensions are dissonant. Denying such dissonance or refusing responsibility for it is frequent in positivistic discourse in the human studies. Such a suppression of awareness implies not only methodological naivete but also false consciousness. As Habermas noted, such inauthentic communication is a basic means for imposing and maintaining relationships of domination. In such relationships there is typically little recognition of either the rights of subordinates to share in the establishment of the basic rules of the interaction or the responsibility of superordinates for having established them. The superordinate rhetor typically seeks to restrict communication to the denotative content and forbid discussion of the terms of the relationship that she has imposed.[9]

Social Science as Persuasive Discourse

Having spoken of the rhetorical character of social thought, I now undertake a more detailed rhetorical analysis of both everyday speech and social-science discourse itself. I suggest that social research is constructed rhetorically, that it is a set of meanings created in response to problems that arise in specific political and historical contexts.

This project is facilitated by the findings of ethnomethodology, a radically reflexive approach to empirical social research. I shall employ the method of speech analysis used by ethnomethodologists to interpret accounts people give in everyday life. Then I will turn this method toward sociological accounts given by behavioral scientists. The results, I hope, will show that sociology is itself a way to construct reality through language, not unlike the way we construct reality as we interpret our workaday worlds.[10]

To illustrate the parallel between the way we produce accounts in everyday life and the way social scientists produce accounts, I draw

on an analysis of a New York City radio talk show done by Howard
Schwartz and a study of Emile Durkheim's *Suicide* done by Michael
Overington. One text is literally pedestrian and the other is figur-
atively scientific. By comparing and interpreting these texts through
paraphrases and quotations, I hope to reveal parallel rhetorical structures in the discourse of Durkheim and that of the talk show host,
suggesting that social science, like everyday speech, is a contingent,
invented account designed to persuade a particular audience in order
to achieve a certain effect. Let us turn to the transcript of the show:

> CALLER: I have a gripe.
> HOST: What's the gripe, dear?
> C: Well, eh, the trains. You know, the people—Uh, why do
> they not respect the so-called white cane? In other words,
> if they see me with the cane traveling the city et cetera,
> why do they not give me the so-called right of way?
> H: Well they probably do, once they see it. Hu, the trouble
> is—
> C: No, they don't, Brad.
> H: How d'you know?
> C: Because I've been on the trains before and they don't care
> whether I live or die.
> H: Well—
> C: (interrupting) Uh—
> H: Dear, wait, wait, wait, wait!
> C: Go ahead.
> H: Now, N—
> C: (interrupting) Okay—
> H: Don't ask a question and then answer it.
> C: Go ahead.
> H: Uh, you see, what happens, 'specially with New Yorkers,
> is that they get all preoccupied with their own problems—
> C: Yes.
> H: —with the fallout and the pollution and the landlord—
> C: Yeah, mm hm.
> H: —and they don't—
> C: (tries to interrupt)
> H: Now, wait a minute, let me finish.
> C: Go ahead.
> H: And they don't notice.

We can interpret this as an instance of a sociological problem in
everyday life: People should defer to a blind woman and yet they don't.

Why not? To answer this question the host invents a theory. He hy-pothesizes that the people in the New York subways must be New Yorkers, and by sympathetic identification he imagines what the pre-occupations of such persons might be. They have "worries" that "make them blind to her blindness—they are 'preoccupied,' they 'don't notice'. . . . What an elegant explanation! She above all people should appreciate the difficulties of being blind!'" (Schwartz 1980:32).

Obviously the facts of the matter—whether the subway riders are all New Yorkers, and whether they really worry about pollution and the landlord—are not known precisely. But they don't need to be; the announcer's theory and the degree of exactitude of the data needed to support it have only to be appropriate to the requirements of the sit-uation. The announcer's account is built on the spot, during the course of an interaction, exactly when it is needed, using the time, evidence, knowledge, and background assumptions that are avail-able. It is for the particular situation that the explanation is con-sciously being constructed. And in fact the announcer's response is designed to fit the problem as the caller has verbally presented it, as the following symmetries suggest (Schwartz 1980:33):

1. She speaks in generalities.   He replies in generalities.
2. Her problem is a complaint.   His explanation is an excuse.
3. She has problems.   They have problems.
4. She is blind.   They are blind.

I now want to argue that there is a fundamental affinity between this pedestrian explanation and the scientific account of suicide given by Emile Durkheim. There is little dispute that Durkheim's treatise is one of the most important sociological works ever produced. Indeed, knowledge of and respect for *Suicide* is a sine qua non of professional acceptability for the budding sociologist. Yet the grounds of *Suicide*'s classic status are not obvious. Durkheim's statistical data were gener-ally available in prior work, and his theory of suicide is conceptually ambiguous, tautological, and not genuinely tested. Nonetheless, as Pope said after his careful documentation of the flaws of this tome, "*Suicide* remains a monument" (Pope 1976:204; see Overington 1978b:1). My question is, How come?

The answer to this question is that *Suicide* is a rhetorical tour de force, a brilliant political use of language in response to the "problem" Durkheim confronted (Overington 1978b:1). In his discussion of the rise of the Durkheimians in French universities, Terry Clark (1972) described the intellectual and social situation that surrounded the appearance of Durkheim's book. In this situation, three factors were salient. First, at the time that *Suicide* appeared there were other groups of sociologists working whose approaches were different from Durkheim's. Second, important bureaucrats in the Ministry of Education were anxious to reform French higher education and to expose young pedagogues to some kind of scientific anticlerical morality. Moreover this concern for reform marked the ascendancy in public and intellectual life of men like Durkheim—bureaucrats and academics rationally committed to scientific morality and republican meritocracy. Third, the professorial and curricular structure of French universities was rigidly unresponsive to change. "To find a place for itself, sociology had to be flexible enough for its adherents to find appointments in philosophy and pedagogy in competition with philosophers, pedagogues, and psychologists" (Overington 1978b:4).

The logical aspects of Durkheim's argument have been amply discussed elsewhere (e.g., Douglas 1967; La Capra 1972; Pope 1976; Wallwork 1972). Yet considering this logic rhetorically in terms of its larger context, the situational problem that Durkheim faced and the response that he made to it display a striking parallel to the symmetry noted above between the blind woman's problem and the radio host's explanation:

Problem in Durkheim's Context	*Response in Durkheim's Text*
1. Senior bureaucrats in the Ministry of Education sought a secular, anticlerical ethical calculus as a basis of pedagogy and republican morality.	Social facts are things; suicide (though an ultimate moral choice) can be understood naturalistically and analyzed with strictly scientific, statistical methods. "The antithesis between science and ethics disappears. To govern our relations with men, it is not necessary to resort to any other means than those which we use to govern our relations with things" (1960:36). "Our principle is to extend scientific rationalism to human conduct in showing that, considered in the past, it is reducible to relations of cause and effect which a no less rational

operation can transform into rules for the future" (1965b:ix). "[Our task is to] discover the rational substitutes for these religious notions which for so long have served as the vehicle for the most essential of moral ideas" (1963:3, 9, 7–8).

2. Republicanism, capitalism, and meritocracy had to be shown to be preferable to monarchism, feudalism, and moral dominance by the Church.

"Organic" solidarity is characteristic of the machine age, whereas "mechanical" solidarity is typical of preindustrial society! Organic solidarity promotes personal development and social interdependence. "Our society must restore the consciousness of its organic unity. . . . No doubt these ideas will become truly efficacious only if they spread into the depths of society, but for that it is first necessary that we elaborate them scientifically in the university. To contribute to this end to the extent of my powers will be my principal concern" (1888:48–49).

3. Present difficulties had to be accounted for.

Present difficulties, each as anomie, are merely transitional. "We are going through a stage of transition and moral mediocrity. The great things of the past which filled our fathers with enthusiasm do not excite the same ardour in us . . . but as yet there is nothing to replace them. . . . In a word, the old gods are growing old or already dead, and others are not yet born" (1965:475).

4. Durkheimian sociology required a special place in the universities of France.

Durkheimian sociology is different from and superior to other sociologies. It is both moral and scientific, yet it is distinct from either philosophy or psychology. "To sum up, the distinctive characteristics of our method are as follows: First, it is entirely independent of philosophy. . . . In the second place, our method is objective. . . . The third trait that characterizes our method is that it is exclusively sociological [and neither psychic nor organic]" (1965b:Conclusion; see also 1909:755–56).

The classic status of Durkheim's *Suicide* can be interpreted as a product of brilliant rhetorical intervention.[11] Though his manifest explanation of suicide was weak, Durkheim offered a powerful latent interpretation of French society of his time. And under the banner of this interpretation, the Durkehimians did firmly implant themselves in the French university system, and Durkheim's recommendations for French civic pedagogy were widely influential (Overington 1978b). Said one supporter, "The introduction of the teaching of sociology in our normal schools . . . marked a most important date on the sundial of republican spiritual power" (Thibaudet 1927:222–23). Said one critic, "The requirement that M. Durkheim's sociology be taught in the two hundred normal schools of France is among the gravest perils to which our country is subjected" (Izoulet, quoted in Bougle 1935:168n). "Such has been the influence of Durkheim in our University that he seems to have monopolized sociology. . . . In our discussions, in our manuals, Durkheimian sociology and sociology *tout court* seem to be more and more synonymous" (Lacombe 1926:35).

The optimistic liberalism, naive corporatism, and mystical scientism of Durkheimians did not survive the slaughters of World War I, the panic and depression, the fall of Blum, and the capitulation to Fascism. After World War II, Durkheimian sociology began to be replaced by Marxism, phenomenology, and existentialism—ideas imported from Germany. Durkheimian thought is still powerful in France among historians and anthropologists, who do not study their own society. But sociology in France for a long time has not been very Durkheimian. Instead, macrosocial analyses were taken over by Marxist philosophers, social-psychological investigations by existential phenomenologists, and empirical studies by economists and urban planners. With the emergence of a techno-administrative style of governance under Giscard d'Estaing and François Mitterrand, however, Durkheimian sociology experienced a revival. In England, with great political stability and a liberalism more conservative than that of France, Durkheimian ideas came to dominate the scientific study of faraway primitive tribes, but was little used for understanding modern society, where social-reformist discourse and technical-economic analyses prevailed. In Germany, Durkheimian sociology has had little impact, given the very different political context of social-science discourse in that nation (Drouard 1982; Hawthorne 1976; Padioleau and Eymeriat 1982).[12]

In the twentieth century it has been above all in the United States that *Suicide* has retained its validity, for in America historical conditions still obtain that are parallel to those to which *Suicide* so brilliantly responded. That is, in the United States, science continues to serve as a legitimating rhetoric for the modern state, the need for a secular morality remains with us, and the desire of sociologists to serve as social priests from their university temples is as avid as ever. Indeed, in his American incarnation, Durkheim becomes even more positivistic than in the French original. *Suicide* and *The Rules for the Sociological Method*, for example, are studied and cited far more than *Primitive Classification* and *The Elementary Forms of Religious Life*. Moreover, it is rarely noticed that Durkheim's greatest insights have little to do with his official method (see Brown 1978b:21) and that, on the crucial question of the existence and knowability of an external natural world, Durkheim, though superficially an agnostic, in fact follows Kant in denying "that we can ever obtain such knowledge, since the categories are always interposed between the individual and the postulated reality. A person can know only society, can think only as a member of society. None [according to Durkheim] can assert that the material world exists" (Worsley 1956:49; see also the epigraph of this chapter).

Like the radio host, Durkheim developed an explicit explanation that conveyed an appropriate implicit interpretation of his setting. Durkheim's response fitted the problem as it presented itself to him, and the fact that his theoretical practice violated his methodological pronouncements, that his hypotheses are conceptually flaccid, and that his theory is either unsupported or untestable—all this makes little difference. The Italian expression, slightly altered, is apt: "E vero *perche* e ben trovato." It is true *because* it makes a good story.

Coda

I have made use of the concept of rhetoric to comment on sociological discourse. Seen rhetorically, the central role of linguistic construction in science, art, and everyday life becomes highly visible. The notion of discourse as the creation of a world also raises the question of power. Which worlds might be more or less useful to the powers that be or to aspiring non-elites? What privileges might users of various paradigms for discourse wish to protect? How is the capacity to create such worlds differentially distributed in society? Who controls the means of ideological production? What is the proper role of intellectuals in the dialectic between theoretical and political praxes (Brown and Lyman 1978:6–9)?

A political phenomenology of language sees persons as makers of their worlds through symbols. But it also shows that no symbol has ultimate priority over others: Alternative symbol systems yield competing definitions of the world. Thus, what might be called a politics and an ethics of paradigms emerges, not only over scientific paradigms as such, but also over all paradigms that authorize public discourse and action. In this framework, "normal" politics can be seen as conflict within an agreed-upon universe of discourse, whereas "revolutionary" politics is the struggle over whose reality—whose truth—is to define the political community.

In these struggles, the social thinker has a special role to play as a manufacturer of those accounts by which adherents of competing paradigms advance their claims. This is true of moral or utopian discourse as well as of conventional social-science speech. Today's fictions are tomorrow's factions. Utopian narrative and political praxis are linked through social mimesis, because the narration of the world—the linguistic representation of society—is an authorization of our existence. The insights gained from theories of rhetoric thus have direct consequences for our moral and political action as social scientists. By transvaluing both positivistic objectivism and romantic intuitionism, the rhetorical understanding of social theory invites us to exchange the moral nihilism of one-dimensional thought for textual emancipation and political self-direction.

Five

Rhetoric and the Science of History
The Debate between Evolutionism and
Empiricism as a Conflict of Metaphors

THE HISTORY OF "REALISM" is a history of literalists who give absolute
priority to one lexicon and exclude all others. For the literalist there is
only one correct way of writing, painting, or doing science; all others
are distortions, ideological, and "rhetorical." Literalism is a view of
representation that has forgotten its own dependence on a sociohistorical, and hence relative, community of discourse. It presupposes a
copy theory of language in which word and object are supposed to
correspond directly. Cratylus in Plato's dialogue expressed this view
when he asserted that words "naturally" reflect the world. Literalism
in modern philosophy of science, however, began in the seventeenth
century with Bacon's attack on words that have more than one definition or referent. Since then fact and fiction have been distinguished by
this criterion; factual statements are those that have a single, mir-
rorlike relation to empirical objects (Rorty 1979).

There have been two implications of the literalist criterion for a
language of science: to develop a unidimensional lexicon for scientific
notation, and to purge scientific discourse of terms with equivocal
meanings (McCanles 1976:279; Barthes 1967). For example, in his
History of the Royal Society Thomas Sprat inveighed against the
"many mists and uncertainties [that] these specious *Tropes* and *Figures* have brought on our Knowledge," and called for a "return back to
the primitive purity, and shortness, when men deliver'd so many
things, almost in an equal number of words. . . . a close, naked, natural way of speaking" ([1667] 1959:114). According to Descartes
science is not science when it seeks to persuade, since scientific arguments, when correctly formed, *compel* assent (1952:31–2). Such
absolutism also had consequences for our understanding of rhetoric,
and of metaphor as its major trope. Thus metaphor, which is explicitly

symbolic and polysemous, was seen by Newton as noting more than "a kind of ingenious nonsense" (Newton, quoted in Bush 1950:40) and by Bacon "rather as a pleasure or play of wit than a science" (Bacon 1864:9:62).

Discourses like positivism that have hegemony in a culture are almost by definition literalist, in that their domination depends in part on their discrediting other forms of representation. Recent developments in the theory of knowledge, however, have shown that the early positivist hope for a precisely confirmable language was doomed to fail. We are now aware that metaphors and other tropes are "necessary and not just nice" (Ortony 1979), since they are indispensable to constituting the basic subject matter of science (or anything else) and to forming theories about it (Grassi 1980). Metaphor is our fundamental way of noting similarity and difference and of providing new slants on the primary object of interest by illuminating it through a secondary one (Black 1962; Hesse 1972:252; Simons 1981). In this view, the primary object is not strictly known in advance and then illustrated or reframed with reference to tropes (Zeitz 1984; Kuhn 1979). Instead, phenomena become objects of scientific discourse by virtue of the metaphor that makes them accessible to cognition.

This formulation reverses the traditional positivist view that science is literal and factitious and metaphors are poetic and fictitious. Instead, the literal and the metaphoric are seen as two moments in a dialectical process. Since metaphor is a way of describing something in terms of something else—and especially of describing the unknown in terms of the known—the creation of metaphors as well as their use in intellectual creativity requires that some terms be taken as nonmetaphorical, that is, as literal. The literal was not always known as such. Once upon a time it began as metaphoric, for example, when Descartes took the world *as* a machine. Metaphors, if they make it socially, become literal expressions. In this framework, it is literal and not poetic discourse that is mythic. All discourse is poetic in that it uses metaphors and other tropes, either generatively or in a petrified form. Myth, by contrast, is discourse that has forgotten its own poetic origins and has become literal and absolute (MacCormac 1976).

The relationship between the literal and the metaphoric also depends on perspective: what is literal when seen from within a dominant perspective may be viewed as metaphoric from another, external, perspective. Since we normally use our own assumptions as a resource for investigations within our own perspectives, and not as a topic of investigation from another perspective, we can easily blind ourselves to the as-if, metaphoric character of our own assumptions. Until the late nineteenth century, for example, few could imagine that the world was not a machine. *"Hypotheses non fingo,"* Newton had said, and most of his followers agreed. Hence the metaphoric quality of his theories was not available for apprehension except retrospectively, after Newtonian physics had been supplanted by another metaphoric model of the universe.

The foregoing remarks set a context for an analysis in metaphoric terms of the debate in historical science between evolutionary functionalism and experimental empiricism. Seen rhetorically, the first paradigm is an elaboration of the root metaphor of organism, the second, of mechanism. For most evolutionists there really is a total History that evolves in homogeneous time and that is described by evolutionary theories. Conversely, for most empiricists there really are discrete historical events that are knowable in terms of various mechanisms and causes. Each group of practitioners claims a literalness for its own position, and empiricists scathe evolutionists for using metaphorical models.

My metaphorical-metalogical analysis construes this debate to be founded in error or bad faith. Each protagonist misunderstands the nature and limits of his own linguistic-logical processes, as well as those of his opponent.

The image of the world as organism is deep and continuous in the Western tradition. According to evolutionists, "The world embraces in its constitution all that it is destined to experience actively or passively from its beginning right on to its end; it resembles a human being, all of whose capacities are wrapped up in the embryo before birth" (Seneca 1910: sec. 29). "Our science therefore comes to describe at the same time an ideal eternal history traversed in time by the history of every nation in its rise, development, maturity, decline, and fall" (Giambattista Vico [1744] 1972:62). "The thesis [of evolutionists, accordingly] is that the savage state in some measure represents an early condition of mankind, out of which the higher culture has gradually developed or evolved, by processes still in regular operation as of old" (Edward Burnett Tylor 1878). Thus, "If one goes back to a primitive society, one finds the beginning of the evolution of what we call institutions. Now these institutions are, after all, the habits of individuals . . . handed down from one generation to another. And we can study the growth of these habits as we can study the growth and behavior of an animal" (George Herbert Mead 1956:23). Similarly, "a world system . . . has the characteristics of an organism, in that it has a life-span . . . that life within it is largely self-contained, and that the dynamics of development. . . . through stages . . . all largely internal" (Immanual Wallerstein 1974:347).

To identify the common elements of these seminal statements is to sum up the main components of the biological metaphor:

- Natural things change according to the law of their nature or telos, as opposed to things that happen by chance.
- Change is natural, regular, continuous, purposive, directional, necessary, and self-generated. *Natura non facit saltum:* nature does not make leaps.
- Differences among examples of the same natural class of things can be explained as a consequence of their being in different phases of the same evolutionary pattern; that is, the more "primitive" examples have either started later or have been arrested in their development by some impediment. Hence, contemporary "primitive" societies reveal what contemporary "advanced" societies were like at an earlier stage of growth.

Students of historical sociology and the history of ideas have shown this biological metaphor to be a fundamental assumption underlying most of Western social thought. Franz Boas and William Maitland in the late nineteenth century, Frederick Teggart and Margaret Hodgen in the early twentieth century, and Robert Nisbet and Kenneth Bock today have all been critics of those thinkers—from Plato to Talcott Parsons— who have made use of the organic metaphor. Their experimental-empiricist critique is as follows: The dualism between natural processes and accidents or impediments has led to a search for causes of processes of change outside of specific historical events. By namiing the subject matter "natural" before investigating it, "laws of development" are invoked to determine which aspects of the phenomenon should properly be considered part of its development and which, being accidents, should not. This orientation has led to the habits of dismissing inconvenient data as irrelevant and of using the assumption of biological growth as a classification system for those data that happen to fit. Rather than seeking regularities by comparing discrete things or events, laws of development are established a priori. They are not arrived at inductively from data; instead they become the prinicple for selecting the very data they presume to explain. Such a method is tautological, in that the thing to be explained (society) and the thing that is supposed to explain it (society's coming to be) are both known by the same indicator (the nature of society). Hence although this approach resonates well with the teleological method of common sense, it is unacceptable as modern empirical science. By contaminating independent and dependent variables, the evolutionists rendered their theories untestable.

One curious aspect of this attack is that empiricists claim to be speaking literally, to be explaining factual histories through causal generalizations, rather than, like the evolutionists, to be inventing a fictive history through metaphorical models. Yet the empiricists have also fabricated their histories on the basis of a metaphor. In the sixteenth and seventeenth centuries, with the work of Galileo, Newton, Bacon, and Descartes, life went out of nature and physical imagery began to replace the imagery of the organism. Nature, and soon history, persons, and society, were seen as machines. One of the first explicit transfers of mechanical thinking to the human realm is in Hobbes' *Leviathan:*

> For seeing life is but a motion of limbs, the beginning
> whereof is in some principal part within; why may we not
> say, that all *automata* (engines that move by springs and
> wheels as doth a watch) have artificial life? For what is the
> *heart* but a spring; and the *nerves*, but so many strings; and
> the *joints*, but so many wheels, giving motion to the whole
> body, such as was intended by the artificer.(1957:5)

This tradition was continued in philosophical radicalism which, as Halevy put it, "was nothing but an attempt to apply the principles of Newton to the affairs of politics and morals" (1955:6). For example, James Mill in his *Analysis of the Phenomena of the Human Mind* undertook "to reduce everything to constant and in some sort mechanical relations between elements which should be as simple as possible." Such ideas were so widespread that they even found expression in the works of such dialectical thinkers as Marx and Freud. Invoking the model of physics, Marx claimed to represent "the economic law of motion of modern society" as a natural law (Marx 1946:16-17). Equally striking is Freud's early "Project for a Scientific Psychology," the goal of which was "to furnish us with a psychology which shall be a natural science . . . to present psychical processes as quantitatively determined states of specifiable material particles and so to make them plain and void of contradiction" (Freud 1954:1:355). Whereas neo-Marxists and neo-Freudians have revised these early mechanistic metaphors, they persist with little change in the forms of orthodox Marxism, statistical sociology, and behaviorist psychology.

The metaphor of mechanism eventually penetrated into the study of history, which in the nineteenth century had still been closer to literature than to science. Peter Gay expressed this shift in his comments on "style" in historical scholarship: "This pressure toward objectivity is realistic because the objects of the historian's inquiry are precisely that, objects, out there in a real and single past" (1974:210). A similar position was asserted by Perry Anderson:

> The premise of this work is that there is no plumb-line
> between necessity and contingency in historical
> explanation. . . . there is merely that which is known—
> established by historical research—and that which is not
> known: the latter may be either the mechanism of single
> events or the laws of motion of whole structures. Both are
> equally amenable, in principle, to adequate knowledge of
> their causality . . . [to] rational and controllable theory in
> the domain of history. (1974:8)

Historical sociologists are even more forceful than historians in seeking to assimilate historical understanding to causal analysis on the model of mechanics. "The most important phase of historical work," said Weber, "namely, establishment of the causal regress, attains validity only when in the event of challenge it is able to pass the test of the use of the category of objective possibility, which entails the isolation and generalization of the causal individual components" (1949:176). The "ultimate objective" of such an approach, declared Theda Skocpol "is, of course, the acutal illumination of causal regularities across sets of historical cases" (Skocpol 1979:39; see Nichols 1985).

This conception of history—as a nomothetic theoretical enterprise seeking causal laws explaining objective facts—is legitimated by contemporary positivist philosophy. The mechanistic metaphor at the root of this approach is defended by logicians' analysis of the Aristotelian tautology, by Carl Hempel's discussion of covering laws, and by Gilbert Ryle's demonstration that to be a cause a thing must be an event and not a process or a law. Empiricists also have tried to demonstrate the utility of this mechanistic approach in substantive historical writings, such as Teggert's *Rome and China* or Hodgen's *Early Anthropology*. Their mode of explanation assumes that change occurs when a critical event takes place outside the thing to be explained. Such an event may come from another society (e.g., trade with China changed the Roman Empire). Within a single, hermetic society, however (e.g., Japan in the eighteenth century), the event will be found in one institutional area that causes change in another. Thus, in asserting a commitment to experimentalist methods of controlled comparative observation and verification, the empiricists reject the functionalist assumptions of telic rationality in social order and of functions that explain institutional or social-system evolution.

Contrary to the views of the participants, however, the debate between evolutionists and empiricists is not a conflict between poetic fiction and prosaic explanation, between metaphoric phrase making and literal thinking, or between pseudoscience and correct science. Instead, it is a conflict of root metaphors, a miscomprehension of two different forms of linguistic-logical encoding which is caused by each side's insensitivity to its own processes of poetic construction.

All historical scientists, whether evolutionists or empiricists, operating with various root metaphors, create historical time periods that reflect their professional interests and cognitive concerns. These may lie in tracing processual sequences in a homogeneous series, as with evolutionists, or in denoting regularities of occurrence between discrete types of events, as with empiricists. In no case, however, can the perspective of the historical scientist be identical to that of the historical actor. No historical actor arrives at the dawn of a great historical period proclaiming, "Today we start the Hundred Years War" (Douglas 1980:18). This is because "great historical periods" are retrospective symbolic constructions by historical scholars which are unavailable to the historical actors themselves. Given that historical science is inherently retrospective, no one perspective can justly claim to be the only possible correct way of creating or explaining historical time.

The teleological perspective of evolutionism supplies principles for organizing history into periods and linking these periods in a narrative account (Campbell 1984). This narrative in turn provides rules of relevance and irrelevance for the writer's theoretical practice. Chekhov said of rules of relevance in drama that "If a shotgun is hanging on the wall in the first act, it must go off in the last." Similarly, if a junior officer, Captain Nolan, appears early in the text on Britain's war with the Ottomans, it is because this will later explain the Charge of the Light Brigade. The denouement of dramatic action—the outcome or telos of narrative accounts—provides evolutionary historians with a principle of selection for what will be taken as relevant data. To accuse such scholars of not considering all the relevant data is a red herring: either the accusation is a truism, since more detailed evidence is always desirable; or it misses—indeed, it clouds—the point, since evolutionists, guided by a different root metaphor, are using different rules of relevance for data than those invoked by experimental empiricists.

From the empiricist's perspective, any version of this narrative logic uses the posited effect to determine what will be the cause (Fisher 1978). Seen in linguistic terms, this logical error of evolutionists becomes an error in translation by empiricists, since the teleological procedures of the evolutionists are not only self-consistent, but are also indispensable to narrative history itself. Such histories, even though they are given a low epistemological status by empiricists, nevertheless provide the factual basis for the empiricists' own controlled experimentalist logic. Empiricists thus depend on teleology even while damning it.

This teleological basis for historical construction appears to be necessary. In forming a period around some telos, for example, we fictitiously set off a given historical field and highlight some of its contents. In being conceived through this artificial conceptual fabrication, the historical material thereby isolated acquires a beginning, a middle, and an end. As Collingwood said,

> We fabricate periods of history by fastening upon some, to
> us, peculiarly luminous point and trying to study it as it
> actually came into being. We find our eye caught, as it were,

by some striking phenomenon—Greek life in the fifth
century, or the like; and this becomes the nucleus of a group
of historical inquiries, asking how it arose and how it passed
away. . . . Thus we form the idea of a period, which we call
the Hellenic period; and this period will resemble the
Byzantine period or the Baroque period *in being a period*,
that is in having a luminous center [an essence or species
nature] preceded and followed by processes whose only
interest to us at the moment is that they lead to and from
it. . . . Thus the historical cycle is a permanent feature of all
historical thought: but whenever it occurs, it is always
incidental to a point of view. The cycle is the historian's field
of vision at a given moment. (1969:173)

The empiricists are correct in charging that evolutionists engage in
the fictional construction of time periods and historical sequences.
But they are in error if they think that such fictions can be eliminated.
The states of affairs that the evolutionist constitutes as the beginning,
middle, and end of a course of development can never be real or actual in any ultimate sense. But neither can the states of affairs constituted by empiricists as events, causes, or effects. Both evolutionists
and empiricists are engaged in poetic construction—albeit with different root metaphors. No form of history can ever be simply a recording of what happened in the transition from one state of affairs to
another. All historical science, as Hayden White said, "is a progressive redescription of sets of events in such a way as to dismantle a
structure encoded in one verbal mode in the beginning so as to justify
a recoding of it in another mode at the end" (1978a:98). In evolutionary explanations, such transcoding precisely comprises the "middle"
of its narratives. Teleological thinking is indispensable to historical
scholarship in the sense that its essentialism is presupposed in any
inquiry that presumes to have, to discover, or to create a determinate
subject matter. Such determinateness is above all a feature of experimental empiricism. The blanket rejection of teleology by empiricists
accounts in part for their difficulties in establishing what is a period
and what is an event.

But even if historical science depends on teleology, this is not to say
that all teleological thought is scientific. Here we can distinguish historical science from scientistic prophesy. The first uses teleology to
periodize and narrate the past, to make the past determinate. The

second invokes teleology to determine the future. Much evolutionist thought is scientific prophesy, of course, and here the empiricist critique is correct, at least insofar as evolutionists claim to be engaged in experimental science. In the nineteenth century the cosmic predictions of social Darwinists like Herbert Spencer provided "a secular providence and a naturalistic theodicy which reassured the frightened and helped coerce the unwilling as the industrialization of western society took place. Sociology was . . . employed . . . to justify an ongoing process as part of the order of nature" (Peel 1974:201). With a similar logic but opposite values, Marx homogenized all of history around the process of class conflict and the telos of proletarian liberation. In so doing, however, Marx rendered himself incapable of explaining the many deviant cases in the scientific terms of his theory. As a historian and a journalist, Marx was well aware of such factors as ethnicity, nationalism, and the like, and of how these might impede the changes he hoped for. Yet his explanations of these factors are tacked onto his theory and are not deducible from it. Marx's difficulties flowed from his having posited a telos that was to be realized outside of historical time. Thus the logical difficulty with evolutionary functionalism as a secular science is not that it is teleological, but that it often posits the telos outside of history, in the future instead of in the past (Mink 1978:134). In this sense Simmel was correct when he said that "historical materialism is a form of epistemological idealism" (Simmel 1977:199).

This brings us to another major criticism of evolutionist thought: its positing of a telos for Humanity or Society as a whole. Even if we do not reject teleological thinking in principle, and even if the telos of evolutionists refers not to the future but to the past, there still remains the biologistic assumption that social change is a normal, uniform, and continuous property of a total society. Evolutionism presupposes criteria that define progressive epochs, as well as an immanent process that links the fragmentary and temporally discontinuous realizations of this ideal progression so that particular histories can be unified into History. Time is seen as homogeneous, and so is the substance that is evolving. "If we discover that this progressive movement proceeds from different, distinguishable substances, we could deny that it qualifies as progress. . . . In other words . . . the concept of progress in history . . . presupposes a homogeneous subject to which progress can be ascribed" (Simmel 1977:182-83).

This view is clearly useful to a people bent on establishing their own superiority and justifying their domination of the rest of the world—for example, the British imperialists of the nineteenth century. From an empiricist viewpoint, however, the presuppositions in evolutionism of homogeneity, continuity, and essence are exactly what needs to be determined empirically. As a mode of explaining historical events, the evolutionary method makes comparison a procedure for homogenizing World History rather than for explaining similarities and differences in particular histories.

The evolutionists' presumption of a total Humanity or Society is also unacceptable to mechanists on empirical grounds, as Christopher Dawson noted, because "humanity is not an organized society with a common tradition or a common social consciousness. All the attempts that have hitherto been made to write a world history have been in fact attempts to interpret one tradition in terms of another, attempts to extend the intellectual hegemony of a dominant culture by subordinating to it all the events of other cultures that come within the observer's range of vision" (Dawson 1957:273). "This . . . is true," agreed Arnold Toynbee, "of the presentation of world history in the Old Testament, in Hellenic literature, in the Chinese dynastic histories, and in Western historians' works" (Toynbee 1961).

Evolutionists, however, have logical and empirical replies to this criticism. Their logical reply is Kant's argument that we cannot make sense of the *res gestae*—the whole record of human experience within which lies any particular historical research—unless we can identify a single theme, a "regular movement," in terms of which "what seems complex and chaotic in the single individual may be seen from the standpoint of the human race as a whole to be a steady and progressive though slow evolution of its original endowment" (Kant [1784] 1949a; see Mink 1978:136). If we want to conceive of a history of humanity or of human society as a whole, we must constitute our subject as having some essence or property that has developed in time. And the same assumption is required for any particular history.

Evolutionists also argue empirically that, at least in recent centuries, there has been one system of interactions—a single global order that includes virtually all particular human societies. Wallerstein expressed this neatly:

> If given societies went through "stages," that is, had a
> "natural history," what of the world-system itself? . . . It
> was at this point that I abandoned the idea altogether of
> taking either the sovereign state or that vaguer concept, the
> national society, as the unit of analysis. I decided that neither
> one was a social system and that one could only speak of
> social change in social systems. The only social system in this
> scheme was the world-system. . . . There had been only one
> "modern world." (1974:7)

Gerhard Lenski has made similar points. The empiricists' criticisms of evolution, he said, apply to theories of the rise and fall of specific societies, but they do not apply to the "new" or "general evolutionism," which concerns itself with humanity as a whole. "Evolutionists today are taking more seriously than did their predecessors the essential unity of human evolution." For contemporary evolutionists "the unitary character of human life is becoming ever more apparent" (Lenski 1976:562; for examples see Boulding 1964; Heilbroner 1974; Lenski and Lenski 1978; or Wallerstein 1974). Moreover, continued Lenski, this new evolutionism is empirically grounded: "There is a growing tendency among evolutionists to define socio-cultural evolution as growth in the store of symbolically coded information and its consequences. Such a definition has no built-in assumptions about moral progress or any other form of human betterment: these remain empirical questions" (Lenski 1976:561). For example, to disprove the theory that there is long-run directionality in such phenomena as population size, level of technology, or complexity of social systems, critics must show that at the global level there is no trend with respect to central tendencies or the upper limits of the frequency distribution (Lenski 1976:552).

For the experimental empiricist, however, these assertions bristle with difficulties: the distinction between specific and general evolutionism, the alleged newness of general evolutionism, the claims of new evolutionism to be empirically grounded, the assertion of neutrality concerning moral progress or human betterment, and the theory of long-run directionality. Let me discuss these one by one.

First, concerning the distinction between specific and general evo-

lution, Marshall Sahlins (1977) distinguished "specific evolutionism," which uses case studies and focuses on single societies or
civilizations, and "general evolutionism," which is concerned with
frequency distributions in the totality of human societies. Though
there is surely a difference in the techniques of data collection in these
two approaches, their basic logics remain identical: both specific and
general evolutionism focus on the development of wholes. Whether
the whole in question is a single society or the totality of societies does
not change the organicist presuppositions brought to the inquiry.

Second, concerning the newness of general evolutionism, general
evolutionism is new only in the limited sense that the concept of humanity, or total human society, has become more comprehensive and
inclusive with greater contact between peoples. A limited developing
totality and an expanded developing totality are still developing total-
ities, however, and there is nothing new about this basic assumption
in the "new" evolutionary study of social change.

Third, concerning the new empirical grounds for evolutionism,
Lenski is correct in stating that contemporary historical scientists are
able to draw on a vastly enriched body of data, produced not only by
historians but also by archaeologists, demographers, anthropologists,
and others. But the enriched body of data is not a defense of evolutionist logic, for the logic cannot be validated by these masses of data.
Empiricists say evolutionism is not a testable theory. Instead it is a
metatheoretical paradigm through which investigators define what
will be taken as data or evidence in the first place.

The metatheoretical quality of evolutionism is also connected both
with Lenski's claims to value neutrality and with his asserted "theory
that there is long-run directionality" in certain phenomena. This theory is in fact a nontheory, since it provides no explanation. It is rather
an assumption presented as a finding, since any attempt to theorize
change over the long run must assume a long-run pattern or directionality as its subject matter. And surely in such an approach one will
be able to find empirically some features that display such directionality.

The key theoretical questions that remain, of course, are which
features of directionality we should be most interested in looking at,
how they operate, and why. Instructive here is an anecdote about the
Kwakiutl Indian whom Franz Boas sometimes brought to New York

to serve as an informant. The visitor "was indifferent to the sight of skyscrapers and streets crowded with cars. He reserved his intellectual curiosity for dwarfs, giants, and bearded ladies who were exhibited at the time in Times Square, for automats, and for the brass balls ornamenting the base of staircase banisters. For reasons which I cannot go into here, all this involved his own culture; and it was that culture alone which he was trying to recognize in certain aspects of ours (Levi-Strauss 1976:27).

This culture-boundedness seems inescapable. When we seek to measure something that is meaningful, it perforce must be meaningful to us—that is, it must be measurable in terms of the system of reference that we use. Like the Kwakiutl that examined dwarfs and banister balls, the new evolutionists see a long-run directionality in the accumulation of technology and the increase in coded information—precisely what we would expect of visitors to the rest of the world from a postindustrial, information society. Similarly, in the nineteenth century, when powerful machines were being used to escalate the wealth and dominion of Western nations, the quantity of energy available per inhabitant and the degree of division of labor were the preferred measure for long-run directionality, providing thereby a hierarchy for ranking societies or economies subordinate to those of Northern Europe. But imagine what long-run directionality would be discovered if the historical sociologists were Bedouins or Inuits? Then perhaps the criterion would be the ability to triumph as an autonomous culture in the most hostile physical environment. In that case the long-run directionality for total society would be one of steady decline. If the theorists were traditional Hindus, their criterion might be the degree of philosophic integration between physical and moral realms, or if Islamic, the degree of solidarity between religious and political institutions. And so on. Given the necessity of some cultural point of view through which criteria of measurement may be rendered theoretically meaningful, it seems epistemologically unsophisticated and cognitively irresponsible to claim that evolutionism "has no built-in assumptions about moral progress or any other form of human betterment" (Lenski 1976:561).

One final point on the theory of long-run directionality. Few would contest the theory if theory were taken to mean merely a report on scientific observations. Theory, however, usually implies an explanation of such observations—not just a statement of what happened, but also of how or why. For empiricists, such an explanation must specify the mechanisms that caused the long-run directionality in question. Evolutionists who claim the status of modern social scientists generally accept this requirement, but in doing so they render their evolutionism redundant. Sometimes, as in Marxism or in Darwinism, the theory of growth is fused with an account of the mechanism of that growth, as well as with an account of the internal, or even external, dynamics of each of the stages. These features might make the theory acceptable to experimental empiricists, even while obscuring the logical inadequacy, from their viewpoint, of the growth theory as an explanation by itself. But obscure or not, having begun by mixing metaphors—the organism and the machine—evolutionists end up with contradictory logic.[1] For empiricists, an explanation of long-run directionality must specify how this directionality is generated—in evolutionist terms how the various stages generate each other. But once we state this generative principle in mechanist terms, that is, once we have specified the causal connection between the various stages, then the development series and indeed the evolutionary theory itself become redundant. On one hand, without a definition of the mechanisms of change from one stage to another the theory is inadequate; on the other, given such a causal connection between evolutionary stages, the evolutionary series as such becomes no more than a list of successive conditions. Thus from an empiricist viewpoint, evolutionism remains either incomplete or unnecessary and hence inadmissible as historical science (Gellner 1965:15).

However powerful this attack may be, it still fails to overcome the critical appreciation of teleology advanced by Immanuel Kant in the second main section of his *Critique of Judgment*, the "Critique of Teleological Judgment." The existence of organic bodies, Kant argued, is something that the mechanical logic of the physical sciences cannot explain. Organic bodies require a explanatory method of their own, the principle of teleology, which alone can comprehend the fact that "an organized natural product is one in which every part is reciprocally both means and end" (Kant 1949b: sec. 66). Teleological thinking is not scientific in a strict sense; it can only be employed by reflective judgment to guide "our investigation of . . . [organic bodies] by a remote analogy with our own causality [that is, our purposive conduct] according to ends generally" (ibid.). Teleology thus occupies an uncomfortable place between theology and natural science. We do not trust its validity, yet we need it to describe the world around us. Such an ambiguous separation must be maintained, however, if we are to keep the study of the mechanical aspect of nature in accord with what we can observe, measure, and experimentally compare.

I have used a rhetorical perspective to analyze two forms of sociological discourse. It should be clear that my purpose in undressing the organismic and mechanistic metaphors is not to embarrass metaphoric thinking but to reveal the figurative aspect of all historical science. And once it is understood that these are metaphors, their relative adequacy may be more clearly seen. Mechanism is a good place from which to see the tautological nature of much biologistic thinking. Conversely, the biological metaphor is better able to deal with immanent factors, intentionality, and systems transformations than is mechanism. Features peculiar to both these metaphors can be limned by light from other metaphoric perspectives.

Numerous philosophers have argued that such ordering schemata are a prerequisite to any rational thought or indeed to making sense of perception itself. In this way root metaphors are frameworks for interpreting meaning within which sensa become facts, facts become concepts, and concepts become discourse. This metaphoric basis of thought was discerned by Nietzsche, and it was noted again by Meyer Abrams:

> Any area for investigation, so long as it lacks prior concepts
> to give it structure and express terminology with which it can
> be managed, appears to the inquiring mind inchoate—either
> a blank, or an elusive and tantalizing confusion. Our usual
> recourse is, more or less deliberately, to cast about for objects
> which offer parallels to dimly sensed aspects of the new
> situation, to use the better known to elucidate the less
> known, to discuss the intangible in terms of the tangible.
> (1953:31)

For example, the *organicist* approach reconstructs and integrates selected elements of the historical field into components of a synthetic process. Actions or events are explained to the extent that they can be

ordered around some common telos that defines the nature and purpose of each particular element. The logic here involves the establishment of a hierarchy of reality or meaning organized around a superordinate telos. The evolutionary approach in historical science is an
instance of such organicist thinking in that it posits—evolutionists
would say discovers—a stage of development that has been or will be
arrived at by history. This schema is then used to determine what will
be considered a part of History and what will be its significance. It is
in terms of the evolutionary whole, in other words, that the historical
parts are constituted and comprehended.

In contrast, the metaphysics of *mechanism* is clearly expressed in
the early modern philosophy of science: it is reductive, naturalistic,
and nominalistic. Its style is analysis rather than synthesis, and reduction to primary elements rather than elevation to a transcendent telos.
It is as though the organicist view had been turned on its head; in
place of the parts being instances of the whole, as the parts of the
body take their essence from their function in a larger system, the
whole is seen as an instance of the parts, much as a machine exists
as such because of the aggregative causal actions of the elements
within it.

Seen rhetorically, the central role of linguistic construction in science becomes visible. As John Lyne noted, the overarching purpose of
such an inquiry is to make academic discourses better serve public
needs, not in any technocratic or policy-analytic sense, but more
broadly and deeply, by enriching rather than denuding the grounds of
civic understanding and decision. It may be more difficult in our time
than in Aristotle's to make knowledge illuminate experience, but the
central question remains: "How do we recover *phronesis*, practical
wisdom for public affairs, in a technological age? The various research specialties of the modern day 'knowledge industry' tend to
shield themselves from public judgment by their self-isolating vocabularies and by their territorial claims of expertise" (Lyne 1985:71;
see Bellah et al. 1985). If we as practitioners of these specialized vocabularies can gain a sense of our own rhetorical practices, we might
be better able to shape social science as a discourse which fosters civic
life.

With this understanding we may reconstitute the relationship between organicism and mechanism to each other and to their respec-

tive domains of application. Both organicism and mechanism are at the same time literal descriptions of reality and fictional metaphors. The relation between the literal and the metaphoric is dialectical. Like essence/appearance or factual/fictional, each term presupposes and implies the other. By not acknowledging this dependency, literalists render themselves incapable of understanding their own creative process, whereas metaphoricists are unable to explain how their tropes relate to experience. Of course, both creativity and experience are linguistically mediated. Hence, we are not speaking of an opposition between language and reality, but of a dialectic within a symbolic reality. As McCanles put it: "Only when it is recognized how all discourse in being metaphorical may yet operate 'as if' it were literal can literal meaning become possible and scientific demands for stipulative, univocal meaning and reference be met. The "let's pretend" ambiance usually relegated to what we call fictions thus spreads itself out to enclose nonfictive discourse as well." (1976:285)

Science aims at a target which its own arrows create, yet the creating of this target is impossible unless it is assumed to exist prior to this process of creation. Literal scientific discourse must pretend that there is a bedrock of nonlinguistic experience to which words are tethered. But can the world exist for humans before it is named? Can it be apprehended without some symbolic point of view? As I have argued earlier, this is impossible. We can take the world as naked reality only as if we were apprehending it without linguistic garments. This is precisely what literalists do, but in being literal they are engaged in covert metaphoric discourse.

The opposite is also true. The writer of fiction can write about a nonfactual world only on the assumption that a factual reality exists outside his text. Jacques Derrida appealed to this dialectic when he noted that to distinguish metaphors from their literal meanings is itself a philosophic task. "The philosophical categories through which we would study metaphors in philosophy are themselves metaphoric" (McCanles 1976:289; see Derrida 1974:28–29). Thomas Kuhn indirectly also made this point. "Normal science" is by definition literal science, since scientists would not invest in elaborating the dominant paradigm if they did not take it to be a true description of reality. Normal science takes its paradigms as literal, and must so take them if it is to function as science as usual. Scientific knowledge depends on metaphoric ignorance. Yet when sufficient anomalies arise, or when competing perspectives or root metaphors challenge the dominant one, both old and new paradigms appear as metaphors until the old world image is reaffirmed or the new one replaces it. After such sea changes, when the waters are calm again, the dominant paradigm sediments and once more is literal.

Defenders of the positive model of science have sought refuge from such sophistical attacks by separating the context of discovery, where metaphor may be admitted, from the context of justification, which is the domain of logic and proof (e.g., Scheffler 1967). Yet the security of their refuge depends on the defensibility of this distinction. And such defenses have largely failed. The context of justification, many have argued (e.g., Feyerabend 1978; Quine 1960) is itself theory-laden, and as such is infused with metaphors. As Kuhn noted, there may be "good reasons for being persuaded," but "there is no neutral algorithm for theory-choice, no systematic decision procedure which, properly applied, must lead each individual in the group to the same decision" (1972:199,200; see Lakatos 1970; Latour and Woolger 1979; Mulkay 1985). As Simons said: "What emerges from these re-analyses of inquiry is a picture of the scientific process quite different from the model presented by verificationists and strict falsifica-tionists. Scientific theories are rhetorical constructions and their key terms are ineliminably metaphorical. Far from being able to translate metaphorical claims into theory-neutral propositions, scientists appear to be *stuck* with metaphor" (1981). Whether this be for good or ill depends in large part on the practitioners' awareness of this process.

We see from this discussion that the literalists' fear of relativism is a product of their own rhetorical practice. Rhetorical relativism, like positivist absolutism, is a relational term. The choice between these positions is thus an artifact of an unreflective commitment to the metaphor of an ultimate foundation to knowledge. Yet today the defects of foundationalism in epistemology are being demonstrated almost everywhere (Nelson 1983:232).

There is also a practical dimension to these disputes, because literalist epistemologies are antipolitical. Literalists are in the business of compelling, not persuading. And even if it were achieved, such an epistemology could not comprehend politics, which is symbolic and

persuasive, as are other human affairs. Because absolutist epistemologies are legitimations of belief that cannot have ultimate warrant, they are in principle ideological. They covertly advocate an
apolitical reality without assuming responsibility for this highly political act.

Every new cognitive orientation needs an epistemology and an ontology for its legitimation. The positivist opposition of "rational scientific method" to "primitive metaphoric thought" is no exception
(Burke 1969:40-46). Indeed, if we observe the pervasive obduracy of
the defense of positivism, it appears to be itself a kind of myth—"not
merely a story told," as Malinowski said, "but a reality lived . . . not
an idle tale, but a hard-worked active force (1948:100–101). The
absolutist epistemology is also a myth in Eliade's sense of being "always the recital of a creation; it tells how something was accomplished, began to *be*. It is for this reason that myth is bound up with
ontology; it speaks only of *realities*, of what *really* happened, of what
was fully manifested. [The reality that ontology describes is a sacred]
reality . . . saturated with being . . . equivalent to *power*" (Eliade
1959:95).

This involvement of epistemology with power is illustrated by placing Karl Popper's epistemological writings in the context of his political essays. By such a transfer we see that valid knowledge, according
to Popper, can be assured only by embracing objectivity and eschew-
ing ideology, that is, by affirming liberalism and denouncing Marxism. Strictly speaking, Popper's literalist use of language is mythic, in
that myth is language that has forgotten its roots in a sociohistorical
community. Myth presumes that the given meaning is the only possible one, and that the meaning is final, so it blinds itself to the halo of
virtualities in which other possible meanings are floating. Myth makes
scientific theories into speaking corpses. By contrast, theories seen as
metaphors for a given domain keep the memory of their origins in
human life. Rhetorical analysis shows us the difference between myth
and metaphor and reveals how myth gives a natural justification to
historical intentions, thereby making contingent choice appear as
eternal necessity. For example, the status of the bourgeoisie is particular and historical; Man, as represented by the bourgeoisie, is universal and eternal (Barthes 1972:129, 141; d'Unrug and de Bellaing
1982). By dehistoricizing basic categories of experience—Man,

Nature, and so on—myth also depoliticizes speech and conduct. In these terms, of course, absolutism in social science makes it precisely a myth. Through rhetorical analysis, however, we can demythologize social theories and thereby recover their power as illuminating metaphors. Moreover, we become able to face the moral and political dangers, and not just the epistemological errors, of relativism or nihilism. Citizens do require a stable context for intelligible moral and political discourse. Such a shared context is a definition of moral and political community. Yet this context is much like the root metaphors we have been discussing—it needs to be taken as if it were literal in order for normal politics to advance, even though it began and will end in metaphor.

In contemporary rhetorical theory, what we see and say and do is viewed as mediated by symbols. In this perspective, social-science theory is itself a rhetorical construction and is understood to be an instrument of political power. Through persuasive symbolization, the frameworks of reality, discourse, and action are given validity and summoned into existence. The rhetorical analysis of scientific language therefore is not a withdrawal into aestheticism or a subjectivist retreat. Instead it can be a demystification of what has been mystified and a critique of domination. Inquiry into the rhetoric of historical science is a method of self-consciousness that could lead to a new methodological conscience. Rhetorical analysis of social-science texts can become an ideological analysis of their contexts, and in this way can help our implicit advocacy of realities to become more politically and morally responsible.

Six

Social Reality as Narrative Text

Interactions, Institutions, and Polities as Language

Ubi nihil erit quae scribas, id ipsum scribes.
                              Cicero, *Epistolae ad Atticum* (4:8:4)

Forme is power.

                              Hobbes, *Leviathan*

IN ACCEPTING RHETORIC as a context and a tradition, we become more aware that there are alternative ways of truth telling and that we are therefore responsible for the ways we tell our truths. In this sense, the dialectics of discourse accord with the responsibilities of communication. We can better see the limits of our own perspectives and appreciate the strengths of others. In this fashion, a rhetorical view of theory may help us overcome dogmatic oppositions in social thought and in our broader culture. Once we focus on language, we begin to understand that individual consciousness and social structure both emerge from discoursive practice. Language as both social institution and political practice is the active synergy between consciousness and things; it is the genitor of both intentions and structures (Jung 1982:45).

In much of social science, however, there remains a residual dualism, an idea, as Sahlins put it, "of culture as generated on the one hand out of real material interests and of consisting, on the other hand, of symbolic representations" (1977:17). In this unreflective opposition it is forgotten that symbols themselves are phenomena of experience and that human reality is experienced only with the mediation of symbols. Reality is imagined as literal and objective, whereas symbols are seen as metaphoric and subjective. This distinction has value in denoting the status of different types of experiences or the referential relations between them, but it clouds awareness of an alternative view: that the realities to which symbols refer are also symbolic—that is, that they are intended by human actors and apprehended within some shared frame of vision.

This view—symbolic realism—draws on the Renaissance conception of man as maker of his world. It was explored by Ficino, Albertus Magnus, Bruno, Machiavelli, Kepler, and Vico, and found its modern expression and partial distortion in the philosophies of Kant, Dilthey, and Husserl. For Machiavelli human life was an attempt to impose form on chance, to master *fortuna* through *virtus;* for Kepler the task of science was to structure thought to match a preformed world (Yates 1966; Harre 1978). Such ideas were eclipsed by the atomism and mechanism of the seventeenth century, the Protestant opposition to Hermetic and neo-Platonic thought, and the rise of commodity consciousness that separated persons from each other and from their environment. These post-Renaissance conceptions became bases for objectivistic, positivist philosophies and social sciences, along with their subjectivistic, romantic oppositions. In American social science in particular, the interpretation of symbolic meanings has been associated with the anthropology of premodern cultures and the microsociology of consciousness, whereas the explanation of objective facts has been part of the macrosociology of contemporary politics and institutions.

One corollary of this bifurcation is that moral discourse in modern societies has been relegated to the purely private, subjective realm, whereas discourse on social institutions employs an ostensibly non-moral, purely objectivistic vocabulary. Rhetoric is a way of rejoining these domains, particularly through the metaphor of society as narrative text,[1] since this metaphor pays homage explicitly to both the logics of action and the moralities of thought. The image of society as narrative text also suggests intelligible subtexts or plots which reconcile hostile theoretical-ideological positions.

In this chapter I will connect different forms of discourse and different levels of conduct through the textual metaphor. By construing society as a text—as a structure or grammar of rules and communications—I will show that even highly symbolic activities such as etiquette are structured and institutional and that institutions and polities are also symbolic. In turning to the explicitly practical and political dimensions of human experience, I argue that there is a semiotics of sociability that infuses quotidian, organizational, and political life. In this I draw on the language-oriented sociologies that usually operate at these three levels of society: ethnomethodology, symbolic interactionism, and structuralism. Finally I compare the two principal methods of textual-social analysis: hermeneutics and semiotics. I discuss their relative strengths and weaknesses and conclude that as two aspects of the language metaphor they together embrace and could perhaps overcome other bifurcations in our culture.

Propriety as a Grammar for Everyday Practice

The textual dimensions of ordinary social intercourse are illuminated by the work of Harold Garfinkel and other ethnomethodologists. These researchers have performed what they call "breaching experiments," in which the experimenter violates the contextual assumptions or implicit grammar that provide the rules for a given situation. Through such breachings, the latent grammar is rendered manifest, and the experimenter is able to observe how persons repair or reconstruct the situation's normal form. One unexpected finding of such studies is the difficulty researchers have in conducting these experiments. Field workers anticipated that their subjects would be upset by such violations (Garfinkel 1963, 1967; Mehan and Wood 1975:113). But they did not expect that they themselves would experience acute anxiety even in their roles as experimenters. For example, Milgram could get only one of his students to volunteer to ask subway passengers to give up their seats, and even this lone student could not complete the experiment. "I just couldn't go on," he said. "It was one of the most difficult things I did in my life." When Milgram decided to undertake the experiment himself, he had a similar experience:

> A moment of stark anomic panic overcame me. But the man
> got right up and gave me his seat. A second blow was yet to
> come. Taking the man's seat, I was overwhelmed by the need
> to behave in a way that would justify my request. My head
> sank between my knees, and I could feel my face blanching. I
> was not role-playing, I actually felt as if I were going to perish.
> Then the third discovery: as soon as I got off the train, at
> the next station, all of the tension disappeared.
> (1974:71–80)

Similarly, Gregory (1977:3) reported "the bizarre mental state of persons doing these breachings," and their overwhelming need to give some account that might normalize their anomalous behavior. Gregory's students found themselves constructing ad hoc explanations to justify their conduct and by so doing to alleviate their anxiety. Such accounts, or presentations of motives, reconciled the students' unusual behavior with a normal biography (Blum and McHugh 1971). The students' accounts seemed to say, "I'm not the sort of person who ordinarily does these things. I have a special reason that makes it OK." When they failed to find such an account, the students, like Milgram, remained anxious until they could escape the situation they had created.[2]

What are we to make of these reports? From the viewpoint of a semiotics of sociability, we do not see the motive or account as either a source or an explanation of the conduct to which it refers. Instead, both the conduct and the account—both the behavioral construction of the scene and its rhetorical reconstruction—become topics to be explained. As Mills put it, "Rather than interpreting actions and language as external manifestations of subjective and deeper lying elements in individuals, the research task is the locating of particular types of action within typal frames of normative actions and socially situated clusters of motive" (1974b:452). In effect motives serve as plot lines for social narrations (Fisher 1970).

What Mills calls "typal frames of normative actions" and what Gregory refers to as the ground for surface rules of interaction are reminiscent of Saussure's notion that language provides the ground or typal frame for speech. The typal frames or socially situated clusters of motive serve as grammars for verbal accounts by which phenomena are constructed into normal, rational, expectable experience. Much as paradigms provide a procedural grammar for guiding and legitimating scientific activities, so there are paradigmatic grammars that advise members of any group about an infinite range of behavioral displays and thereby provide them with a sense of objective social structure (Cicourel 1974:51; Civ'jan 1977; Shimanoff 1980).

These reflections warrant the view that breaching experiments create anomalies in the grammar of polite interaction. The resultant crises are then normalized by ad hoc arguments that reconstitute the unexpected events to conform to the dominant grammar. By this means the unity of the social text is restored. In contrast, consider the violations of normal forms that were enacted by radicals in the United States and Europe during the 1960s. Here aggressive incivility became an openly political statement about the artificiality of normal forms. Ad hoc adjustments were rejected by radicals who sought instead a cultural-textual revolution.

The Textual Analysis of Total Institutions

The metaphor of society as linguistic construction can be further elaborated with reference to social institutions. By definition, institutions are normal forms of social conduct. Institutions are not things, nor are they merely ways of doing things; they are also grammars that account for these ways of acting. Marriage, the market, or monarchy, for example, are all patterns through which conduct may be routinized and justified. To institutionalize a behavior means not only to regularize its performance but also to provide models, normative justifications, and sanctions. In this sense social institutions, like paradigms in science, are expressive vehicles for exemplary definitions of normalcy and deviance, recipes of duties and obligations, and syntaxes of self and other. "Just as a language is a system of signs whose values are interdependent or diacritical," said John O'Neill, "so every institution is a symbolic system in which the individual incorporates himself and through which his actions acquire a typical style" (1970:58–59).

What has been said of institutions generally is truer still of formal organizations, especially "total institutions" such as mental hospitals, prisons, or concentration camps. Seen through the textual metaphor, there is a basic affinity between the sociological portrayal of total institutions by Erving Goffman and their literary representation by Alexander Solzhenitsyn.[3] In their respective mimeses, both Goffman and Solzhenitsyn describe social-textual language systems that are designed to preclude free speech and a freely created identity and environment.

Total institutions are those in which "all aspects of life are conducted in the same place and under the same single authority. They are places in which one's activities are always in the company of large batches of similar others, where time is tightly scheduled, where there are explicit rules and a body of officials, all according to a single overall plan (Goffman 1961:6).

In a weak sense of our textual metaphor, total institutions have a code or language of their own. In a stronger sense, they are a code; that is, they constitute a textual grammar and enactment, a system of signs as well as significations, a language as well as speech. It is this stronger sense that I will try to sustain.[4]

Just as there are different levels in scriptual texts, so there are different levels in behavioral or institutional texts. For example, in total institutions there are explicit written texts, such as bureaucratic records, the file kept on each inmate, or the house organ that gives the official version of the institution. These scriptual texts are explicit, official, and (because written down) more transpersonal and historical. Another level of institutional text is the verbal code and performance, the actual language and speech of the organization. A third level might be called gestural—the system of communication in which meanings are conveyed through nonscriptual and nonverbal props and actions.

We may illustrate the operation of these codes by considering the constitution and functioning within them of such basic categories as time, space, and number. Just as novelists sculpt time to achieve desired mimetic effects, so in total institutions there is a chronotopos, as Bakhtin (1968) would have said, that helps construct the reality of organizations. The *One Day in the Life of Ivan Denisovich*, for example, illustrates the new code of temporality that he has entered. Getting through the day and making it to the next day—the *durée* of one long day—becomes the horizon of experience for inmates. The vocabulary of expectations is truncated, temporally narrowed, made negative; and the self is thereby diminished. Because time is suffering and terror, opportunities for killing time (in reverie, joking, and playing cards) bring merciful relief. And since time is the property of the institution, the inmate struggles to steal some moments for his own time, as a symbol of, as well as a resource for restoring, a noninstitutional identity. For the institution time is ordered, rigid, and controlled. For the inmates time is wasted, lost, or destroyed; it is time that must be put in or done. It may be easy time or hard time, but it is always the institution's time, time taken from one's life. Thus, for example, in Chinese thought-reform prisons, one has no time of one's own:

> It is Chinese custom to allow defecation and urination only at one or two specified times each day—usually in the morning after breakfast. The prisoner is hustled from his cell by a guard, double-timed down a long corridor, and given approximately two minutes to squat over an open Chinese latrine and attend to all his wants. The haste and public scrutiny are especially difficult for women to tolerate. If the prisoners cannot complete their action in about two minutes, they are abruptly dragged away and back to their cells.
> (Hinkle and Wolff 1956:153)

Herman Melville provides another example of how time, and with it life, are measured, or measured out, on a daily basis. "In the American Navy," wrote Melville, "the law allows one gill of spirits per day to every seaman. . . . To many of them, indeed, the thought of their daily tots forms a perpetual perspective of ravishing landscapes, indefinitely receding in the distance. It is their great 'prospect in life'" (Melville n.d.:62–63).

Perhaps such control of time is most extreme in thought-reform prisons, where the institution owns the inmate's past as well as his present and future. In the process of remembering things past, even the most innocuous details of the prisoner's former life are reinterpreted in time present as symptoms of counterrevolutionary attitudes or actions (see Lifton 1956:182–84). Moreover, since all time is official time, intimacies are in principle contrary to the institutional code and hence time for them is restricted with special severity. Thus in *The First Circle* the boundaries of time are felt most in the most intimate moments. When Nerzhin meets his wife, for example, their time is so limited that they must count their every word; what in the code of normal life would be a spontaneous outpouring becomes in the prison code a careful calculation of emotions that in their nature do not admit to such calculation.

Like the chronotopos, the shape of space is also a basic code in social texts. And like time in total institutions, it is totally controlled by the established authority and minutely constricted for the inmates. The spatial code is in effect so narrowed that it leaves neither physical nor psychic room for real human activity. In *The First Circle* spatial boundaries are always close, making even the most ordinary activities a contortion. Nerzhin and Simochka are forced to hide their affair in a booth for voice instruments; Nerzhin meets his wife in the screened box. Space is divided into binary possibilities. Inside/outside, inmate's/staff's, "to go to the cold cell/to be pardoned, to work in the freezing cold/to be spared, to work when ill/to be admitted to the infirmary" (Pomorska 1980:164; see Perelman and Olbrechts-Tyteca 1969:415–59). The space belongs to the system, not to the inmates. They do not move within it; instead they are moved. Space is specialized not merely according to functions but also to express the official hierarchy of privilege, "with one ward or hut acquiring the reputation of a punishment place for especially recalcitrant inmates, while certain guard assignments become recognized as punishments for staff" (Goffman 1961a:52).

What is personal space in the code of normal life is translated into the code of the total institution, thereby abolishing former significations and imposing the institution's own order of meaning. Thus the ritual distance that on the outside signifies status differences based on race, age, or ethnicity, is collapsed into a new social topography. An upper-class English prisoner described such a redefinition of his status as he entered the new code of space: "Another warder came up with a pair of handcuffs and coupled me to the little Jew, who moaned softly to himself in Yiddish. . . . Suddenly, the awful thought occurred to me that I might have to share a cell with the little Jew and I was seized with panic. The thought obsessed me to the exclusion of all else" (Heckstall-Smith 1954:14).

The lack of control of space by inmates can result in physical as well as social contamination, as is suggested in this scene from a concentration camp hospital:

> We were lying two in a bed. And it was very unpleasant. For example, if a man died he would not be removed before twenty-four hours had elapsed because the block trusty wanted, of course, to get the bread ration and the soup which was allotted to this person. . . . And so we had to lie all that time in bed together with the dead person. . . . In most cases the dead men would soil themselves at the moment of death. . . . People who died from phlegmonous, suppurative wounds, with their beds overflowing with pus, would be lying together with somebody whose illness was possibly more benign, who had possibly just a small wound which now would become infected. (Boder 1949:50)

Even one's interior physical space may be under the control of the institutional elites, as was suggested by a young woman released from a Chilean prison, who referred to "*my* rapist," the guard whose job it was to regularly violate her. Similarly, "in some total institutions the inmate is obliged to take oral or intravenous medications, whether desired or not, and to eat his food, however unpalatable. When an inmate refuses to eat, there may be forcible contamination of his innards by 'forced feeding'" (Goffman 1961a:28).

The social etymology of this semantics of space can be drawn from Goffman's distinction between frontstage and backstage and from Durkheim's conception of the sacred and the profane, for both of these distinctions are expressed directly in personal territory. The low-status, profane inmate is all frontstage and totally exposed. Everything that he does is not only visible but is scrutinized by others. In contrast, the sanctity and inviolability of high-status officials is expressed and preserved by a large backstage into which they can withdraw unfollowed. Surrounded by a large protected space, the body of doctors or wardens is protected from profanation (see Harre 1978:156; Lyman and Scott 1967).

The organizational operation of numbers is another example of how verbal and nonverbal communication constitutes the text of social reality. As categories without contents, numbers provide an ideal vocabulary for emptying the personal identities of inmates. Thus Pomorska noted,

> The basic sign system in every place of confinement is that of
> number instead of proper names, in a concentration camp as
> well as in a hospital. The annihilating function of such a
> system is that it makes people faceless and indiscernible,
> which is what both Zamjatin and Orwell predicted. To act
> within this sort of code is to have a life indistinguishable
> from that of the person next to you. Solzhenicyn often
> mentions the fact of "going around stamped with a number"
> as the most abusive part of the system. In . . . *One Day in
> the Life of Ivan Denisovich*, . . . [when it is discovered] that
> Shukov . . . did not get up for the bell, . . . the chief warden
> shouts his *number*. Later, at any unpleasant encounter of
> Ivan Denisovich with the camp supervisors, either his own
> number or the numbers of other *zeks* are shouted, e.g., in the
> foremen's station where the protagonist washes the floor, or

during each *razvod* dispatching to huts of the brigade, or
during *shmon* when the guards time and again shout ritual
numbers: "the first, the second, the third, the fourth."
(1980:165)

That identities and activities in total institutions are "by the
number" is further shown by the routine of one jail for youthful
offenders:

At 5:30 we were wakened and had to jump out of bed and
stand at attention. When the guard shouted "One!" you
removed your night shirt; at "Two!" you folded it; at
"Three!" you made your bed. . . . All the while three
monitors would shout at us: "Hurry it up!" and "Make it
snappy!"
We also dressed by numbers: shirts on at "One!"; pants at
"Two!"; socks at "Three!"; shoes at "Four!" Any noise, like
dropping a shoe or even scraping it along the floor, was
enough to send you to the line. (McCreery, quoted in Hassler
1954:155)

Thus we could say, again following Pomorska, that "the numbers
belong to the language of those who oppress and who try to annihilate
the personality of the oppressed. In abolishing a name they take away
the living essence of a human being given by the act of naming, for this
act equals that of predication—the nucleus of the creative power of
language. Predicating or naming, we create the reality" (1980:165).
This is expressed throughout the world in rites of birth and other
passages—to give a new name is to create a new person. By the same
logic, each proper name, even if statistically common, is unique for its
bearer, thereby making him or her an individual.

The numbers impose the official code in still another way: they
permit guards to read the prisoners from afar, and thereby control
them. In Ivan Denisovich's camp, prisoners were made to paint numbers onto their clothes, leading Ivan to conclude that "The number
for our man is nothing but evil: the supervisor will notice you from a
good distance, the guard will take note and mark you down; and if
you do not renew your number in due time—you go to the punishment cell again." But even before being sent to the punishment cell,
the prisoners are already locked in an ironclad system of communication.

Time, space, and number are thus read as constituent forms of the social rituals that they express and embody. Places and periods are structured to convey meanings about selves and social settings. Indeed, anything that is structurable—even if only in a binary fashion—can bear a meaning. Thus a line drawn in the playground sandbox may demark their side and our side, just as a line drawn with barbed wire and cement can demark inside and outside. It is through such structuring that physical properties such as space and time become social signs. Similarly, numbers acquire their social signification not by their inherent logical structure, but by being structured in juxtaposition to supposedly unstructured, spontaneous, non-numerical human beings.

The particular structuring of the total institution is that of an over-determined text, filled with coercively enforced codes. It is a narrow and constricted world in which characters are uniform because they can articulate themselves only through rigid rules and reified symbols. In the social texts as represented by Goffman and Solzhenitsyn, however, "speech" (in Saussure's term) still may prevail over "language," for the calculatedly oppressive institutional code also prescribes the possible escapes from it (Kogon 1958:254). Within the mental hospitals and prisons, in these lower depths, persons emerge again as naked agents. By resisting or evading institutional authority, inmates again become the authors of themselves, albeit in an immensely truncated sphere. The oppressive code restricts their speech to its binary essence—good or evil, life or death. But it is the very limitations of this authorial space that give a primordial authority to inmates' choices.

Politicae Sub Specie Semioticae

The normalization of textual action or social interaction require that certain rules of construction not be continually called into question. This also applies to political conduct. Just as practice within a specialized institution is conducted through its reigning grammar, so public action within a political community is made possible by the grammars—constitutions, common laws, or traditions—through which political thought and conduct may be expressed. By this way of thinking, transformation of the grammars of a polity is a definition of revolution. Thus the political rhetor seeking to create a revolution must shift the fundamental assumptions by which the presently given world is defined. He must proffer an alternative notion of the nature of reality and the ways we can seize it—that is, must offer an alternative public language, an alternative way of encoding and decoding the world (see Bennett 1977; Fisher 1970).

An example of a revolution in this sense is the convulsion in the collective grammar of political practice that occurred in England at the beginning of the modern era. The Faustian ambivalence of the Renaissance gave way to the Revolution of Saints. Calvinism provided a new grammar for politics and nature, for self-control and collective self-direction (Walzer 1965, 1967; Craig 1970:193). Similar revolutions in political grammars probably could be noted in the theories of the Enlightenment philosophes and the French Revolution, in Marxism-Leninism and the Soviet Revolution, or in Maoism and the Great Proletarian Revolution. André Breton made a similar point when he observed that there would be no proletarian literature in the Soviet Union until the nature of language had been modified (Breton 1967:113–15).

Once such sea changes have occurred and the waters again have settled, people tend once more to take the background rules for granted. Again they hold certain truths to be self-evident. Indeed, in the holding of these truths, they again become a "we," a community of civic discourse, characters in a unified text. The revolution has served as a rite of passage, and those who have undergone it experience a new gestalt. They and their world are no longer the same. The new vision is not convincing because it describes the world more precisely. The vision is compelling because it *creates* a world that is more existentially adequate (see Strong 1978; Wolin 1960).

To see the polity as text is to understand it as a process of communication in which each new item of information is interpreted in terms of other messages already pronounced, as well as in terms of the reciprocal reaction it engenders on the part of the political addressee. The grammar in which the text is written guides perception and establishes the range of what will be taken as a real or possible fact. In this way, happenings are organized into events through the attribution of meanings. And dialectically these meanings provide for the facticity of experience and orchestrate it into the textual grammar of that polity, a grammar that is itself the rules by which those meanings are generated. By uniting persons in a system of political communication, the textual grammar constitutes them as a polity. Membership within this system of communication, of course, brings with it the possibility of conflict between persons who speak the same language but different dialects. What is most meaningful in one class or gender position, for example, might be intelligible but unimportant in another. Different readings of the common text may stem from different levels of interpretation, different segmentations, different perceptions of primacy between the segments, or different punctuations of causality.

Such an interpretation of polities is illustrated by the efforts of Peter the Great to rewrite the text of Russian society.[5] One interpretation of this period is that Peter was using a European language of polities wholly alien to that of pre-Petrine Russia. But another interpretation is also possible, that "post-Petrine culture was more traditional than is usually thought, in that Peter negated the existing code without creating a new one." In this view, Peter's Russia "was constructed not so much on models from Western culture (although it was subjectively experienced as Western) as on an inverted structural plan of the old culture" (Lotman and Uspenskij 1985:54). What is clear is that the masses of Russians strongly disapproved of Peter's reforms. As Uspenskij pointed out, many documents of the period attest to this negative popular view of Peter. By analyzing them "we can disclose the directly formal, semiotic state of affairs behind such a reaction" (Uspenskij 1977:108).

The dependence of popular perception of Peter's actions on a political grammar of interpretation is particularly obvious in such matters as Peter's marriage to Catherine, his assumption of the titles "Father of the fatherland" and "the First," and such cultural innovations as the forced shaving of beards and the adoption of German in place of Russian garb. The uproar caused by Peter's marriage, for example, hinges on the semantics of the word "father." Peter's son, the tsarevitch Aleksej Petrovic, was Catherine's godfather, and thus when she entered the Orthodox Church she took the name "Alekseevna," that is, "daughter of Aleksej." Because of this, Catherine's spiritual relationship to Peter was that of "granddaughter." The fact that Peter was getting married for the second time, or that he had forced his

living wife to become a nun, was not nearly so unprecedented or out-
rageous as the spiritual incest and blasphemy against fundamental
Christian laws that his marriage to his "granddaughter" Catherine
represented.

Moreover, in addition to such titles as "Emperor" and "the Great,"
Peter also took the title of "Father of the fatherland." This of course
is a direct translation of the Latin *pater patriae* used by Roman em-
perors. Whereas in the Roman political grammar pater patriae indi-
cated a fitting spiritual fatherhood of the people, in its Russian translation this appelation signified a usurpation of the spiritual role of the
Orthodox Church. For in pre-Petrine Russia, "only a member of the
church hierarchy could be a spiritual father, and in turn the title 'father of the fatherland' could only be applied to an archpastor-bishop
and primarily to the patriarch. And indeed that is how the universal
patriarchs of Constantinople and Alexandria were referred to"
(Uspenskij 1977:108). To put his message in italics, as it were, Peter
adopted the title "Father of the fatherland" just when he abolished
the patriarchate and designated himself as "Supreme Judge" of the
Ecclesiastical College. Given the political grammar of the time, these
plays on the term "father" by Peter were read accurately by his sup-
porters and detractors alike.

Peter's message—interpreted of necessity as a blasphemous assumption of spiritual primacy—was reiterated in his command that
he be named without patronymic, that is, his insistence that he be
addressed as the father of himself, as "Peter the First" rather than
"Peter, the son of ———" In pre-Petrine Russia, spiritual authority
came from origins, with the first being the highest, just as Constantinople and Moscow were considered to be the "second" and the
"third" Rome. By demanding that he be addressed as "the First,"
Peter ordered that he be considered a saint or spiritual genitor—not
merely the founder of a worldly political order, but a godly one as
well. This was underlined, on the one hand, by Peter's allowing himself to be called "God" or "Christ" and to be worshipped almost
religiously and on the other, by Peter's mocking disdain for traditional religious rites, as in his "All-Jest Synod" or in the mock wedding he arranged for the patriach, performed by a real priest from the
Cathedral of the Archangel. Given the political grammar of pre-Pe-

these messages had an inevitable interpretation: Peter was the Antichrist.

Likewise, the forced shaving of beards and the adoption of German clothing were not merely symbols of modernization but also, and more precisely, inversions of the iconography of the epoch. There is of course a grammar to hair and clothing in every culture. In the early days of Rome, for example, the difference slave/free was expressed by the contrast shaven/bearded—until a technical revolution made shaving much less disagreeable, encouraging Hadrian to decree that henceforth slaves be bearded and their masters not (Barthes 1967; Cooper 1971; Harre 1978:160). In the case of pre-Petrine Russia, however, the inversion of the heraldry of hair was even more dramatic, since in the religious representations of the period only demons shaved and wore Western dress. The naked face commanded by Peter was thus an officially required heresy and, being read as such, was strenuously condemned by the Church. The same was true of Western clothing. In the pre-Petrine period, foreigners living in Russia were forbidden to wear Russian clothes, whereas German clothing was used for masquerade costumes. Peter changed these signs into their contraries: henceforth Russians were forbidden to wear Russian clothes except mockingly, as at the weddings of the court jesters Sanskij and Kokoskin, or as a punishment for schoolboys. The opposition between Russian and Western dress was preserved, therefore, but the signification was inverted.

These examples could be extended, but they are sufficient to permit a textual interpretation of Peter's efforts to transform the Russian polity. In these terms, Peter's actions did not constitute a social revolution so much as an antisignification within the same social-textual boundaries. His actions make sense as negations or contraries of the dominant pre-Petrine signs, but all the while operating within the same syntactic system. In this reading, Peter's revolution was not a revolution at all. Instead of creating a new language for political conduct, Peter's deeds publically declared him to be the Antichrist, an image that was inscribed in the political text beforehand. The inorganic combination of Russian and Western, Christian and godless, and spiritual and despotic operated within the same traditional text. Only now this text was deeply bifurcated, filled with a self-negation that was to be felt for many years to come.

Of Metaphor and Method

What are the limits of the textual metaphor? What does it imply for the methods of logic of the social sciences? Paul Ricouer said that

> the notion of text is good paradigm for human action . . . . [because] human action is in many ways a quasi-text. In becoming detached from its agent, the action acquires an autonomy similar to the semantic autonomy of a text; it leaves a trace, a mark. It is inscribed in the course of things and becomes an archive and document. Even more like a text, of which the meaning has been freed from the initial conditions of its production, human action has a stature that is not limited to its importance for the situation in which it initially occurs, but allows it to be reinscribed in new social contexts. Finally, action, like a text, is an open work, addressed to an indefinite series of possible "readers." (1968:160–61).

If societies are like texts because both treat human action, how, then, are we to treat humans as acted upon? That is, if textual analysis is essentially hermeneutic analysis of meanings objectified in intentional conduct, how can it address those aspects of society that are superintended or determined, aspects that need to be explained and critically assessed, not just understood? Should sociologists abandon their enterprise to philologists? Or does social-textual analysis embrace explanations of causes and laws as well as interpretation of reasons or intentions? By these questions may be judged the relevance of the textual metaphor for social science as a whole.

My responses to these concerns are animated by the larger telos of this volume: to advance a theoretical-cultural practice that assumes the primacy of human authorship. There are two basic ways to provide a warrant for this assumption. The first strategy is to enter the fortress of positivism and show that, like interpretation, positivist science is itself a verbal art. This was my aim in *A Poetic for Sociology* (1977), and it also has been the project, at least implicitly, of Nelson Goodman (1951), Paul Feyerabend (1978), and Richard Rorty (1972). I will not repeat this argumentation here. The second strategy is not to show explanation to be interpretive, but the reverse: to show that text interpretation properly includes explanation. I will argue this point by two tactics: by responding to criticisms of the hermeneutic

method, and by showing that text analysis includes not only hermeneutics but also semiotics as its methods of explication.

Wilhelm Dilthey (1957-1960) remains a major theorist of hermeneutics as well as a prime source for responses to criticisms and
misunderstandings of the methods of social-textual analysis. One line
of criticism of Dilthey, of hermeneutics, and of the textual analysis of
society is that it denies the utility of scientific sociological methods.
But this allegation is untrue. Dilthey did argue that hermeneutic interpretation is crucial in the human studies (1957:7:220–27); yet his
interpretive procedure was not opposed to science in being pretheoretical or antideductive. On the contrary, the hermeneutic circle
of social-textual interpretation brings in natural facts and generalizations wherever appropriate. Dilthey gives numerous examples of how
interpretations must be constrained by theoretical knowledge of the
natural sciences (1957:5:139, 281; Makkreel 1985:239). Historical
reconstruction may involve knowledge of metallurgy in order to date
weapons or coins; archeology may require a knowledge of structural
engineering; art history may require a knowledge of optics and chemistry. But such scientific knowledge cannot be central to the human
sciences, for they depend on hermeneutic procedures for the very definition of their subject matter. Unlike the natural sciences, which may
interpret various sets of events, the events for the human studies are
themselves interpretations, or more precisely the objectifications of
the interpretations of other persons.

A similar but more subtle and ambivalent criticism of hermeneutics
has been launched by such neo-Marxist writers as Horkheimer (1939)
and Habermas (1968), who have criticized Dilthey's hermeneutics for
its "bourgeois" features: methodological individualism and its concomitant idealism. Horkheimer's assessment, though ungenerous, reflects an intuitive sense of the boundaries of hermeneutic thought.
Implicit in Horkheimer's criticism is a distinction between what might
be called humanistic as opposed to social-structural levels of analysis.
In terms of Rousseau's paradox, "Man is born free yet is everywhere
in chains," Dilthey advanced a program of universal self-analysis
through history with respect to human freedom. In contrast, mac-
rosociologists such as Marx, Weber, or Durkheim were more interested in the chains that limit individual freedom, and this led them
to structural analysis of the social scarcities in which all persons are

involved. What such distinctions overlook, however, is that the social forces that limit persons' autonomy—to the extent that these forces are social—may have their origins in some persons' consciousness. The "rationalization of production" or the "competition for foreign markets" may narrow the freedom of workers; and for analytic utility these forces may be treated as impersonal naturalistic events, much as climatic changes can be consequential for historical action. Yet such a heuristic is in no way inconsistent with the hermeneutic assumption that such events, if they are to be understood, must be seen as deriving from actions taken by individuals. One group of persons may impose their definitions and intentions on other groups; but this in itself provides no logical justification for reifying the actions of the stronger group into forces.

Even with this proviso, however, much remains of social reality that is not malleable to any person's intentions and indeed it is just such constraints that provide the field for human praxis. In Sartrean terms, society is not only praxis but also practico-inert; it is like nature. Thus to the extent that society is the product of conscious human intentions, a Diltheyan hermeneutic will better encompass what is salient. But to the extent that history is made "behind the backs and against the wills" of even powerful persons, then structural and dialectical modes of social-textual analysis are also needed.

If these are limits to hermeneutic interpretation, they do not require a rejection of the metaphor of society as text. For it is precisely within the textual metaphor that the antinomies of interpretation and explanation and of freedom and constraint may be held in double vision. This is because textual analysis offers its own mode of explanation: semiotics. That is, in addition to hermeneutic interpretation that focuses on semantics and pragmatics, textual analysis of society also engages in structural explanation that focuses on syntactics and grammatics. Unlike the rupture between the discourse of interpretation and explanation within the social sciences generally, however, these two discourses may be dialectically conjoined in the metaphor of society as text. To develop this point I need to sketch a theory of language in light of structuralism and semiotics.

Semiotics has two principal sources: the pragmatic phenomenology of signs invented by Charles Peirce (and later vulgarized in American symbolic interactionism), and the structural linguistics of Ferdinand de Saussure. A brief excursis on the latter will serve our purpose here.[6] Saussure's seminal innovation was to distinguish the structure of significations as encoded in the system of language from the history of meanings as expressed in speech. On this distinction a science of purely synchronic systems of differences, oppositions, and combinations was founded. This science—structural linguistics—was developed by the Geneva, Prague, and Danish schools, first by decoding the phonemic components of which words are constructed; then by extending the method to the lexicon and sentences of natural languages; then by applying it to units of speech larger than the sentence, such as the story or the myth; and finally by extrapolating the linguistic model to such nonlinguistic sign systems as the worlds of fashion, food, faces, families, females, and the physical environment (Ricoeur 1978:152).[7]

Given two central assumptions of the structuralist method—that spoken language is a sign system among many possible sign systems, and that sign systems have a hermetic, autoreferential character—space is cleared for a fullblown semiotics of society. Verbal sign systems—such as tales or myths—openly call for textual analysis. But in an equally strict sense, so do nonverbal systems of signs. Thus, what Levi-Strauss said of structures of kinship is no less true of etiquette, total institutions, or political communities:

> Marriage rules and systems of kinship are considered a kind of language, that is to say, a set of operations designed to ensure a certain type of communication between individuals and groups. That the "message" is here made up of the *women of the group* who *circulate* between the clans, dynasties or families (and not as in language itself by the *words of the group* circulating between individuals) does not affect the basic identity of the phenomenon in both cases. (1963:69)

The major disjunctions of the social sciences as a whole, then, seem to be reproduced within social-textual analysis itself:

positivism	versus	romanticism
explanation	versus	understanding
objectivity	versus	subjectivity
distantiation	versus	identification
language	versus	speech

```
    syntactics   versus   semantics
        system   versus   life world
 structuralism   versus   hermeneutics
```

It thus appears that our initial questions were formulated in a misleading way. The important question is not how textual analysis can be reconciled with positivist sociology, but how romantic and positivistic ways of knowing can be sublated within the textual (or any other) metaphor of society. I believe that the textual metaphor recommends itself as a situs for such sublation on both moral and logical grounds: morally, because this metaphor reinforces the conception of human agency, the recognition of which is a cultural precondition for any possible ethics; logically, because whereas the textual metaphor can include structural, deterministic, and causal explanations, nonlinguistic metaphors of society such as the machine or the organism eschew an understanding of human will and reason. A sociology of human freedom presupposes an analysis of the scarcities and constraints that form the context for human choice. But the reverse is not true. Deterministic sociologies do not logically require a theory of human agency for their completion.

The sublation of positivist and romantic ways of social-textual analysis is not possible without their modification. First, romantic hermeneutics needs to be augmented with a critical, depth hermeneutics that stresses miscomprehensions, thwarted intentions, and false consciousness, as much as it stresses conscious intention as a focus for hermeneutic interpretation (Bourdieu 1977; Gadamer 1975; Habermas 1968). This recommendation implies a corresponding shift in the structuralist conception of language. That is, to direct hermeneutic inquiry toward *mis*understandings is to implicitly challenge the semiotic view of the text as a set of self-contained codes, the machinelike operation of which would in principle obviate the possibility of such misunderstanding. As Jonathan Culler (1977:32–54) has shown, such a structuralist view reifies the conception of language and invites arbitrary attributions of signification.

One way around this difficulty, following Emilio Betti, would be to revive Humboldt's distinction between *Sprache* (language) and *Rede* (speech, discourse). These concepts prefigure Saussure's distinction between langue and parole, but without Saussure's reification of the former and denigration of the latter. Instead, for Humboldt language is an *ergon* that objectifies itself in *energeia*, in living speech. Drawing on Husserl's distinction between actuality and objectivity, the relationship between Humboldt's *Sprache* and *Rede* can be understood as a dialectical interaction between meaning intentions of the speaker and the meaning inherent in the object, or form. As Betti (1955:111) put it, "if one considers the speech act as a mediating activity, then the totality of language appears as the living actuality of the linguistic formulation of inner experience. Language is, therefore, actualized in speech as thought and position-taking, and speech transforms language into a living presence." (1955:111)

All language is figural and nonreferential, yet we must consider it only partially so. We must insist that some uses of language are metaphorical and others are not, thereby denoting some things as real, replete with identity and presence, whereas others are mere fictions. As Rousseau noted in his *Essay on the Origin of Language*, the assignment of a literal meaning may blind us to the purely hypothetical quality of all linguistically generated activity, yet such blindness is necessary for our sight and for our capacity to cognize things as real.

Such illusions are the very stuff of social reality. As Goffman has shown, social action is directed at "maintaining the definition of the situation" in order, in effect, to suppress its fictive character so that other activities/fictions can be conducted within it. "Definitional disruptions would occur much more frequently were not constant precautions taken." The grammar of social life requires that "others" be "forced to accept some events as conventional or natural signs of something not directly available to the senses" (Goffman 1959:2). Hermeneutic interpretation keeps this structural grammar in the background in order to focus on the meanings that are generated within it. Semiotics keeps the intended meanings in the background in order to focus on the structures by which they are generated.

Semiotics and hermeneutics are thus dialectically interdependent. Semiotics does not automatically tell us what is important in a social text. It becomes most helpful after we have identified what needs explaining. It is not a tool for the interpretation of meaning or intention, but rather a method for organizing the interpretable and the results of interpretation (Culler 1981). Semiotics is not concerned with the decoding of individual utterances or actions, but with the laws, conventions, and operations that allow meaningful utterances to take place and be understood. Whereas hermeneutics asks "What does it mean?" semiotics inquires "How are such meanings possible?" (de Man 1973:28; MacCannell 1976:5).

The potential meanings of an action/text are always fuller than intended by the author, because the future contexts and consequences of such actions are always more ample than the possible intentions of the original actors. Hence the interpretation of the social text involves not merely a hermeneutic recognition of the actor's intended meaning, but also a semiotic cognition of the unintended, often unstable, presuppositions and outcomes of conduct. As Bleicher noted:

> Sociology cannot be reduced to a *vershehen* psychology since
> only a limited part of human actions are consciously
> undertaken. It is equally impossible to rely on a naturalistic,
> generalizing approach since this would lead to the neglect of
> the historical specificity of these phenomena. . . . The
> differences here are fundamental ones: on the one side the
> mediation of the interpretation of meaning through a subject
> that is itself located within a context of traditional meaning;
> on the other side, the investigation of structures within a
> system of signs that functions according to objective laws and
> independently of an understanding subject. (1980:44, 216)

Yet each of these antinomies requires the other not only for its completion but also for its very essence. The hermeneutic reduction to meaning, or the poststructuralist deconstruction of meaning, all require some totalization as the background to their reductions. For example, though the very diversity of interpretations of a social text may show that all interpretations are in some sense arbitrary, it also shows the opposite, for insofar as these are understood to be interpretations of the same text they are presumed to be mutually intelligible within a common frame of reference and, hence, nonarbitrary (Graff 1982). In the same sense Deleuze's conception of the schizophrenic text or Derrida's notion that all frameworks are fictions of power both depend on some initial appearance of wholeness and continuity that already exists and which they seek to undermine or shatter. This mutual interdependence, of interpretation of meaning and semiotics of structure, is further illustrated by the debate between Jacques Derrida and John Searle (see especially Derrida 1977; Searle 1977, 1983).

According to Derrida, the conventions of intelligibility are "by essence violable and precarious, *in themselves* and by the fictionality that constitutes them." Yet as Searle pointed out (and as can be argued from Derrida's own earlier writings), Derrida's absolute relativism provides no standpoint from which such conventions could be labeled a fiction. That is, no matter how hard we try to put intelligibility into question, we can only do so from some standpoint of intelligibility. Otherwise we are talking nonsense. Structures of sense making are inescapable in that all interpretations, even those that challenge intelligibility, depend on some assumed framework or grammar from which meanings can be generated. Derrida is right to point out that absolute objectivity is a chimera, and Searle is right to note that absolute relativity is self-defeating. But why should we have to choose either?

These considerations return us to the problem stated at the outset of this chapter: the transformation of both positivist and romantic thought through the medium of textual analysis. For if hermeneutic thought destroys the fiction of absolute objectivity in positivist social science, semiotic thought reveals the structural limits of a purely subjective interpretive sociology. Such a subjectivistic sociology—in the romantic rather than the positivist mode—interprets social behavior in terms of motives that are identical with the subject's own assessments of the situation. Sociological meanings thus become equivalent to linguistically articulated meanings; that is, they are assumed to be isomorphic with the verbal statements by which the actor orients himself. But even a subjectivistic hermeneutic recognizes that interpretation in terms of motives is not the same as explanation in terms of cause. Motives or intentions do not cause actions; instead they provide a teleological account for them. Subjective-interpretive social science has demonstrated that intentional action is relatively autonomous of nonintentional, natural constraints, and that it must be accounted for by rules rather than laws. Yet the question remains: Whence come these rules? And it is here that semiotic thought reveals that a purely subjectivistic meaning-interpretive sociology is itself a kind of myth, in that it posits a world of speech outside the rules of language.

Semiotic analysis of social texts has its beginning and end in human speech. But hermeneutic analysis of meanings that are intended in speech cannot be a merely subjective interpretation, because the linguistic context of meaning is always larger than the contexts of meanings that may have been subjectively intended by the original actors. Indeed, it is only through analysis of the rules of discourse that we can come to know what possible meanings the original actor may have intended. By setting limits on both objectivistic and subjectivistic ways of knowing, textual analysis gives birth to a new freedom, a freedom suggested by Dilthey and expanded by contemporary critical theorists and semioticians, a freedom that emerges dialectically in and through a field of constraint.

Textual analysis of society not only reveals that received forms of knowledge are determined by the structures of language; it also shows them to be invented through acts of speech. In this sense the textual view draws on the tradition of Western humanism, though this humanism is now transvalued through self-reflective criticism. Marsilio Ficino invoked this heritage when he defined the person as both finite and free, as a "rational soul participating in the intellect of God, but operating in a body." That to be human is to be both subject and object was also recognized by Pico della Mirandola in his essay "On the Dignity of Man." Pico did not say that man is the center of the world, but only that God placed man at the center of the universe so that he might be conscious of where he stands, and so become "with freedom of choice and with honor, . . . the maker and molder of himself" (Pico 1956:7).

Whatever luggage the term humanism may have acquired since the Renaissance, one moment of its meaning remains the person as a conscious and intending actor capable of exercising *virtus*—a moral courage in life that combines virtuosity with virtue. In such a view, moral agency is understood as the capacity to create culture. This capacity is central to being human, and as linguists and philosophers have shown us, every person has acquired this ability by the time she has learned to speak (Vygotsky 1962). The textual metaphor invites us to investigate our linguistic constraints and capacities, because it sees persons as carriers of preformed linguistic structures as well as agents who perform culture and speech. By simultaneously addressing both structure and agency, such an approach not only can unmask overdetermined encodations; it also offers hope for developing practical definitions of morally and politically competent discourse— the modern virtus of speech. Textual analysis of society is central to what Habermas (1970) and Stanley (1978) regard as the next stage in the moral evolution of Reason: the development of a rational ethic of civic communication.

My representation of society as text is thus intended neither to bury positivist social science nor to praise romantic human studies, but instead to affirm them both, once they are reconstituted and conjoined on a more sophisticated and reflective level. For the textual metaphor invites us not only to reject the naive copy theory of traditional positivism but also to renounce the naive intuitionism of traditional romanticism. Instead, our attention is now focused on the dialectical interplay between rules and actions, *Sprache* and *Rede:* the constraints and freedom of persons writing, being written into, and reading their worlds.

Seven

Narrative Fiction as Social Text
Literature, Literary Theory, and the Self
as Social-Symbolic Act

> Fictional worlds are metaphors for real worlds, metaphors that may
> themselves become literal descriptions. Fictional worlds make and
> unmake and remake real worlds in recognizable ways, in ways that
> may again be re-cognized as real.
>> Goodman (1978:105)

> The narrator is the voice of the symbol. His role is to mediate the
> individual consciousness and the collective consciousness, symbols
> of reality and symbols of utopia.
>> Krysinski (1977:58)

As SOCIETY CAN BE SEEN as a factual text, so fictional texts can be
viewed as social-symbolic acts, as representations of possible selves
and societies. With the collapse of moral agency in public life, however, contemporary civic culture has been eviscerated of narrative
forms, and meaningful plots are ever harder to find in society and in
fiction. From Cervantes to Balzac to the contemporary antinovel, the
scope of narrative has steadily narrowed. Correspondingly the scope
of information, commercial entertainment, social science, and ideology have widened, so much so that today traditional narrative is
almost dead. To explain its demise is to account for the collapse of
intelligible moral-political discourse in our culture.

I will take narrative to mean an account of an agent whose character or destiny unfolds through events in time. Thus "The king died
and the queen died" is no narrative; but "The king died, and the
queen died of grief" is a narrative, because the latter events are linked
to the earlier ones, revealing character through actions and forming a
plot. Plot gives integrity to the actions as a whole as well as to the
characters represented. Plot is the means by which essential features
of human existence are expressed through specific events. By organizing actions into a logically unfolding development, the author can
show in a palpable fashion the tension between what the character
takes or wishes himself to be and what the world tells him that he is.

Plot conveys a moral meaning by encoding in actions some item of wisdom that auditors can decode into their own lived experience.

What is the social situation in which narratives may thrive? If narratives are accounts of agents whose character or destiny unfolds through actions and events in time, then the existence of narratives presupposes a social order of meaning in which significant action by moral agents is possible. Narrative requires a political economy and collective psychology in which a sense of lived connection between personal character and public conduct prevails. But such a presupposition is less and less valid in advanced industrial cultures, and this is why narratives have become an endangered species. Their habitat has been destroyed, and they now live mainly in laboratories and zoos. To develop this thesis I will show narrative to be an emblem of a larger social text, first by advancing a rhetoric of aesthetic forms, then by tracing the development of the modern novel as an aesthetic form and subjecting it to a rhetorical analysis. Finally I will argue that narrative, despite its travails, remains essential for a humane civic discourse.

Toward a Rhetoric of Aesthetic Forms

From a rhetorical viewpoint, the production, reception, and interpretation of works of art are inextricably embedded in particular communities of discourse that are defined by shared presuppositions, similar expectations, and common grammars of expression. Such a rhetorical view of art differs from most contemporary approaches. The sociology of culture in America—for the most part positivist studies of career paths, networks, and organizations—could be related as much to the production and consumption of autos as of art. Conversely, European sociology of art, though sensitive to history and philosophy and informed by connoisseurship, lacks the empirical rigor and systematic grounding typical of American social science.

One way to overcome these twin limitations is to invoke Kuhn's conception of paradigm to refer to genres or aesthetic forms. Such a transposition has in fact been suggested by Jonathan Culler: "Recently . . . genres have been treated as normative conventions that permit the possibility of creating meaning, codes for encyphering and decyphering experience. Understood this way, genres are seen to function somewhat as paradigms operate in science—they are shared canons of representation and interpretation that render experience valid and significant" (1977:11). The use of Kuhn's concept in the domain of the arts is also warranted by our postpositivist, postromantic understanding that the barriers between science and art are weaker than we once thought. This is not because science is an art or because art is a science, but because both are now envisioned as socially constructed systems of symbols. As such they are distinct domains within the sphere of the social and the cognitive (Goodman 1978:102).[1]

Everything that we can signify is subject to human understanding, even though such understanding is as varied as our methods of symbolization. Works of art make (and take their shape from) artistic worlds, as scientific theories do from scientific worlds. Members of such worlds, as Kuhn said, "have undergone similar education and professional initiations. . . . [and] have absorbed the same technical literature and drawn many of the same lessons from it" (1972:177). Like scientists, artists cannot make their works in any way they choose. Production in both science and art requires patronage, audience, and techniques appropriate to any particular work. The proper unit of analysis for a sociology of art is therefore not so much specific works as it is genres, schools, art worlds, or paradigms. These are reflected but not wholly contained within any work itself. The stress on genres or paradigms focuses analytic attention on the social-contextual and historical forces that impinge on artistic production, particularly in times of paradigm shifts, when the conflict between aesthetic/social visions is more readily understood as a conflict between political or economic factions. The idea of genres as aesthetic paradigms thus stresses the cognitive, institutional, and political aspects of art, not merely its psychological or aesthetic functions. Paradigms are a means of imposing control as well as a resource that dissidents may use in organizing their awareness and action. They are what Kaplan (1964:11, 61) called logics in use, the chief use being that of social control within a community of practitioners. The artistic activities of such communities are what constitute "normal art," the orderly continuity of the genre, school, or mode of interpretation.

Seen in this light, every form of literature or of literary criticism has political import, for all texts draw upon a larger cultural context that they help to maintain or to transform. The author's personal intent has little to do with this dependence of text on context. More important is the form or genre through which the author realizes her intentions. The genre is a definition of the world, and it provides the frame for deciphering what the author's intentions might have been. The author might even fade into a montage of audience, interpretations, textual connotations, and critical invasions. What we call the "author" becomes an artifact of her text as this text is defined in a social matrix of discourse. The author's identity, like that of the narrator within any possible story, is itself inconstant, for it depends on readers' conceptions of the author's role and intentions, which change with each generation or social group (Polanyi 1958).

Just as discourse fictionalizes the author, it may also fictionalize the audience, in the sense that the audience, like the author, is cast into a role by the text. Thus, for example, the rhetorical tradition in Western letters, allied with logic and dialectic, fictionalized the audience as organized in agonistic structures—as defenders of theses, legislative adversaries, or hawks and doves. With the rise of positivism and the decline of rhetoric, however, the audience was cast into a different role. Positivism does not employ a conflict methodology but instead assumes that all of its facts are construed through a single observational theory. And as faith in argumentative reason was replaced by faith in positivist science, the prudent citizen assumed in previous discourse was replaced by a rational man stripped of sagacity, passions, and emotions. Indeed, even his body was removed, leaving a pure *cogito* in place of a living public (see Ong 1975; Mead 1934; Ferguson 1973; Christie 1977; Feyerabend 1978).

In times when a given paradigm is regnant, the authorial intention or audience interpretation may appear self-evident. But in times of paradigm conflict it becomes clear that meaning, even in normal discourse, is paradigm induced. The author must employ language that is inherently polysemous. The exact range of such ambiguities is given to the author by the cultural tradition and contemporary community of speech in which she finds herself. Given the multivalency of her speech for various audiences, she cannot control all the plausible meanings conveyed by her text. Borges said that every writer creates his own precursors in that his work modifies our conception of the past. Similarly, every writer's work is created by its future: by the interpretations of future audiences which read the text through a different linguistic code. And the new meanings thereby drawn from the text may be outside any range of ambiguity that the author could have intended.[2]

Most authors live in their own time, reinforcing or extending contemporary assumptions. In contrast, great authors are born posthumously (as Nietzsche said of himself): they write for an audience that does not yet exist. Their authorial greatness lies in their having authorized a new vision of ourselves and our world, in having initiated a genre and engendered a public for their work. When the poet Hugo von Hofmannsthal, for example, read a certain essay by Walter Benjamin, who was then completely unknown, he called it *"schlechthin unvergleichlich"* (absolutely incomparable). The trouble for Benjamin was that Hofmannsthal was literally correct, for there was nothing else in existing literature to which Benjamin's work could be compared (Arendt 1968:3). Unlike most authors, who reaffirm current perceptions, Benjamin summoned forth an alternative definition of the world and thereby authorized a new form of social existence.

That artistic authors, audiences, and schools are socially defined is illustrated by Bernard Berenson's creation, and then destruction, of the artist Amico di Sandro.

> The history of his other creation, Amico di Sandro, is a gruesome tale of disinterested infanticide. There was, Berenson felt, one artist whose style combined the features of Sandro Botticelli and Filippino Lippi, with a dash of Ghirlandaio; he wasn't any of these but he leaned most heavily toward Botticelli. Berenson christened him Amico di Sandro and attributed a group of pictures to him. . . . [Amico's] market value in America went up steadily. One of the greatest American collectors paid altitudinous prices for him. . . . But then Berenson began to disapprove of Amico. His patient and laborious studies finally persuaded him that Amico was too good to be true. Nobody, Berenson felt, could be that good—so consistent, so distinctive. In the strong solution of Berenson's scholarship, Amico disintegrated. Berenson divided him into three parts: he gave part of him back to Botticelli, part to Filippino Lippi, and part to Ghirlandaio. The effect on the American collector who paid so high for Amico was catastrophic. (Behrman 1952:156–57)

The point I am making with this anecdote is not merely that style makes the man, but that style and authorship are both created from a social community of discourse that includes the influences of other works, canons of quality, social reception, and the historical traditions of interpretation. The stylistic and other features of a work that denote membership in a school or genre are not merely products of a given author. More importantly, authorship and stylistic features are themselves products of social categories into which are grouped (or by which are constituted) authors and works. In the story above, Berenson "made" an artist to whom he attributed the coherence he discovered (or invented?) in a collection of works as a style. When further assessment and an expansion of the sample destroyed the coherence visible within the earlier formulation, Berenson just as quickly "unmade" its author (see Silvers 1981:270; Hernadi 1981).

Through the methods of rhetoric we can understand artistic (or scientific) revolutions as processes by which original, poetic modes of representation become literal and prosaic. Conversely, art (or science) describes reality only to the extent that its metaphoric construction of experience has become frozen. Realistic representation appears as such only when a given genre or paradigm has become commonplace, a dead metaphor that is taken as a literal description. Realistic art or science is not convincing because it is realistic; instead it is realistic because we have already been convinced.[3]

The history of art, like the history of science, abounds with examples of absurdities later taken as truths, that is, of metaphors that were spritely when new but that have become frozen. *Créer un poncif*—to create a commonplace—this was Baudelaire's ideal: to invent something so unprecedented it would at first be taken as absurd, only to have a discourse form around it which would transform the initial absurdity into a banality. Similarly, "the world as a machine" for Descartes became "the world is a machine" for Newton. In this way a metaphoric half-truth of artistic or scientific invention may become institutionalized as a whole doctrine—not merely accepted, but indispensable to the further experiments done under its aegis. "Knowledge of the socio-historical context of a literary work or genre is not therefore an 'extra' to be kept in the margins of rhetorical analysis. In general, whether one is aware of it or not, such knowledge furnishes the starting point for interpretation itself" (Moretti 1983:8).

As long as a dominant paradigm reigns without challenge, and as long as artists and lay people use the same grammar of representation, aesthetic mimesis may remain as fully integrated into culture as religious discourse was integrated into archaic society. But if anomalies are noticed, if alternative grammars of representation come into use, and if the messages conveyed through the regnant paradigm lose their existential justness, then artists and savants become alien to the dominant culture. As the social armature begins to crack, the seedlings of new modes of representation fall into its fissures. If the new roots spread out softly and quickly, the stonework of society may hold. But it is also possible that the old codes will break down before the new ones are in place. Then things will fall apart, and what the society had unreflectively taken as reality will collapse into a rubble of icons once thought to be immutable reflections of the real. Instead of reinforcing the previously regnant paradigm, "literature becomes a process of demystification, an unmaking of the sanctified views of the epoch revealing, for example, the exploitation beneath the affluence or the despotism behind the united front. Henceforth, no language is considered *per se* as *the* metaphor for translating . . . reality" (Gavronsky 1979:3).

The Vagaries of Narrative as an Aesthetical-Rhetorical Form

The first step in the demise of narrative was the invention of the novel, for this was a major break with earlier, oral forms of narrative that presupposed a community of experience between rhetor and auditors. The epic, the legend, the fairy tale, the *skaz*, and even the novella can all be told in one sitting. This distinguishes the novel from the story telling or play enacting of all premodern cultures. The storyteller draws on his own experience and those of others and makes this material into experience for the persons who are copresent as he unfolds his story. In contrast, as Benjamin remarked, "the novelist has isolated himself. The birthplace of the novel is the solitary individual, who is no longer able to express himself by giving examples of his most important concerns" (Benjamin 1968:87; see Ong 1977:21). Indeed, the solitary reader, reading a book read by many other such solitary readers, is an image of the world to which the novel is proper: the modern world of mass privacy (Holquist and Reed 1980:419–420).

Since the Renaissance, Western culture has been increasingly "novelized" in just this sense. With the growing adherence to the Baconian dictum that "knowledge is power" and to the Cartesian belief that science would make us *maître et possesseur de la nature*, an inner estrangement appeared in Western culture. On the one side were positivists, with their reified or reductive conceptions of reality and knowledge. On the other side were romantics, who stressed the higher truth of art as a representation of inner feelings or emotions. And with romanticism the novel received its major ideological under-pinnings. Friedrich Schlegel defined the novel as the romantic book and, by naming both Dante and Shakespeare as novelists, he achieved a retrospective novelization of European literature.

By the seventeenth century, when God left the throne from which he had ordered the universe, given a name to each thing, and told good from evil, the world was thrown into moral and epistemological crisis. The one unified divine truth issued into a myriad of particular human truths, each contending for faith and each representing an alternative form of life. Descartes attempted to restore certitude by finding a foundation for knowledge in doubt itself. By contrast, Cervantes accepted the multiplicity of partial perspectives and embodied this diversity in his imaginary characters. Thus was born the novel, and with it a principal vehicle for the articulation of modern consciousness.

Little by little the unbounded universe that Don Quixote had set out to explore became smaller. In the eighteenth century, Diderot's *Jacques le fataliste* is also on a journey in an unbounded space, but in the nineteenth century this openness is filled by civil society, by law, business, politics, and other social institutions. Time, too, becomes constricted. "Time, in Balzac's world, no longer idles happily along as it does for Cervantes and Diderot; it is propelled along the rails of History. Later still, the horizon closes in yet further for Emma Bovary, and comes to seem like a cage . . . . Dreams and daydreams surge into the monotony of the quotidian. The lost infinitude of the outside world is replaced by the infinite expansion of the soul" (Kundera 1984:15).

As space and time are reduced there is also a reduction of meaning.

Contemporary modes of representation express the premise that man is unknowable and the world is absurd. The question is no longer what is self and reality, but how is meaning created and how are identity and society constructed. Past (causality and motivation) and future (telos and destiny) are collapsed into the present (acceptance of absurdity and choice). From Homer to Tolstoy, war had a clear, intelligible meaning—Helen, or Russia, was being fought for. But in the contemporary period the *Good Soldier Schweik* and his comrades go to war without knowing why, or even caring. Socially stable meaning died first as a given, then as a possibility, and then finally as a significant category of human existence. This exhaustion of meaning is expressed in prose forms by the radical dislocation of the temporality of language itself. Contemporary narratives tend to subvert their narrativity in favor of a self-referential structure. The narrator becomes the reader and, as Proust said, "every reader reads himself" (Proust 1948:209; see Issacharoff 1976; Kundera 1984).

In a world where, as W. I. Thomas (1966) said, "there are rival definitions of the situation and none of them are binding," ordinary persons become more and more like Hofmannsthal's imaginary Lord Chandos: "I have lost my ability to concentrate my thoughts or set them out coherently." Persons' lives are characterized by a "thrown-ness-into-Being" (Heidegger 1980), in which, as Thomas Wolfe said, "solitariness is by no means a rare condition, something peculiar to myself or to a few specially solitary human beings, but the inescapable, central fact of human existence." Many contemporary persons could reply, as did Ulrich, Robert Musil's *Man Without Qualities*, when asked what he would do if he were God: "I should be compelled to abolish reality." Hemingway expressed this metaphysical dispair in the flat outdoorsy prose of *A Farewell to Arms*:

> Once in camp I put a log on top of the fire and it was full of
> ants. As it commenced to burn, the ants swarmed out and
> went first toward the center where the fire was; then turned
> back and ran toward the end. When there were enough on
> the end they fell off into the fire. Some got out, their bodies
> burnt and flattened, and went off not knowing where they
> were going. But most of them went toward the fire and then
> back toward the end and swarmed on the cool end and
> finally fell back into the fire. I remember thinking at the time
> that it was the end of the world and a splendid chance to be a

messiah and lift the log off the fire and throw it where the
ants could get off onto the ground. But I did not do anything
but throw a tin cup of water on the log, so that I would have
the empty cup to put whiskey in before I added water to it. I
think the cup of water on the burning log only steamed the
ants.

Such a rejection of meaning and sociality is paralleled by the rejection of narrative objectivity. This may take the form of Musil's "active
passivity," Joyce's stream of consciousness, Gide's *act gratuit*, or
Eliot's "Shape without form, shade without color / Paralysed force,
gesture without motion." Nathaniel West's *Miss Lonelyhearts* (1933)
also expressed this morbid, almost pathological, despair of what is
called reality. "Men have always fought their misery with dreams,"
but today the dreams "have been made puerile" by commercialized
culture. "Among the many betrayals, this one is the worst." Similar
thoughts are expressed by Celine's Ferdinand, who sees life as *Death
on the Installment Plan*, and for whom "having been born" was the
great mistake. To be merely a man, writes Georges Bataille in *L'Expé-
rience intérieure*, is intolerable. "He who is not 'dying' from being
only a man will never be anything but a man." For such writers,
society no longer beckons with the promise of fulfillment. Characters
no longer embark with great expectations on a journey of self-cre-
ation. Instead they may wake up one morning as a giant beetle. Society barely offers a surveyor's job. What can K do when confronted by
court and castle? He cannot even dream, as Madame Bovary had
done, for his condition is too awful, absorbing even his imagination.
Like Camus's *Stranger* (1946), nothing seems sweet or sure except
death itself.

The corrupted dream finally destroys not only itself but all vision-
ary possibility. Like Celine's Ferdinand or Kafka's K, "West's Lonelyhearts is portrayed as *both* profoundly serious and disgustingly
diseased. He is a clinical case with a 'Christ complex' yet a perceptive
man who, by questioning 'the values by which he lives,' moves toward
saintly compassion" (Widmer 1980:69). As Musil's Ulrich says, "One
is faced with a simple choice: either one must run with the pack . . .
or one becomes a neurotic."

Traditional society accepted power, hierarchy, and authority in
principle and, describing these in religious terms, cured the ills of the

soul through mortifications of the flesh. By contrast, modern liberal society has so mystified relations of domination that its spiritual illnesses become privatized, to be treated by therapy. Yet in such a situation, the person who chooses mental illness is perhaps the only free being left, a committed personality whose sickness is a social protest against the false and manipulative social order as well as an expression of it.

As judgments of good and evil are replaced by those of profit efficiency or political expediency, moral evaluation of things and people comes to be calculated in terms of utility or adjustment. In this context, persons are no longer punished because they are evil but because they are sick, that is, because their conduct interrupts the normal, efficient flow of activities in the dominant system. Thus inefficacious conduct is deemed a behavioral disorder, whereas the epitome of mental health is adjustment. As Herbert Spencer asserted, "All evil results from the nonadaption of constitution to conditions" (1886:73). Just as crime becomes an illness, so it logically follows that illness is a crime. This was parodied in Samuel Butler's *Erewhon*, a fictional society where morality is defined in terms of utility, and "Ill luck of any kind, or even . . . loss of fortune, . . . is punished hardly less severely than physical delinquency."[4]

The movement in Western literature and society from idealist individualism to individual pathology is implied in Cervantes's *Don Quixote*, developed as comedy in Diderot's *Le Neveu de Rameau*, turned to pathos with Melville's *Bartleby* or Dostoevsky's *Underground Man*, and brought to despair with Celine's Bardamu of *Journey to the End of the Night* (1932). Instead of realizing their destinies through the system, which was still possible for Balzac's Eugene de Rastignac or Stendahl's Julien Sorel, the contemporary character is adverse to society, alienated, and "psychotic."[5] The realistic novel of the nineteenth century celebrates individualism and still finds society a proper field for personal praxis. Novels of this period are filled with orphans, bastards, foundlings, and parvenus—self-naming heroes and heroines who literally make themselves (Ermarth 1984). This penchant for self-created heroes is seen today in popular narratives, from *Horatio Alger* novels to *Rocky* films. Yet such stories have become fraudulent, masking rather than revealing contemporary social structure and experience. As the exercise of power is bureaucratized and mystified, public discourse is reduced to spectacles, acclamations, and cliches.[6] Optimism in society and in literature is replaced by skepticism, and skepticism by nihilism. The serious novel has shifted from representing the best hopes of society to revealing the worst fears of the individual. Yet this nihilism is at the same time a humanism, for it implies in its radical and self-destructive will to truth that society should be a place fit for authentic human life.

Rhetorical Criticism of the Contemporary Novel

Literary genres are normally conservative; transformations of literature involve genre revolutions. Such a revolution appears to have occurred with the dethronement of narrative as a literary form, though no new form has yet assumed the scepter. Narratives are still being written, but today they catch fish that are already dead. Results: a proliferation of new literary forms and new critical foci, a satirization or reification of the apodictic properties of narration.

The writer of the traditional narrative sees further and speaks better than we do, but she is seeing through the same frame and speaking in the same code as the rest of us. Moreover, the functions of such a writer have been largely preempted by information, entertainment, social science, and ideology. The bureaucratization and atomization of society have thrust most writers in front of English classes and most readers in front of television sets. Contemporary experiences that were formerly reported in novels are now transmitted more by journalists and ethnographers than by writers of fiction. Simply telling stories or even gaining an insight from everyday life no longer gives a writer something to say. The premium is rather on stylistic innovation as such, on making language itself the topic of the text.

Unlike writers of conventional narratives, postmodern authors invent new ways of reading the world. Instead of reconstructing the world in terms of an earlier, conventional code, they deconstruct conventional experience through new forms of encoding. Such writers focus not on objects as they are pregiven but on how they might be made to reveal themselves as mediated by a new linguistic apparatus. As in the surrealists' automatic writing, the rules of the word game are made up as one writes. Such texts are therefore opaque to the uninitiated; being able to comprehend them separates the igno- from the cognoscenti and the clods from the connoisseurs. Each form of writing has its risks. The normal, traditional narrative is in danger of becoming a *Reader's Digest* condensed book, of inspiring boredom because it tells what we already know. In contrast, the postnarrative is in danger of becoming a gnostic text; close reading may even nullify comprehension.

In both avant-garde literature and avant-garde criticism, the narrator disappears and language predominates. The focus of both author and critic is on neither plot nor character but on the linguistic devices used to construct the literary text, particularly as these devices reflect a social, historical, and political context. Deconstructionist criticism seeks "the eclipse of voice by text" (Hartman, 1979). "The slippery doctrine of *écriture* . . . has delivered literature into the hands of linguistics and set out to eliminate the author in favor of language itself" (Shattuck 1980:29). "Language is not the predicate of a subject [that is, of a conscious agent. Instead, language] . . . *is* the subject" (Barthes 1966:70, my italics).[7]

Formerly, criticism tended to be either positivistic or romantic; it saw literature as directly determined by various forces, as in vulgar Marxist or Freudian analyses, or as directly expressing the genius of the author. By contrast, contemporary criticism is neither positivistic nor romantic in the traditional sense; instead, it is dialectical. Its goal is to deconstruct texts so as to reveal how historical forms of consciousness are constructed and, for neo-Marxists, how such forms misrepresent actual social relations of domination. Such a criticism rejects the objectivistic determinism of positivism as well as the subjective humanism of romanticism. At the same time, however, it affirms a more sophisticated science and a more sophisticated humanism in two ways. First, it undertakes a critique of the basic forms, categories, and methods of literary and, thence, of social and historical consciousness; and second, through such a critique, it confronts men and women with the choices inherent in their actual historical possibilities.

The emancipatory function of art, then, is to provide critical distance—a distance that combines the apprehension of nearness with the comprehension of farness. Realistically represented contents cannot in themselves represent essential realities but only surface appearances as these present themselves in already established categories of perception. Conversely, a purely formal expression cannot represent essential properties of experience because it is devoid of phenomenal referents. In contrast to both these extremes, contents may be articulated into a formal order through which, so organized, they acquire a power of signification that represents the inner significance of the social order. Thus, for example, when Aeschylus introduced a second actor, he accomplished an innovation not merely in form, or content of what the second actor said. The new dramatic conflict in dialogue also revealed a profound essence of personality that undoubtedly emerged with the democracy of the Athenian polis. As Lukács noted, "Aeschylus' genius lay 'simply' in discovering the maximal literary expression for the maximal revelation of life. Dramatic dialogue became infinitely varied in the course of time, but the interrelationship of life content and dialogue form remained constant within the changes introduced over thousands of years" (1971:21).

In our present circumstances, aesthetic form and political contents are similarly interdependent. The apparent antirealism of the postnarrative text is in fact brought to ripeness by its real object, a society so emptied of inner human meanings as to have become unreal to its members. Such aesthetic transcendence is thus a political statement—a critique of taken-for-granted reality. The liberating powers of memesis are lost, however, if art does not respect its own formal properties. Unformalized contents—no matter how correct they may be ideologically—are merely didactic, socializing propaganda. Art becomes an educative, emancipating practice when it develops that which is already latent within the auditor—his or her own powers for awareness and action. In order to speak to the particular experience of each auditor, however, art must express the essential elements of human experience that are contained within the particular contents that are represented. Such an essentialization of experience is achieved through the embodiment of form in particular contents and the mastery of contents through their formalization. In this confluence of form and contents the artist can reveal for sensuous apprehension as well as cognitive comprehension the universal properties of particular experiences. Indeed, "A work which does not exhibit its sovereignty vis-à-vis reality, and which does not bestow sovereignty upon the public vis-à-vis reality, is not a work of art" (Brecht 1967:7:411). "In order for a text to expect in any way to render an account of the reality of the concrete world (or the spiritual one), it must first attain reality in its own world, the textual one" (Ponge 1965:48).

Like sociological texts, fictional writings incorporate within their own discourse the crises of our culture. In the human studies, there are battles over hard and soft methods, causality and interpretation, or value neutrality and engagement. Similarly, in fictional texts there is a dichotomy between conventional writings whose meanings are vapid mystifications and antinovels whose display of arcane technical virtuosity is meaningless to a broader public. Language is bifurcated into the false extremes of positivism and romanticism. Positivism encouraged the bureaucratization of social processes, whereas romanticism preached a withdrawal from this alienated public world into a higher, private realm. Both of these tendencies have drastically reduced the public space for practical moral action and hence for public narrative discourse.

The conception of narrative structure as the basis of integrity in moral life is clear in Benvenuto Cellini's autobiography. Cellini declared that "All men of whatever quality they are, who have done anything of excellence, or which may properly resemble excellence, ought, if they are persons of truth and honesty to describe their life with their own hands" (Cellini [1558] 1946). Cellini is more than confident of his excellence, which he takes as having arisen from the discipline of work. The passage also implies that craftsmen tell the truth "with their own hands" (unlike a priest for example), so that people may grasp the truth for themselves. "The presence in society of an ethic of workmanship, thus conceived, is the precondition for the transformation of his life into a significant story. To practice this ethic of workmanship is the chief obligation one owes to other people. The Renaissance man. . . . is still primarily a man who defines himself by his substantive works" in front of an audience of other people (Kavolis n.d.:8).

Narrative is an iconic social representation of moral action, an expression and preparation, therefore, for the largest such representation—the democratic political community. By contrast, in the contemporary moral order, behavior is judged in terms of adjustment to the dominant technological system. Yet, as Habermas pointed out, "even a civilization that has been rendered scientific is not granted dispensation from practical [moral] questions; therefore a peculiar danger arises when the process of scientification transgresses the limit of technical questions. . . . For then no attempt at all is made to attain a rational consensus on the part of citizens concerning the practical control of their destiny" (1973:255). The attempt to control one's destiny is, of course, the stuff of which narratives are made. As the public space for such moral action has diminished, there has been a corresponding decline in narrative discourse.

When Descartes juxtaposed the *res cogitans* to the *res extensa* he hinted at the dystopian potentials of a world in which all public questions are defined as technical ones. But Descartes could not imagine that man in his being could become wholly the object of other people's expertise, or that there would exist an expert other than the person himself, an expert who was himself being managed by yet another expert. With the shift to industrial production, however, artisans became either unskilled workers or expert technicians, and engaged in crafts only as a private hobby. The scientization or privatization of craft production, and the loss of linkages between the soul, the hand, and the eye, was thus a loss of social space in which whole and consistent moral being—character—could be enacted.

The invention of the novel was itself a response to the increasing impossibility of conveying an integral vision of self and society in the modern era. Even in the beginning, as in *Don Quixote*, the realistic heritage of the novel was an ironic one—a derealization of the conventional in order to rerealize it in a more cogent and illuminating form. Today, however, such irony appears as a last defense against the totalization of culture. Kafka, for example, used irony to express the difficulty of forming an identity—either through art or outside of it—with his image of the Nature Theatre of Oklahoma. "The . . . Theater will engage members for its company today," said the poster. "If you want to be an artist, come forward! Our Theater can use everyone and find the right place for everyone!" (1962:272). The only requirement for the new artists was an impossibility: to enact their former identities. "When you name yourself," wrote Brecht in *A Man's a Man*, "you always name another."[8]

The divorce of individuals from society shattered the possibility of an integral biography. It is thus for good reason that narration is hardly possible today; for to narrate means to have something to say that is at once special and universal—"individual," in Adorno's sense of the term. "Prior to any statement which is ideological in content, already ideological is the narrator's claim that the course of the world is essentially still one of individuation, that the individual, with his emotions and feelings, is still up to competing with destiny, that the inner life of the single human being is still immediately capable of accomplishing anything" (Adorno 1958:63).

Conceived in this fashion, the history of the novel is a history of ways in which the self can be told, a history of universal types for particular identities. "It is for this reason that the novel makes the self a historically significant subject. . . . The novel's persistent function . . . is to mitigate the laws that govern the 'proper' categories of biography, thus keeping open possibilities of individuation available nowhere else in society" (Holquist and Reed 1980:423).[9] But today the individual is merely the private, whereas the universal now exists only in the scientific, public sphere; and because of this separation both the private and the public are reduced to standardized generalizations that express the essence of nothing while imposing themselves on everything.

As the shared community of human experience has disintegrated in modern societies, so has the web binding narrative and life. In this context, the antinovel or postnarrative text bears witness to the problematic nature of contemporary meaning, identity, and experience. Today art and art criticism share a common supposition that the disintegration of the human community renders any narrative articulation of reality partial or inauthentic. The narrative as a telling of self and world has become an antinarrative that sees self and world as unaccountable. "The position of the narrator," Adorno said, "is characterized today by a paradox: it is no longer possible to narrate" (1958:61). As the technicians and functionaries we have largely become, we think of the processed representations of our experience as "the real world." Yet if a real world is one in which intentions are reflected in actions and actions have ethically significant consequences, few of us today live in a world that is real (Stanley 1978:253). The facts and data and information of our everyday lives require a narrative rather than technical rationality to become integrated with our moral existence and hence to gain their full intelligibility. In the absence of such a public narrative discourse, the novel remains true to its realistic heritage by renouncing realism, since today realism only reproduces the deceptive facade of inauthentic social relations. " 'Things happen one way and we tell them in the opposite sense,' observed Roquentin in *La Nausée*. The orders of living and telling have become incompatible. 'One has to choose: live or tell' " (Brombert 1980:490–91).[10]

Storytelling was formerly a craft that required sensuous involvement, shared traditions, practiced gestures, and the transmission of lore and skills. The same forces that shattered craft production in industry also shattered the craft production of tales, because these forces destroyed the *textum*, the web of community and hence communicability of collective experience. Henceforth persons were as isolated in their worlds of work as in their conceptions of themselves. With this disintegration has come a reintegration, not of community, but of the cybernetic state. The authority structure that once unified author and auditor has been replaced by a new unification authored by the corporation, the military, and the party. As things fall apart on the human level, they are transformed, reintegrated, and reproduced on the bureaucratic level.

Today "the various phases and trends of anti-art or non-art share a common assumption—namely, that the modern period is characterized by a disintegration of reality which renders any self-enclosed form, any intention of meaning (*Sinngebung*) untrue, if not impossible" (Marcuse 1978:50). Inconsistency of roles, publics, and intentions is a central feature of modern society, a society characterized by instability of identity, by the difficulty of achieving an integral biography, and by the reduction of the person to a factor of production. All these conditions are inhospitable to narratives—to the conceiving or comprehending of texts about the unfolding of the character and destiny of agents. Now public discourse is characterized by the inauthentic communication that Bateson called a "double bind." If one challenges the hierarchic relationships as defined by the implicit norms of the communication, one is being "irrational" or "crazy." Conversely, if one remains "rational" and restricts ones responses to the explicit content, one is accepting a relationship of domination. One rhetorical strategy in such a situation is to impose a counter–double bind: to communicate inauthentically authentically, to use lies, in Kierkegaard's sense, in the service of truth, for example by using craziness or absurdity to affirm sanity and reason. This might be done by structurally inverting the oppressive communication to denote rationality while connotatively making this rationality absurd. Reality is thereby exposed through fantastic portrayals. Artists have done exactly this in such statements as Duchamp's teacup lined with fur or Cage's forty-five-minute-long *Lecture on Nothing* (1959).

As a voice heard through the din of processed culture, postnarrative aesthetic expressions persist in seeking to establish an otherness, a negative space in which the conventional is derealized, in which necessity is shown to have really been a choice and apparent choices to have been imposed by force or fraud. As the reified categories of official ideologies become less and less valid existentially, there is a shift in the forms and contents of artistic expression. Objects that were once represented aesthetically as a form of pleasure or instruction now are deconstructed as emblems of the dominant culture. The bidimensional, all-at-once representation of cubist art, for example, reveals the hollowness of the linear, progressive representation of bourgeois culture. Similarly, the sacred American car is demystified when pictured by Roy Lichtenstein, as is the baseball glove when hyperbolized by Claes Oldenberg. As popular music has become noise, serious composers protest by making noise into music: "Since the theory of conventional music is a set of laws exclusively concerned with 'musical' sounds, having nothing to say about noises, it had been clear from the beginning that what was needed was a music based on noise, on noise's lawlessness" (Cage 1981). In like manner, trash art says that our primary experience may be found in junk rather than in ideal athletes or sloe-eyed madonnas. When the consumer culture refuses art by making it a disposable commodity, art strikes back by turning refuse into art (Widmer 1975:33; Gavronsky 1979:3).[11]

The conflictual or absurd quality of contemporary existence undermines traditional distinctions between surface and depth, appearance and reality, and truth and falsehood. For example, in surrealist novels, time as usually ordered is disordered into banal minutiae that are inaccessible to comprehension by linear temporal conventions. Or, as in surrealist pictorial art, the hours and minutes of melted watches drift into infinite empty landscapes. Cubists are visual deconstructionists, as Nietzsche was a philosophic deconstructionist. In cubist paintings distinctions of surface and depth are reallocated. All aspects of a once-concrete, readable object are now presented simultaneously, each aspect both reinforcing the presentness of the others and contradicting their conventional logic, order, and meaning. But what does reality in society or realism in art now mean other than a temporary and fragile agreement? And how can one have faith in the possibility of any certain truth? Relativism, the multiplicity of valid, competing truths, slides toward cynicism, the disbelief that there is any truth or value.

As science and the novel evolved they became an opposition. The one spoke of an outer world of things, the other of an inner world of choice. Yet these opposites share a basic affinity, not only of mutual implication as front depends on back, but also as two aspects of the same metaphysic: neither positivist science nor the late modern novel accepts a distinction between appearance and reality. For both the existent is reduced to the series of appearances which manifest it, appearances that are neither interior nor exterior.

> They are all equal, they all refer to other appearances, and none of them is privileged. Each appearance refers to the total series of appearances and not to a hidden reality which would drain to itself all the *being* of the existent. . . . To the extent that men had believed in noumenal realities, they have presented appearance as a pure negative. . . . But if we once get away from what Nietzsche called 'the illusion of worlds-behind-the-scene' and if we no longer believe in the being-behind-the-appearance, then the appearance becomes full positivity; its essence is an 'appearing' which is no longer opposed to being but is on the contrary the measure of it. (Sartre, 1943:xliv-xlvi)

Those at the far edge of modernity—surrealists, antinarrative writers, postmodernists—take modernism literally, but with a calculated and parodistic naiveté. By literalizing the belief that spirit can shape matter in art or in society, postmodernists reduce surface and depth to a relativized sameness.[12] By assuming a stance of utter seriousness the postmodernists playfully inquire how the medium produces its messages, or how mind produces matter, only to discover that the medium of creation is itself less a spiritual force than a noisy interaction of surfaces that don't quite fit. Of course meaning is not really dead. It is merely differently encoded. Now not through visual perspective, narrated time, or moral career, but through the exemplified relations among concrete elements that the work displays literally. Flaubert's defining Emma through her sensory apprehension of a pot of boiling beef is perhaps the beginning of this metaphysic of the mundane. Surrealists and postmodernists carry this process several steps further. Much as Cicourel, Garfinkel, and other ethnomethodologists have unmasked the arationality of everyday reality simply by examining it in scrupulous detail, so artists like Magritte, Escher, or Dali demystify spirit by revealing the mysterious depths of the literal process of making sense. In his *Portrait of Gala* (1935), for example, Dali starkly renders three distinct planes,

> with no effort to link them illusionalistically, [thereby calling]
> attention to their interaction purely as surfaces in complex
> relations of identity and difference. Incongruity is the
> dominant feature of the painting. . . . This materialism is not
> a naturalism; it maintains mystery, but the mystery must be
> earned entirely within empirical models of perception. Then it
> becomes the idealist who fails the spirit of art by ignoring the
> mind's dependencies on the effects of perceptual and semantic
> surfaces (or codes) in tension. (Altieri 1983:6, 3)

The world intended by postnarrative art is not world of mere fantasy. "It is 'unreal' not because it is less, but because it is more as well as qualitatively 'other' than the established reality. As fictitious world, as illusion, it contains more truth than does everyday reality. For the latter is mystified in its institutions and relationships. . . . Only in the 'illusory world' do things appear as what they are and what they can be" (Marcuse 1978:54). Fictional portrayal and political praxis are thus linked through social mimesis, because the representation of the world is the authorization of our existence. Art can reveal our present conditions and authorize the creation of new ones.

That political authority is itself linguistically and culturally authored is understood by repressive statesmen and progressive artists. "Words wreak havoc," said Sartre, "when they find a name for what had up to then been lived namelessly." Social orders are nominally secured through the myth that the obtaining version of reality is the sole legitimate one, self-sufficient and complete. For those defending established power, "The selected view of the world must be seen as the *only possible* view; it must be identified with the real world. All other versions of reality must be seen as whimsical and arbitrary and, above all, in *error*" (Goode 1969:83). At this conjuncture the revolutionizing writer seeks to commit such great "errors" that our collective treasure, our language, is reclaimed and purified. Within her own order of representation the writer can escape the iron cage of language on her own parole, shattering frozen categories and suggesting new, possibly more adequate, forms for self and society. It is through such artistic illusions that the word and the world progress.

Narrative as a Paradigm for Civic Communication

Any paradigm for civic communication must join efficiency in systems with significance in the life world. That is, it must enable us to govern our polities in a rational manner to insure collective survival, while providing us meaning and dignity in our existential experience of ourselves. Hence such a discourse must be adequate not only on the scientific-technical level but also on the moral-political level. I believe that despite its travails, narrative offers such a mode of civic communication. To show this I must argue for two subsidiary assertions: that the logic of science and technology can be subsumed under narrative discourse; and that moral-political life takes a narrative form.

To show that scientific or technical rationality depends on narrative logic, I will defend three claims—that narrative logic is universal and that hence other logics are derivative of it; that epistemological crises in the philosophic tradition of positivist science are conflicts of narrative traditions; and that paradigm shifts in science itself are reformulations of cognitive traditions in terms of narrative logic.

Unlike formal rationality, which requires special training and is culture-, class-, and gender-specific, the logic of narrative appears to be a human universal. Because human beings are linguistically constituted animals, all persons come to know narrative discourse through normal socialization. This conception is expressed in Kenneth Burke's notion of life as an "unending conversation" (1957:94–97), in Michael Oakeshott's idea of culture as "the conversation of humanity" (1962:199), in Martin Heidegger's view that "We are a conversation . . . conversation and its unity support our existence" (1949:278), and in Walter Fisher's argument "that symbols are created and communicated ultimately as stories meant to give order to human experience . . . in communities in which there is sanction for the story that constitutes one's life" (1984:7).

In the same spirit, students of comparative archeology, literature, and anthropology report that "the story exhibits narrative probability and fidelity across time and culture" (Jacobsen 1976). "Far from being one code among many that a culture may utilize for endowing experience with meaning, narrative is a metacode, a human universal on the basis of which trans-cultural messages about the shared reality can be transmitted. . . . The absence of narrative capacity or a refusal of a narrative indicates an absence or refusal of meaning itself" (Hayden White 1980:6). "The narrative use of language is not a property of subordinate cultures, whether folk, or working class, or the like, but a universal function" (Hymes 1980:132). Narrative enables us to understand the actions of others and endow them with meaning, because it is through narratives that we live and understand our own existence.[13]

This relationship between narration and experience was taken for granted in traditional societies. The sirens who tempted Ulysses had to sing to save their lives. In their chagrin at seeing Ulysses sail past, they threw themselves from their aerie into the sea. Similarly, the characters in the *Arabian Nights* are obsessed with stories; if the narrator fails to narrate she dies. And within specific stories the Caliph may say, "If you tell me a story more amazing than this one, I shall pardon your slave. If not I shall have him put to death." Elsewhere the Caliph is asked, "Will you give us the gift of life if I tell you the adventure which befell me yesterday . . . ? It is surely more amazing than this man's story." "If it is as you say," replies the Caliph, "I shall grant all four of you your lives." In traditional societies narrative signified life, and the absence of narrative, death (Todorov 1977:58, 73–75).

If narrative is a universal logic of human life, what is its role in crises of epistemological faith? Can we show that epistemological crises in philosophy and paradigm shifts in science can be subsumed under narrative logic? To answer the questions, following MacIntyre (1980), we might examine the radical doubt of two exemplary figures in the philosophy of science, Hume and Descartes. Hume described his own philosophic despair:

> The understanding, when it acts alone, and according to its
> most general principles, entirely subverts itself, and leaves
> not the lowest degree of evidence in any proposition, either in
> philosophy, or common life. . . . The *intense* view of these
> manifold contradictions and imperfections in human reason
> has so wrought upon me, and heated my brain, that I am
> ready to reject all belief and reasoning, and can look upon no
> opinion even as more probable or likely than another. Where
> am I, or what? From what causes do I derive my existence,
> and to what condition shall I return? Whose favour shall I
> court, and whose anger must I dread? What beings surround
> me? and on whom have I any influence? I am confronted
> with all these questions, and begin to fancy myself in the
> most deplorable condition imaginable, inviron'd with the
> deepest darkness and utterly depriv'd of the use of every
> member and faculty. (1941:1:267–69)

Hume's epistemological crisis was not resolved in the terms that he had hoped for, for he established criteria of reason and knowledge that no system of belief, "in philosophy or common life," could possibly meet (MacIntyre 1980). Hume did not ask what form of reason would be adequate to the questions he posed in terms of the specific social-historical context in which he found himself. Instead he wanted answers that would be always and universally true. Such knowledge is available only to God. By contrast, the knowledge that humans may possess is always mediated by language, always construed through some point of view, and hence always limited and partial. Hume invited despair because he failed to provide himself with a narrative account of his own historical situation, an account which would have recognized the projective dimensions of language and provided him with usable canons of adequacy for his rational discourse.

Descartes thought he had resolved his epistemological crisis purely in reason. In fact his resolution is founded in logical error, religious faith, and historical amnesia. The ergo sum of Descartes's foundational axiom—I doubt (think, reason, etc.), therefore I am—does not follow from its premise. All that can be concluded logically from the existence of doubting is that there is doubting, not that there is a doubting being, an agency of this doubt. Moreover, having established the cogito, Descartes has no way of assuring himself in reason that cogitation and reality have anything to do with each other. And so he relies on his faith that a benevolent God must link reason with the world.

Descartes did not really doubt everything. Self and God remained necessary albeit undemonstrated categories of his system. And how could these categories be validated by formal reason alone? Descartes was susceptible to facile resolutions because he depended on, but did not acknowledge, the very intellectual tradition within which he was working. He was able to resolve his epistemological doubt because he did not engage in historical doubt. He did not even put into question that he was cogitating within a tradition of Latinate rationalism, that what he took as spontaneous representations of his own mind were reproductions of sentences and phrases from his forgotten but still imprinted childhood schoolbooks, that he had inherited a certain epistemological ideal, and that for him knowledge was akin to vision (MacIntyre 1980:60).

In sum, the frailty of Descartes's resolution of doubt is due to his failure to formulate his problem in terms of a narrative account of his own historical situation. Had he done so, he would have seen that his epistemological crisis was a crisis in a particular intellectual tradition, and that its resolution required a reformulation of that tradition. In other words, the crisis and its resolution would have been couched in narrative terms. Epistemological crises are experienced by individuals but take place within historical cognitive traditions. The mode of articulation and awareness of these traditions is narrative logic. Resolutions of epistemological crises of individuals therefore will be either impossible, as with Hume, or specious, as with Descartes, as long as they are not cast as part of a narrative of the relevant tradition and its adequate reformulation.

Much the same is true of paradigm crises. Just as Descartes and Hume recounted their own epistemological crises as though they had occurred outside any tradition, so contemporary philosophers of science such as Feyerabend, Hanson, Kuhn and Polanyi discuss paradigm crises as moments of abrupt discontinuity with tradition. In doing this, however, they fail to account for the continuity of intellectual traditions which is the precondition for the intelligibility of their own historical narratives. Tradition is of course not a unitary monolith that presses against the present. Instead, as anthropologists and historians have shown us, it is as diverse as the present, because every group in the present may seek to legitimate its contemporary claims by advancing its particular version of the past. And since scientific paradigms constitute and are constituted in traditions, struggles between paradigms become debates over which tradition is the more legitimate or adequate one. Such discourse of traditions is a form of historical reasoning that takes a narrative form. In times of the dominance of a particular scientific paradigm, narrative discourse may be dismissed by a positivist mode of logic. But when paradigms clash, the intelligibility of each to the other, and the victory of the emergent one, depends on narrative form. The shift from one paradigm to another is not merely a psychological gestalt switch or an unreasoned leap in the dark. Rather, it is a leap into the logic of narrative, a construction (or reconstruction) of a cognitive tradition in order to make sense anew (MacIntyre 1980:69).

These ideas are hinted at in Lakatos's notion of a research program, of which "the appraisal is rather of a *series of theories* than of an isolated *theory*" (1974). What is often taken as a single theory is on closer inspection "a growing, developing entity, one which cannot be considered as a static structure" (Burian 1977; MacIntyre 1980). This growing, developing series of theories must be assessed over time. Hence falsification of particular discrete and static theories gives way to narrative accounts of the temporal development of research programs. Theory and method dismiss narrative and tradition and thus make themselves unaware of their own sources of intelligibility. By contrast, narrative and tradition respect the rights of theory and method, but see them as subsumed within a larger social-historical context. Customs—that is, traditions within scientific communities—govern such canons as falsification, the rules for linking observations with generalizations, and the degree and even the very definition of exactitude that may be required. When these customs compete, the resolution of their antagonisms is conducted through narrative discourse.

Culture is even more besieged with conflicts than the traditions of philosophy or science. The epistemological crises in philosophers like Hume or of princes like Hamlet have become the confusions of Everyman today. Culture—the shared schemata that constitute and regulate action and make it intelligible to oneself and to others—has lost its narrative form. The stars have shifted and we can no longer plot the coordinates of identity, polity, and cosmos. Narrative discourse has been replaced by scientific-technical calculation, and with this we have lost much possibility for moral unity in our individual lives and historical unity in our moral traditions. As moral meanings become fragmented, society becomes unsusceptible to emplotment.

For Aristotle the function of rhetoric was not to pursuade an ignorant public of the rightness of policies made by their leaders, but to help citizens enact morally defensible decisions. The public was presumed to share a sense of how their own moral histories were involved with the moral life of the community, and how their personal choices extended the impersonal teleology of the Greek tradition. The classical rhetorical audience was "entrusted with the responsibility of critically assessing the original vision," and thereby serving as "the ultimate guardian of moral action" (Frentz 1985:4,16).

These presuppositions are untenable in advanced modern societies with their liberal-individualistic (or statist-communistic) conceptions of morality and polity. With the increased specialization of modern society and knowledge, the actions of private citizens are increasingly cut off from the public realm, which is more and more dominated by technicist discourse. By contrast, narrative public discourse is radically democratic because it is available to every socialized member of the community. But when mastery of the language of specialists becomes the admission ticket to participate in public debate, moral argument gets submerged under ideological discourse concerning expertise, technical discourse concerning facts, and bureaucratic discourse concerning feasibility. All such discourses denude public life of ethical consideration, turning moral-political concerns into policy issues to be considered only by experts (Fisher 1984:12; Farrell and Goodnight 1981). "Public" comes to mean that the arguments of experts are publicized, rather referring to the public as an informed citizenry collectively making its decisions. Technical rationality as public discourse thereby renders the public irrational. It makes experts hierarchically superior to and more competent than citizens. Citizens are reduced to spectators who have no rational criteria for judging the competing actors or their performances. From the perspective of narrative, however, as Fisher noted, the experts are story-

tellers and the audience are active participants in the meaning
formation of the stories:

> The proper role of the expert in public moral argument is
> that of a counselor, which is, as Benjamin notes, the true
> function of the storyteller. His or her contribution to public
> dialogue is to impart knowledge, like a teacher, or wisdom,
> like a sage. It is not to pronounce a story that ends all
> storytelling. The expert assumes the role of public counselor
> whenever she or he crosses the boundary of technical
> knowledge into the territory of life as it ought to be lived.
> Once this invasion is made, the public, which then includes
> the expert, has its own criteria for determining whose story is
> most coherent and reliable as a guide to belief and action.
> The expert, in other words, then becomes subject to the
> demands of narrative rationality. (1984:13)

The intelligibility of our moral and political life depends on the
restoration of narrative discourse. This is because the sense and
meaning of individual acts are construed through attributions of
motive and intention that depend on temporal contexts of roles and
identity and on the larger moral traditions of which these contexts are
a part. Though they might be cast in terms of psychological science,
attributions of motive presuppose a narrative logic that gives moral
meaning to particular acts and unity and continuity to particular
lives. Narrative thereby links personal conduct with the possible impersonal good of the community by showing that past actions are
causes of the present and that the future is a potential extension of
present conduct (Frentz 1985:5).

Yet today any possible public narrative discourse must be characterized by an awareness of its own impossibility. There is no telos
outside of human experience around which human conduct might be
organized in narrative form. But perhaps we may say that the quest
for such a telos is the moral telos of contemporary humanity. Such a
telos seems appropriate, not as an absolute ground, but as a Kantian
regulative principle of collective human life. As we observed in chapter 5 and as Ken Wilber noted, "if we assume that history has some
sort of *meaning*, then we must also assume that it points to something
other than itself, which is to say, something other than individual men
and women" (1981:1). In this sense, said Frentz, "the narrative unity
of an individual's life and the historical unity of moral traditions

would be narrative quests in the fullest Homeric sense, quests for universal moral truths" (1985:15).

There is one trope that is itself a logic of discovery for such a quest, and that also constitutes itself on the awareness of the impossibility of literally "telling it like it is." This trope is irony, today perhaps the only possible form of emancipatory public discourse.

Eight

Literary Form and Sociological Theory
Dialectical Irony as Emancipatory Discourse

> In the face of the gruesomely serious totality of institutionalized politics, . . . irony . . . become[s] a necessary dimension of the new politics. . . . . The rebels revive the desparate laughter and the cynical defiance of the fool as a means for demasking the deeds of the serious ones who govern the whole.
>
> Marcuse (1969:63-64)

THROUGHOUT HER LIFE Hannah Arendt sought to define a mode of thought and discourse that would of its own nature be illuminating and liberating. Having witnessed the barbarization of reason in Nazi Germany, yet still committed to the Enlightenment ideal of the power of reason for good in the world, Arendt's work explored the relationship between thought and politics and expressed the hope that a humanizing form of discourse could be discovered to support a humanizing political practice.

This chapter, like the book as a whole, is a contribution to Hannah Arendt's project. I advance dialectical irony as a literary mode of social thought, a form of intellectual action that can help liberate us from the one-dimensional thought of orthodox social science and of oppressive social conditions. After discussing the background of irony, I will show how it came to be seen as a uniquely dialectical trope, one that demands participation and completion by its publics and in so doing enlightens them. I will then suggest that social theory, when it is good theory, illuminates its audience and its subject matter with dialectically ironic insights. I conclude that such a mode of awareness is appropriate not merely for social scientists but for all who presume to intervene in the conduct of human affairs, that is, for all true citizens of modern states.

What recourse is there for the social thinker who knows himself to be made of signs, who sees society as a collective syntax, and yet who fears to speak for the love and despair of language? I think the choices are three. He may confine his voice to the monotone of positivist method, and so alienate himself from his moral being. Or he may choose what Steiner called the "suicidal rhetoric of silence," in the tradition of Deidreich Bonhoffer or Walter Benjamin. Or he may make his voice an emblem of the larger crisis, conveying in his discourse the fragility of our efforts to comprehend in thought the contradictions of our age. He can try to show that, like men and women, words have endured great suffering in our times, that they have been drained of significance by repeated indignities, that their power of truth can be restored only by respecting their potential for lies.

This third choice embraces and transcends the first choice and the second. Its method is dialectical irony. Such a mode of expression contains both the public assertion of positivism and the private withdrawal of romanticism. It combines science with silence. Irony is not merely stating the opposite of what one means, for by such a definition irony would be no more than lying. Instead, the ironist is, in Neitzsche's sense (1960), a liar in the service of truth. He simultaneously asserts two or more logically contradictory meanings such that, in the silence between the two, the deeper meaning of both may emerge. This deeper meaning is dialectical. It does not inhere in either the initial literal assertion or its negation; it is rather the tension and completion set off between them that constitutes dialectical ironic awareness.

Irony and dialectic are two ways of expressing the same processes of perception and conduct. Irony is the linguistic form of dialectical thought, because its use presupposes an awareness of the possible misuse of language (Nelson 1977:13). "Irony thus represents a stage of consciousness in which the problematical nature of language itself has become recognized. . . . It is therefore dialectical . . . not so much in its apprehension of the process of the world as in its apprehension of the capacity of language to obscure more than it clarifies. . . . This is why characterizations of the world cast in the Ironic mode are often regarded as intrinsically sophisticated and realistic. They appear to signal the ascent of thought in a given area of inquiry to a level of self-consciousness on which a genuinely enlightened— that is to say, self-critical—conceptualization of the world and its processes has become possible" (White 1973:37). My intent is to bring this literary term, irony, as a penitent to its philosophic confessor, dialectic. And in hearing their dialogue, social thought may find a voice of its own that conjoins the existential immediacy of literature with the normative rigor of logic.

The marriage of dialectic and irony was arranged only in the modern era. The two terms had grown up in different families and played in different parks. The earliest meaning of irony comes from classical usage. In the Attic comedies at the time of the Peloponnesian Wars, the symbol of irony was the fox. "Sly, smooth deceiver—that is his character." Socrates and his friends also used the word in this fashion, and never to refer to the Socratic dialogue. Aristotle spoke of irony not as an instrument of logic but as a sword for cutting down opponents. Cicero and Quintilian enriched the term by describing it as a habit of genuine thought and conversation. "Among the Greeks, history tells us, Socrates was fascinating and witty, a genial conversationalist; he was what the Greeks called *eirōn* in every conversation, pretending to need information and professing admiration for the wisdom of his companion" (Cicero 1947:1:30; see Sedgewick 1948; Knox 1961:5).

In the Renaissance and through the eighteenth century much of the vulgar connotation of irony disappeared, and the term took a greater depth and nuance in referring to a verbal or literary device, as in Mark Anthony's insistence that Brutus is an honorable man. Similarly Voltaire's Candide or Montesquieu's Persian peasant are naifs who praise current mores in a damning fashion, whereas Swift's Gulliver lauds foreign institutions so as to damn his own.

Another mode of irony, that of conduct or events, appears only in modern usage. For example, in *The Concept of Irony, with Constant Reference to Socrates* (1965), Kierkegaard explains that in his manner with others, in his presentation of self, and in his choice of life or death, Socrates was a master ironist of conduct.[1] Contemporary examples of irony of conduct include put-ons by hipsters, anarchistic artists, or theatrical revolutionaries. All such enactments juxtapose mutually exclusive frameworks. For example, when Abbie Hoffman requests people to, "Hold this dollar bill while I go into that store and steal something," he is conjoining law-abiding trust with the morality of a thief.[2]

The irony of events is similar to the irony of conduct, only here the agent is some impersonal force. The irony of events is formed by the fickleness of fate, the hand of God, or the dialectic of history. A man avoids Death by fleeing to Samarra, only to find his appointment was in Samarra after all. A despot suppresses dissent in order to keep the peace, only to find that this very suppression creates unrest. The action is not played face to face, but in the larger theatre of history.

Dialectical irony encompasses and completes all the other forms (Brown 1977:176–78; Burke 1969:503; Muecke 1969:137–47; States 1971; Worchester 1960). It is at once logical and practical, an irony of text and of action. Dialectical thought or conduct always reflects back upon itself. By reinvolving its presuppositions in its presentation, dialectic fuses the objectivity created by the author's methods with the subjectivity of his critical reflection on his own interests and techniques. This dialectical revolving back upon oneself was first seen explicitly as an ironic movement in the late eighteenth and early nineteenth centuries, particularly in the works of Friedrich Schlegel and his critics Hegel and Kierkegaard (Muecke 1969:177–215; Glicksberg 1969:1–24). At the time these men were writing, the French Revolution had become the symbol and means of a new mobility of people and ideas and of intensified awareness of institutional and ideational choices. This expansion of life alternatives brought with it a concern for contrast, contradiction and paradox, and a tendency to suspend taken-for-granted ideas and to reflect on the problems of awareness itself. The mind, seeking its way in a thicket of competing beliefs, became more conscious of its own operations. The old aesthetic of realistic representation and perfect harmony—a view akin to the closed world of Newton's physics and Calvin's polity—began to give way to a more ambiguous, open conception of art and of life.

Schlegel himself is an example of this transition. Beginning with an admiration for the "objectivity" of Greek art, Schlegel then stood under the influences of Fichte's notion of "absolute subjectivity" (Glicksberg 1969). Schlegel's work can be seen as a playing with these two opposites, a "transcendental buffoonery" in which one perspective continually leapfrogs over the other and in which objectivity and subjectivity converge. The world was seen by Schlegel as the objectification of mind, an expression and an alienation of the consciousness that creates it.[3] And art, which is quintessentially a world created by persons, is also a quintessential expression of these dual features. The task of art as of life, however, is not to choose between alienated objectivity or chaotic subjectivity. On the contrary, the order created in art and life must bring into itself this very chaos; it must not suppress it under a static harmony, but must maintain it in a dynamic structured tension. Life, like art, is perfected "when it is limited at every point, yet within its borders is without limitation and inexhaustible, when it is quite truly itself, everywhere homogeneous and yet exalted over itself" (Schlegel 1938:297:215).

In this view, the person has greater existential status. He does not merely receive sensations; he also unifies that which he receives. But as persons in this way shape the world, so the objectified world shapes persons. There is a dialectical interaction between the finite subjectivity of the individual and the infinite objectification that is culture. We both create and are constrained by social structure and history. This social-historical world can treat our freedom to realize ourselves ironically, but at the same time we can regain our freedom by ironically derealizing the world. If what the ironist says is not what he means, or is the opposite of what he means, he becomes free in relation to his objects, his audience, and himself. The object is derealized and the freedom of the subject and the audience is regained, for what has been derealized is now open to intentional redefinition.

This point is illuminated by Kierkegaard's discussion of phenomenon (the word) and essence (the thought or meaning). Truth requires an identity of phenomenon and essence. But with irony "the phenomenon is not the essence but the opposite of the essence" (Kierkegaard 1965:264). The object is deprived of its reality by ambiguity and contradiction, making possible a reobjectification in different terms. If such a process is extended to existence in general, the result is the reestablishment of existential freedom (Kierkegaard 1944b:4-64). Through irony we can "raise ourselves above self-love and be able to destroy in thought what we worship, thereby entering into a perspective that rises over limited things, even over our own art, virtue, and genius" (Schlegel, *Fragment*, quoted by Muecke 1969:200). The poet must stand above his creation, for only through such distance can he make his work utterly objective and self-contained, yet at the same time an utterly subjective expression of himself.

If Schlegel is the most sensitive exponent of irony as dialectic, Hegel is its most powerful critic. Hegel, like Kierkegaard and others after him, chose to emphasize the buffoonery rather than the transcendental in Schlegel's formulation, and thus accused Schlegel of not seeing that irony is merely the first moment of philosphical inquiry, the "transition point" in the "dialectical unrest" that Hegel himself called "infinite absolute negativity." In Hegel's reading, the romantic irony of Schlegel never gets beyond this negative moment. Instead for Hegel the ironist falls into an infinite epistemological regress, never reaching a synthesis. He is aware of something, then of its contrary, then of his awareness, then of his awareness of his awareness, and so on indefinitely. By such a method everything is turned into illusion, the absolute subjectivity that irony presupposes comes to contradict itself, and "all that is objective and of essential worth" is rendered null (Hegel 1920:1:91-92).

Is Hegel unfair to Schlegel?[4] Hegel does quote passages that support his view of Schlegel as a buffoon caught in endless negativity (for example, Hegel 1942:101n). But other passages could be cited to interpret Schlegel as having found a transcendent synthesis. Such a debate between Schlegelian negativity and Hegelian affirmativity is a bit like that between the potential suicide and the fireman. Is is really useful to take sides? Or can we find a third position such as that of Neitzsche, who remarked that the thought of suicide was a great consolation: it had helped him through many a bad night. A similar formula by which we could agree/disagree with both Hegel and Schlegel would give us magical power, for at one stroke we would have achieved a metaperspective that would embrace the subperspectives of each author and at the same time show that neither of them is completely correct.[5] As Kenneth Burke said,

> Irony arises when one tries, by the interaction of terms upon
> one another, to produce a *development* which uses all the
> terms. Hence from the standpoint of this total form (this
> "perspective of perspectives"), none of the participating
> "sub-perspectives" can be treated as either precisely right or
> precisely wrong. They are all voices, or personalities, or
> positions, integrally affecting each other. When the dialectic
> is properly formed, they are the number of characters needed
> to produce the total development. (1969:512)

When Schlegel was writing he could point only to *Wilhelm Meister* and a few other works as modern embodiments of the ironic world view. Since then irony has been transformed from a rhetorical device to the expressive strategy of a metaphysical vision, "the fruit," as Glicksberg said, "of the growing suspicion that life is essentially meaningless" (1961:11). In addition to expressing a sense of meaninglessness, however, irony is also a strategy for the creation of meaning. In the very process of showing that the taken for granted is devoid of essential human meanings or represses them, irony encompasses and transforms contradictions and affirms human sensibility. Moreover, it integrates conflicting meanings through its negative dialectic, much as does the unsuspected confluence of narrative plots.

"Great modern art is always *ironic,* just as ancient art was *religious,*" said Cesare Pavese, and this is true of social thought as well. "Just as a sense of the sacred was rooted in visions beyond the world of reality, giving them backgrounds and antecedents pregnant with significance, so irony discovers beneath and within such visions, a vast field for intellectual sport, a vibrant atmosphere of imaginative and closely reasoned methods for making the things that are represented into symbols of a more significant reality" (Pavese 1961:161–62; see Hass and Mohrluder 1973; Booth 1974). With the fragmentation of social relations and meanings, however, the literary treatment of irony has also changed. In the eighteenth-century comedy of Sheridan, for example, irony draws on simple principles of value and a clear social consensus; a century later, in Balzac or Tolstoy, irony can be controlled only by an omniscient and highly manipulative narrator; and today in Kafka, Borges, or Barthelme, the irony refers back to the text itself "through the deliberate introduction into both story and discourse of gaps, contradictions, and absurdities" (Scholes 1982:86).

An ironic suspension and transformation of the mundane is also found in the human sciences. As Lyman and Scott put it, "A new wave of thought is beginning to sweep over sociology. . . . The term "absurd" captures the fundamental assumption of this new wave: *The world is essentially without meaning.* In contrast to that sociology which seeks to discover the *real* meaning of action—a sociology of reality, such as the functional meaning of social behavior—this new sociology asserts that all systems of belief, including that of the conventional sociologist, are arbitrary" (1970:1).

Discontented with positivist sociology, such thinkers have focused on the exact methods by which actors construct their worlds or have the worlds of others imposed upon them. Yet this new wave has not swept across the discipline as a whole. Social thought continues to be dominated by a methodological dualism that posits a strict separation between the subject and the object, and gives a standing admonition not to contaminate the data, not to shatter the value-free chrysalis in which the investigator is thought to work. In terms of this dualism, the empirical variables of social theories are taken to represent naturalistic facts. Stated inversely, this entails a suppression of awareness of the philosophic value frameworks that are the preconditions of the meaning and validity of such theories themselves. To examine reflectively the presuppositions of scientific objectivity does not mean that we should give it up, but that, epistemologically, we should transvalue objectivity and value freedom into value commitments in their own right and that, existentially, we should stand accountable for the moral and political consequences of our scientific practice.

Dialectical irony leads us towards such reflexivity, both as social scientists and as citizens. A central aspect of such irony is the relationship it imposes between the social scientist and the social world. Dialectical irony involves making a statement that is open to ambivalent interpretations, that is, interpretations of opposite weights and meanings. The construction of a meaning that is to be taken as the intended one is left to the audience. The ironist must thus be an explicitly social actor in that to practice her irony she requires a public that is (willing to be) enlightened. In order to be ironical, the ironist must impel her publics to make choices about their own categories of perception and evaluation. By her ironic method of derealizing reified meanings, she challenges her publics to create meanings for themselves.

The dialectic of irony has two moments: smiling downward, and jeering upward. The first is a moment of superior power, the second of compassionate rebellion. The first is expressed by Flaubert: "When shall one describe the facts as a vast joke, that is to say, as God sees them, from above?" Karl Solger also spoke of a supreme irony that "reigns in the conduct of God as he creates men and the life of men. In earthly art Irony has this meaning—conduct similar to God's (quoted in Sedgewick 1948:17). This moment of irony opposes knowledge, power, meaning, or happiness to ignorance, impotence, absurdity or misery. These oppositions become ironic through "the self-congratulatory awareness of the victim's absolute un-awareness of the predicament he is in, an awareness that finds ex-pression in 'smiling down'" (Muecke 1983:404; see 1969:216–19).

The second moment of dialectical irony demotes the ironist instead of devaluing the victim. The feeling is "that the god of irony is not God but Satan, not Apollo but Asmodee, or that as ironists, God and Satan are identical" (Muecke 1983:404). Such irony lowers those on high and elevates the usual victims. It is what Thomas Mann called "an irony of the heart, a loving irony; it is greatness filled with ten-derness for little things."

Dialectical irony is thus not merely negative. Its spirit is not merely proud humility that says, "There but for the grace of God go I," connoting pity and amour propre. On a deeper level, as Muecke point-ed out, irony also expresses a fundamental kinship with the victim. It implies a bondedness in which the ironist realizes her own freedom only through unmasking the pretensions of her "victim," but in which the victim regains his subjectivity only through being ironized. We do not laugh at a cretin when the results of his actions violate his intentions; if we do we are attributing to that creature the capacity for planning and reflection. Similarly, we can laugh at the victims of irony only because we have attributed to them the possibility of self-awareness and autonomy. When people's pretensions are treated ironically in this manner, their humanity again becomes accessible to compassion.

To see someone as the victim of irony is to see that person, relative to oneself, as submerged in unreflective absolutism. Yet this relativity of perspectives itself implies a context of meaning created by the iron-ist and constituting her standpoint. Franz Boas described this type of relativizing freedom and self-awareness as a quality both gained through immersion in a foreign culture and indispensible to the study of culture in general: "It is given to no one to free himself from the constraints which life has placed upon him. We think, feel and act loyal to the tradition in which we live. The only way of freeing our-selves is submersion in a new life and comprehension of a mode of thinking, feeling, and acting that has not grown from the same roots as our own civilization, but that has its source in another cultural formation" (Boas 1932:16). What Boas described is an act of ironic imagination. The anthropologist studies savage cerebrations to understand *mentalité moderne* (Lévi-Strauss 1963). Cultural relativity is itself relative to such an act. Unironic anthropologists are not broadened by their travels. Similarly, for the ironist the journey may be metaphoric: "One needs to be Japanese to recognize the farcical contradictions of the Christian civilization. One needs to be an inhabitant of the moon fully to comprehend the stupidity of man and his state of perpetual illusion" (Henri-Frédéric 1931:277–78).

The imaginative submersion in other cultures also was noted by Kierkegaard as characteristic of the ironist. By suspending commitment to pregiven definitions the ironist may lend at least a temporary validity to any situation or historical period. "In this matter the ironist has great skill. . . . Now he strolls about with the proud mien of a Roman patrician in trimmed toga, now he disguises himself in the humble cloth of a penitent pilgrim, now he crosses his legs like a Turkish pasha in his harem. . . . This is what the ironist means when he maintains that one should live poetically, and this is what he attains by poetically producing himself" (Kierkegaard 1965:299).[6] This also is a way for persons within the same society to understand others of different gender, class, or social position.

Kierkegaard knew that such poetic irony could lead one to becoming what Musil called a man without qualities, a man whose "life finally loses all continuity," a person who "wholly lapses under the sway of his moods and feelings." At the same time, however, Kierkegaard recognized that irony can also be a mastered moment, a source of truth and freedom. Freedom in this sense refers to a mode of being, that of active moral choice. Thus the person who votes, criticizes his government, or assumes a new way of life is not necessarily free in the way Kierkegaard used this term. For should the actor have no inward relation to his actions, should he not be commiting himself in his being, to that extent we cannot speak of his being as free. In contrast, the free person is assimilated into the age in which he lives, yet at the same time he is able to rise above it. He is, like Kierkegaard's poetic ironist, "positively free within the actuality to which he belongs" (1965:339).

Kierkegaard's discussion in *The Concept of Irony* is directly related to the contrasts he draws between romantic aestheticism and existential ethics in *Either/Or*. For Kierkegaard, irony is the means of moving from a purely subjective hedonism to a truly ethical existence. The transition from one to the other begins with appreciation of the incongruity between one's inner life and its outer expression, between the subjective and the objective. Through irony the actor grasps the contradiction "between the manner in which he exists inwardly and the fact that he does not outwardly express it" (Kierkegaard 1965). The contradiction between the inward lack of wisdom and the outward presentation of self that seeks to conceal this lack precisely defines the ironic situation. Ironic awareness of the incongruity of mimetic forms is the beginning of the ethical awareness of the incongruities of moral norms. "The ironist, who is in the 'boundary zone' between the aesthetical and the ethical, poignantly expressed these incongruities and thus drives beyond the aesthetical to the ethical" (Schrag 1961:195; see Glicksberg 1969:9–10).

As I have tried to show elsewhere (Brown 1977:171–220), great modern social thought is ironic in precisely this sense—it is critical, dialectical, and self-reflective; it describes outward forms of behavior while implying an inner agency and moral community of persons. Was Adam Smith anything less than ironic when he asserted that private avarice yields public good?[7] And was Marx not ironical when he inverted Smith by saying that class enrichment yields collective impoverishment? Indeed, as an explicitly dialectical sociologist, Marx offered numerous ironic insights. Competition leads to its opposite, monopoly. In oppressing workers the factory system organizes them for liberation. Feudalism yields capitalism and capitalism engenders socialism. Marx the revolutionary treated bourgeois marriage ironically as a system of legalized prostitution (Marx and Engels 1967). A century later the conservative Kingsley Davis treated prostitution ironically as the illegalized system for maintaining bourgeois marriage (1937:744–55).

One of the richest areas of sociology is theory of organizations, and this theory is highly ironic. For example, Michels posited a law by which democratic movements become oligarchic bureaus. As trade unions become successful in building their membership, they need to organize themselves in a disciplined, functionally effecient manner. "Yet this politically necessary principle of organization renders necessary what is called expert leadership. Consequently the power of determination comes to be considered one of the specific attributes of leadership, and is gradually withdrawn from the masses to be concentrated in the hands of the leaders alone. We escape Scylla only to dash ourselves on Charybdis" (1966:62). In the same spirit, Karl Weick noted that to the extent the organization wishes to remain orderly it is unlikely to survive. If an orderly process is appled to a chaotic set of information inputs, then only a small portion of these inputs will be attended to and made unequivocal. "It is the unwillingness to disrupt order, ironically, that makes it impossible for the organization to create order" (Weick 1969:42). In the same fashion, in his study of goldbricking in a machine shop, Donald Roy showed that workers, perceiving the efforts of time-study engineers to control output, engage in systematic subversion. In some settings the more organizational experts seek to rationalize production, the less efficient production is likely to become (Roy 1952:430; see Bensman and Gerver 1963).

Another aspect of dialectical irony is its sensitivity to varying levels of awareness. Once the dialectical relationship becomes known to some of the actors, it may cease to operate. To reap the hidden good behind apparent evil, we may have to remain ignorant that the evil is only apparent. The earliest example of this is probably Plato's awareness that his Noble Lie, the myth of the metals, would insure the stability of the Republic only so long as most people believed in it. Modern students of religion and of legitimation in general have made similar observations. For example, Charles Bennett observed that "if one is to get these spiritual benefits [from religion] one must pray not for these benefits but for rain. The precondition for getting them is that one be superstitious and unenlightened" (1931:58).[8]

Having revealed the positive functions of ignorance for ordinary folks, the next step for sociological dialecticians is to turn this finding back on social-science experts themselves. Robert Merton implied this in his discussion of the pitfalls awaiting the sociologist turned social engineer:

> BASIC QUERY: What are the effects of the transformation of
> a previously latent function into a manifest function
> (involving the problems of the role of knowledge in human
> affairs and the problems of 'manipulation' of human
> behavior)? . . . *To seek social change, without due*

*recognition of the manifest and latent functions performed
by the social organization undergoing change, is to indulge
in social ritual rather than social engineering.* (Merton
1957:51, 81; see Argyris 1968).

Merton's remarks suggest that unintended ironies of social theory
may seep into the practice of intentional social change. The self-ful-
filling prophecies of social movements have their counterparts in the
self-defeating predictions of social engineers. To the extent that the
latent functions upon which their plans depend become manifest,
those plans may cease to work. Moreover, for the "rightminded" social engineer, the pursuit of humane ends seems to require the use of
inhumane means. For example, the cure of souls requires a calculated
program that makes of the patient a soulless object, the alleviation of
poverty calls forth an alienating welfare bureaucracy, and the intervention by experts results in the manipulation of clients. "Moralism
itself generates the rebellion whose quelling is its official mission"
(Skillen 1978:175).

In trying to avoid such unwanted latent functions, however, the
social engineer may become like Kafka's molelike creature in *The
Burrow.* Hoping to get all the data in, he constantly searches for hidden enemies about his nest, never sure whether their absence is due to
their not being there or to their hiding because he is looking (Muecke
1969:135). Thus, the circumspection advocated by Merton can itself
be made ironic. Carried too far, the desire to avoid nasty surprises
becomes surprisingly nasty. Indeed, any desire for absolute knowledge or control is susceptible to irony because all knowledge is mediated, and all efforts to control may constrain the controller.

Many situations occur in which social intervention or manipulation
can be justified as good, of course, and therein lies the irony. If failing
students understood they were being cooled out by counsellors, they
would subvert this manipulation, and would thus overburden colleges
with inept students and set themselves up for greater failure later on
(Clark 1960). If the goals and techniques of therapy were fully known
to patients they would resist treatment. At the same time, however,
such victims of irony can turn irony against the social engineers. Welfare clients, inmates of mental hospitals, lower-level workers, alienated students, and oppressed people in general may learn to "work
the system," thereby manipulating their manipulators and retaining
some measure of freedom.

Modern resistance to manipulation needs a peculiarly modern form, however, for the Noble Lie of Plato has been packaged by contemporary social scientists to have a new, improved appeal. Ruling-class theorists used to express themselves more clearly before mass literacy and enfranchisement forced them to dissemble (Skillen 1978:140). As late as the nineteenth century, elitest thinkers such as Mosca or Bentham show no hint of apology in their recommendations for duping the public.[9] But today their straightforward cynicism has been replaced by intellectual and institutional bad faith. Indeed, the peculiar character of modern oppression is that it is masked as therapy, science, efficiency, or personal concern. Bad faith on the personal level is an illusion of constraint that masks actual choice, or the reverse. On the social level it is the appearance of participation in institutional decision making presented in a way that covers real exclusion. In the early days of capitalism, workers were explicitly forbidden to unionize. Today unions that pretend to represent workers tend to manage them instead. In the nineteenth century, church and reform groups made some efforts at "status acceptance" of the lower classes, but there was relatively little ideology and practice aimed at cooling out subordinates and co-opting their means of protest. Today such official propagation of inauthenticity has become part of the normal structure. It is not only conduct that the corporate state wishes to control, but consciousness as well.

What are the social uses of irony? How might it be a means to liberate us from domination? The political dimension of irony has been treated as absolute negativity (Hegel 1920; 1942), idealist aestheticism (Franklin 1970:35), bourgeois defeatism (Jankélévitch 1950), antipolitical erotic conservatism (Mann 1950:494), a withdrawal tactic of the literary intellectual (Widmer 1975a:120), or a diabolical mockery that ends in rebellion (Alexander Beck, quoted in Tertz 1960:74). In such definitions there are two opposite but interrelated concepts: ritual or safety-valve irony, and free or mastered irony in the Kierkegaardian sense.[10]

Ritual irony has a long history. For example, the majesty of power and glory, yet an irony standing above them, is reflected in the Roman practice of permitting legionnaires to recite satirical verses over the triumphator. The medieval Church also expressed a sense of the relativity of its earthly power by allowing itself to be conceived ironically on such occasions as the Feast of Fools, Easter Humor, or the Feast of the Ass, during which a carved donkey was carried in procession in place of the image of Christ. A redeeming feature of ancient and medieval monarchies was their court jesters, whose function was not merely to make the king laugh, but also to make him laugh at himself (Hyers 1969:208).[11]

A Dutch commercial agent noted a similar rite when traveling on the coast of Guinea around 1700:

> The Devil is annually banished from all their Towns with abundance of Ceremony. . . . This Procession is preceded by a Feast of eight Days, accompanied with all manner of Singing, Skipping, Dancing, Mirth, and Jollity: In which time a perfect lampooning Liberty is allowed, and Scandal so highly exhalted, that they may freely sing of all Faults, Villanies and Frauds of Superiours as well as Inferiours, without Punishment, or so much as the least interruption; and the only way to stop their Mouths is to ply them lustily with Drink, which alters their Tone immediately, and turns their Satyrical Ballads into Commendatory Songs. (Bosman 1705:158; quoted in Rattray 1923:151).

R. S. Rattray saw the same sort of fetes when he visited the Ashanti over two hundred years later. He was given a careful explanation by the high priest of the god Ta Kese of the licensed ridicule he had witnessed:

> Your soul may be sick or you may have hatred in your head against another, because of something that person has done to you . . . our forebears knew this . . . and so they ordained a time, once every year, when every man and woman, free man and slave, should have freedom to speak out just what is in their head, to tell their neighbors just what they thought of them . . . [and] also the king or chief. When a man has spoken freely thus, he will feel his *sunsum* [soul] cool and quieted. (1923:15; see Turner 1969:180)

These examples of ritual irony have two features in common. First, they all refer to the central values of a particular system of belief—the martial honor of a conqueror is challenged by soldiers, the divinity of God is contested by priests, the majesty of the king is mocked by his dwarf or his loyal subjects.[12] Each irony is directed at myths that validate that group's ultimate concerns, and each mocks the symbols that are the source of its legitimacy, its sine qua non of meaning. What is treated ironically is sacred.

A second feature of ritual irony is that it is enacted or controlled by the very persons who are treated ironically. It is as if those in power had a monopoly on the official resources for ironizing themselves. As Goffman put it in his discussion of ritual irony in insane asylums, "To act out one's rebellion before the authorities at a time when this is legitimate is to exchange conspiracy for expression. . . . the very toleration of this skittishness is a sign of the strength of the established state" (1961:109–110). Just as only Jews are "allowed" to tell "kike stories" and only blacks to say "nigger," so it would seem that ritual irony is offered as a kind of safety valve to those who must be already committed to the values of the group. Their irony is a means of highlighting contradictions of logic in order to reaffirm faith. Only believers may make Christ absurd; only soldiers may satirize martial honor; the dwarf is unlikely to abandon his king; Jews and blacks rarely leave their castes. In the manner of Tertullian's dictum, *credo quia absurdum est*, they seem almost to be saying, I am loyal because I am oppressed.

Alongside the practice of ritual or official irony is another tradition, that of unbounded, unofficial, subterranean irony, irony that is radically free. Whereas ritual irony shakes us out of conventional roles and assumptions only to allow us wryly to rejoin them, a mastered dialectical irony shows that any role or assumption is reversible, "any signified may become a signifier, any discourse may be without warning rapped over the knuckles by some meta-discourse which may then suffer such rapping in its turn" (Eagleton 1981:160). The cleric, to take a negative example, whether in ritual irony or dialectical argument, has accepted a pregiven end to his debate. He is free only to choose the means to reenforce the majesty of God. The subterranean ironist, in contrast, is free to choose both means and ends, and indeed he does not assume a priori differences between them. For him ends have consequences, just as means have normative implications, and since this is their dialectical relationship, each can be used to ironize pretentions of the other. Thus whereas the cleric may use irony to serve his notion of morality, the free ironist uses irony in order to liberate us from moralism of any stripe. Unlike the hypocrite, who strives always to appear good although he is sometimes evil, and unlike the "sincere" person who believes he is wholly what he seems, the subterranean ironist desires only to create freedom through his irony. He may thus as easily appear evil in order to relativize his goodness as good to relativize his evil, and in no case can he be accused of believing his own propaganda. His purpose is existential freedom itself, independent of any pregiven determination. In this way, free or mastered irony not only serves freedom; it is freedom.

It should be obvious that this type of irony can be subversive to persons and political regimes that presume they have an absolute right to define reality. Thus, whenever free irony appears, attempts are made to either suppress or co-opt it. For example, efforts to create a cultural perspective contrary to the dominant model, like the mock army of war-surplus-clad hippies, appear next season in the ads for Vitalis. Similarly, the symbology of the woman's movement is used to market vaginal products, thereby attempting to reduce would-be autonomous women to the status of consuming objects. Vacationers in capitalist Holland can take a commercial bus tour called "Visit Amsterdam's Provos," whereas tourists visiting communist Cuba can buy government-packaged baggies of sand labeled "From the Bay of Pigs, where Yankee Imperialism was Defeated by the Glorious Revolution." Arty styles of life and other modes of differentiation, dropout, or dissent are also defanged under the pervasive narcosis of industrial technology and organization (Nelson 1970; Widmer 1975a). Instead of constituting a radical critique of society, they become, like court jesters and feasts of fools, a ceremonial adjunct of practical behaviorism, ritual irony digested by the status quo as part of its healthful diet.

Through such co-option or repression, the modern state reduces the ironic distancing from experience through which critical consciousness can develop. The loss of such inner distance, combined with the overwhelming efficiency of the organized system, blunts the individual's awareness so that she has less and less space in which to voice dissent. Without such space, the power of negative thinking—the power of dialectical reason—atrophies from disuse.

Just as persons need psychic and public space to examine their experience critically, so whole cultures must have such perspectives if they are to transvalue their traditions and let their choices shape their actions. Kierkegaard noted that moral awareness begins with the appreciation of contradictions between phenomenon and essence, or between public conduct and private commitment. Today, however, such contradictions are built into the very logic of the modern state. The bureaucratization of modern societies has been accompanied by a massive shift of responsibility from individuals as moral beings to rules, regulations, and calculations of efficiency that are implemented by persons acting merely as functionaries. Such anonymous action is "beyond good and evil" because in modern bureaucracies to appreciate an action as "good" or "evil" appears to be "merely subjective" (Belohradsky 1981). The neutralization of subjectivity makes a person insensitive to the moral meanings of the actions he performs as an official. Indeed, such subjectivity, sympathy, and moral awareness become temptations that the official must resist. Modern organizations reduce the critical distance through which the objectivity of instrumental rationality might be conjoined with the subjectivity of moral commitment. There is an overdistance from reality that denies the human consequences of offical actions, and an underdistance that considers moral choices as purely private tastes.

Such logic and conduct are exactly antithetical to dialectical irony, and they are precisely what Hannah Arendt had in mind when she wrote of the banalization of modern culture. In the banal culture, terms such as objectivity, efficiency, rationality, and science come to be associated with the public sphere; subjectivity, imagination, moral choices, sensuality and fun are considered private. In such an alienated vision of society and self, the public sphere is equated with mass behavior that can be aggregated into statistical facts. These in turn are ideally manipulable by cost-efficiency techniques. At the same time, the private realm is seen as the arena into which one can withdraw from the mass industrial state. And given the dominance of industrial techniques of organization, decision making, and persuasion, the private arena is increasingly narrowed to contain only that which is irrelevant to administrative interest or irreducible to commercial count. The result is that freedom to enact moral intentions comes to be defined purely negatively, as the right not to participate in the cybernetic society (Stanley 1978). All morally and politically affirmative definitions of freedom become obsolete, and participation in society is restricted either to rituals of co-option masked as dissent, or to those public roles deemed functionally necessary by political elites and social engineers.

Such political schizophrenia cries out for dialectical irony. Such an ironic transcendence presupposes the capacity to imagine things as other than they are, the capacity to derealize the present. To summon forth the contrary of that which is through the power of dialectical irony is the basis of moral freedom and imagination. Both the romantic ideologue and the positivist technocrat lack such an imagination. Dielectical irony lifts us above the view we are given of what the world is or must be. It is the absolute beginning of public life as well as personal life.

Though we still have freedom of speech in the private realm, freedom to communicate publicly has been largely captured by state- and monopoly-dominated media. Such forms of processed communication are incapable of free or mastered irony, which requires the public to experience and resolve ambiguity and contradiction. Instead, as in television, the studio audience is programmed to laugh on cue. The only way to guarantee that they will respond with conspicuous spontaneity is to plan the spontaneity with the utmost care. "A seriously ironic mood would disintegrate this totally masked control, so 'stable' irony or irony pretty well labeled as such [i.e., ritual irony] is all that television can normally tolerate" (Ong 1977:293).

How might dialectical irony help us to realign humane values and contemporary political practice? Or, in Robert Merton's terms, how might it aid the moral sociologist, the active citizen, or the social engineer? Since irony hinges on peripety and reversal—on differences between intention and outcome—it is highly resonant with the contradictions of political life today. Moreover, because irony also stresses the interplay between levels of awareness, the ironist is able to incorporate into his analysis both his own perspective and the perspectives of the people whom he studies or serves.

Ironic awareness can safeguard authority against arrogant presumption. As an ironist, the leader knows that the more he presumes his own greater wisdom, the more he becomes like his clients (or victims) in their naive self-confidence. By virtue of his calling, the political leader or agitator must assume knowledge or skill superior to that of his constituents. But as ironist, such a leader sees these constituents in a real sense as constituting him as leader. His constituents become an active audience or true public for his ironic politics, and their enlightened completion of his acts is necessary for his stratagems to succeed. In just this manner, for example, Cloward and Piven led welfare workers to "naively" apply the welfare code to the letter in order to bring about new welfare legislation.

A similar method can be used when examining metatheoretically the relation of one realm or perspective to another (Wright 1978). For example, we may wish to look at the problem of crime from the perspective of sociology. In this instance we would assume a calculated naiveté. The laws governing behavior and constituting certain actions as crimes would be derealized through ironic bracketing. These laws would be made a topic rather than a presupposition of the inquiry. The researcher would pretend that there is no known difference between criminal and noncriminal conduct. Such a starting point would be the antithesis of the usual objectivist approach. In fact, it would reverse objectivistic assumptions by making the concepts "crime," "criminal behavior," and "criminology" themselves problematic—topics rather than resources of investigation. By thus treating the subject matter ironically, we become able to explore the analytic categories of the conventional approach, to see them as socially and intellectually constructed, and to note the interests that such processes and categories may serve.

Such an ironic method has several advantages. First, it permits us to respect the purity of the paradigm under study, in this case objectivist criminology. By derealizing it as a self-sufficient explanation, we can make it a moment in a dialectic between the theory that is criminology and the practice that is law enforcement and crime. Secondly, such a movement allows us to appreciate the methodological probity of conventional criminologists insofar as they seek to be consistent with their own rules. That is, by unmasking the extraparadigmatic function of orthodox criminology as ideology, we also can more accurately appreciate its intraparadigmatic function as science. In so doing, we become able to respect the agency and honesty of that paradigm's practitioners.

A third advantage is that, having treated knowledge ironically by revealing its hidden interests, we are now better able to explore falsity. The true consciousness of the paradigm's practitioner rests in his adhering to his paradigm's rules. But his false consciousness lies in his presumption that the paradigm rules are ultimately adequate and disinterested. By subjecting this consciousness to dialectically ironic reformulation, the ostensibly apolitical value neutrality of rule-following honesty is revealed to be politically and morally inauthentic. Its small truth becomes a larger lie.

By reducing all modes of consciousness to a relativized sameness, dialectical irony reveals all to be processes of symbolic construction, all to be historical, and none to be ultimately superior to others. Irony teaches that nothing is known absolutely, and that everything is reversed when overextended. An awareness of this would encourage humility in those wishing to shape human affairs. And such a modesty would re-ally social analysis and political activism with humanism, not only in their goals, but also in their acknowledgement of human freedom and frailty, with the concomitant postulates of moral responsibility and tolerance. Irony captures this double-edged humanism in that while it laughs at people's complacent unawareness it also attributes to them the capacity to be aware of their circumstances and to control their fates. Such a perception devolves back upon the ironist herself. To be ironic means that one is conscious that ones own existence is itself a contradiction. "This contradiction is precisely the awareness, on the other hand, of being a finite creature compelled by and subject to the demands of the world and, on the other hand, of being a free, responsible being who can never be compelled or subjected to any external force. The irony is that one *is* a contradiction, that one exists dialectically" (Hanna 1962:281–282).

In most of Western history this two-sided conception of humanism was a value of the aristocratic class. Dialectical irony transvalues this conception for modern societies. As a dialectical movement in the discovery of new cognitive and social forms, irony preserves the aristocratic concept of humanism; yet because it requires collaboration and completion by a public, irony also provides a truly democratic method for critical societal analysis and emancipatory political change.

Notes

Chapter 1

1. The question of why people with different backgrounds, even if they share certain notions about better worlds, can't seem to communicate with each other could be asked with reference to doctors and patients, lawyers and clients, or professors and undergraduates. Are the difficulties of communication between such groups linguistic or cultural, or do they derive from inequalities of power? Probably all of these. One of the points of this chapter, however, is to help identify what part of mutual incomprehension may be inherent in linguistic codes or in specific contexts and practices of speech. Of course political cooperation between different classes and groups does not necessarily require mutual understanding or sympathy, but can be achieved mainly on the basis of a perceived mutuality of interests, as with Jack Sprat and his wife. All these considerations should not be taken as contrary to the argument of this chapter, however, for our purpose here is essentially utopian: to suggest a theoretical framework in sociolinguistics that could guide us towards the undistorted communication of an emancipated polity. Such emancipation is not identical to instrumentally successful political alliances, though presumably it could include them.

Radical pedagogues have argued that educational socialization will become effective and liberating only if schools are restructured to better respond sociolinguistically to low-income children. We might suppose that political socialization will become effective and emancipatory only if political movements are themselves similarly restructured. More fundamental change in the interests of justice might come after all not from either bureaucratic liberalism or revolutionary movements, but from entirely new forms of collective enterprise.

2. "Helping" includes not only political mobilization but also social work and personal therapy. On these see Kenneth C. Hallum, "Social Class and Psychotheraphy: A Sociolinguistic Approach," and F. Hollis, "Casework and Social Class," in F. J. Turner, ed., *Differential Diagnoses and Treatment in Social Work* New York: Free Press, 1965); S. Minuchin, *Families and Family Theraphy* (Cambridge: Harvard University Press, 1974); and H. L. Leonard and A. Bernstein, "Interdependence of Therapist and Patient Verbal Behavior," in Joshua Fishman, ed., *Readings in the Sociology of Language* (The Hague: Mouton and Co, 1968).

3. We use the term "speech act" in a simple sociological sense, which is not quite the technical linguistic or philosophical meaning given by some writers (e.g., Searle 1976).

4. Claus Mueller argued that a restricted speech code introduces "noise" and "acts as a barrier to political communication. . . . Groups and individuals who have internalized and are thus bound by a restricted language code cannot cope with sophisticated messages nor effectively comprehend a complex political environment" (Mueller 1973:95).

5. For example, whereas middle-class parents tend to give reasons that "explain" their commands, lower-class parents more often use categoric commands such as "Do as I tell you," or "Shut up," in which the personal relationship between children and parents is the single point of reference to which the child's compliant or

resisting action might be related. Conversely, when a middle-class parent says "Shut up, you'll wake your sister," or "Keep quiet, one does not interrupt adults while they are talking," the parents thereby establish a structured relationship between the behavior of the addressed child and her sister or innumerable adults. Such a structuring implies principles that transcend the immediate situation, which is construed as an example for a category of situations. Thus, according to Bernstein, there are different orders of meaning, realized through different speech codes, varying according to a family's or person's social locations.

Though Bernstein's research is mainly of working-class Britishers, his methods and findings have been reproduced cross-nationally, as in the case of Peter M. Roeder's studies of modes of articulation among West German children. "Sentence structure of German working-class children was less complex than that of middle-class children, and more grammatical mistakes, particularly in the use of nouns and verbs, were made. Children from a higher socioeconomic status used more qualifying clauses in their sentences and applied adjectives of a more abstract nature" (Peter M. Roeder, "Sprache, Sozialstatus und Bildungschancen," in P. M. Roeder et al., eds., *Sozialstatus und Schulerfolg* [Heidelberg, 1965]).

The comparison of middle-class speech with that of gang members is justified to the extent that social classes are located along a continuum from the lowest to the highest. Significant differences among classes thus become evident only if noncontiguous groups are compared. Such an assumption is true insofar as class is defined ordinally in terms of wealth or income. This seems acceptable so long as we also include differentiations of status and power in our schema of stratification. Only thus would we be theoretically sensitive to racial and ethnic differences within and between classes, national differences across classes within different countries, and so on. Doubtless, language use also varies with age, gender, degree of urbanization, and the like. See Trudgill's review of Bernstein in the *Journal of Linguistics:* 11(1975):147–151; as well as J. van den Broeck, "Class Differences in Syntactic Complexity," *Language and Society* 6(1977):149–181; L. Schatzman and A. Strauss, "Social Class and Modes of Communication," *American Journal of Sociology* 60:4 (1955); and A. Strauss and L. Schatzman, "Cross-Class Interviewing: An Analysis of Interaction and Communicative Styles," *Human Organization* 14:2(1955).

6. The distinction between abstract and concrete speech, while inappropriate if thought of as absolute, is nonetheless useful in some contexts; for example, when speaking neurologically of feral or brain-damaged patients. The dichotomy has been made since the nineteenth century and invoked in an extensive literature in philosophy, psychology and brain physiology. As one anonymous reviewer pointed out, "Goldstein and Gelb use this dichotomy in their discussion of aphasia victims, and Alfred Schutz in 'Language, Language Disturbances, and the Texture of Consciousness,' uses the Gelb/Goldstein hypothesis. In addition, brain physiologists such as Head, Jackson, and Pierre-Marie also distinguish abstract and concrete attitudes. The point of their researches is that severe brain damage to the left cerebral hemisphere (Broca's or Wernicke's areas in particular) creates an aphasia for the abstract or categorical mode of speech—a general problem with naming, but no problem with other more concrete aspects of speech. Penfield uses a similar dichotomy to articulate his findings from thousands of operations on the left cerebral hemisphere. Much of the work done with the feral child or isolate, as in K. Davis or R. Brown, or in Curtiss's *Genie: A Psycholinguistic Study of a Modern-Day "Wild Child"*, 1977,

point to similar disadvantages in cognition as exemplified through inabilities to use abstract speech." This weighty tradition of usage, however, is no defense against the logical difficulties of the abstract-concrete dichotomy when applied to language users who are not feral, isolated, brain damaged, extremely malnourished, or abused.

The abstraction of language suggests another important question that we will not treat here: When does abstraction become reification? This question is implied in debates between the epistemological status of thinking versus feeling, or print-oriented learning versus multisensorial learning, and of learning through schooling versus learning through praxis. For studies that illuminate the cognitive role of the emotions, see Richard S. Peter, "The Education of the Emotions" (1972); and Robert C. Solomon's philosophic explorations of *The Passions* (1976). Concerning print-oriented learning, aside from the well-known works of Marshall McLuhan and his precursor Harold Innis, see also Walter Ong (1972, 1982). Unfortunately, this debate on book learning by sociolinguists and educators is conducted within a very limited scope. What is left out by those criticizing or defending print in the name of direct or indirect experience is the larger philosophical and sociological literature on the nature and political economy of abstraction in general. Some of the obviously relevant contributions of such classical sociologists as Marx, Weber, Durkheim, and Simmel, are discussed by Anton C. Zijderveld in *The Abstract Society: A Cultural Analysis of Our Time* (Garden City, NY: Doubleday, 1970). Many of the points made by Herbert Marcuse about the political economy of language from a Marxian perspective are placed in a broader cultural and historical framework by Walter Ong in his studies of the rise of Ramism.

7. Organic and mechanical solidarity refer to the effects of the division of labor on the modes by which people relate to one another. Organic solidarity points to a social structure in which dissimilarity of function is the main basis of social bondedness; people act through specialized but interdependent social roles, expressing a wide range of different beliefs and sentiments. Individuals joined in organic solidarity are grouped "no longer according to their relations of lineage, but according to the particular nature of the social activity to which they consecrate themselves" (Durkheim 1933:182). The social norms and laws in such a society are constituted of restitutive sanctions, the main function of which is not to punish but to reestablish the normal state of cooperative relations. The *conscience collective* becomes very limited in its power to constrain individual actions, "consensus" diminishes, and rules of conduct and thought become "indeterminate," so that "individual reflection must intervene to apply them to particular cases" (Durkheim 1933:152).

In contrast, a society characterized by mechanical solidarity consists of a social structure based on similarity of functions. It is a system of segments that are homogeneous and similar to each other (Durkheim 1933:181). Society is divided into small compartments completely enclosing the individual (1933:300). In conditions of mechanical solidarity we find "repressive" law that is born from a "passionate reaction" (1933:96) to punish the rule breaker and that imposes "uniform beliefs and practices upon all" (1933:226); it is a way to maintain solidarity by reinforcing collective sentiments and values. Under these conditions, the *conscience collective* is "extensive and strong" (1933:146), determining conduct so that "it is not in view of our personal interest that we act, but we pursue collective ends" (1933:106).

From these short quotations it becomes evident that behind Bernstein's concepts of restricted and elaborated codes are Durkheim's models of mechanical and organic solidarity, implicitness and explicitness, and particularistic and universalistic orders of meaning (see Lawton 1972:102). Particularistic orders are "contextbound" and "tied to a given local structure," whereas universalistic ones are "less tied to a given context," thereby enabling a speaker to enter into a "reflexive relationship to the social order he has taken over." Speakers using elaborated speech variants do not take for granted that the listeners share the same assumptions, history, etc. "Difference lies at the bases of the social relationship" compelling the speaker "to individualize his meanings." He acts on the ground of individualized roles set in the context of universalistic rules. In contrast, when speakers use restricted variants they rely on a taken-for-granted "backdrop of common assumptions, common history, common interest." They realize "communalized" role relations.

Bernstein is in good company in making this too-simplified generalization: Mary Douglas (1970), and Randall Collins (1975:67–79) have also applied Durkheim's distinction between mechanical and organic solidarity of historical societies to the forms of solidarity of classes within contemporary societies.

8. In her ethnography of domestic networks in a ghetto community, *All Our Kin* (1975), Carol Stack argued that the ghetto world is not disorganized, but is organized on bases different from those within the middle class. Stack showed systematic pressure against marriage, for example, but countervailing norms of solidarity within the extended family.

9. One can also state the difference between sacred and profane space in Goffman's terms (1959). Frontstage and backstage are differentially distributed socially. Elites manage the stage as a whole and are usually able to keep their backstage performances private. But publicly they are frontstage, for the legitimacy of their power requires that they maintain good form. Lower-class persons have no such options; virtually all their performances, whether public or private, are enacted backstage—the realm for spontaneity, particularism, and subversion.

In between the elites and the lower orders are middle-class professionals, whose very professionalism is achieved through collective manipulation of backstage and frontstage. The process of professionalization involves the collective construction of an idealized frontstage image of a certain group of practitioners. For example, influence peddlers become lobbyists or even legislative representatives; undertakers become morticians. Each group attempts to shunt off its dirty work to subordinate occupational categories in order to legitimate its own claims to superior money, status, or power, and it justifies all this in the name of rationality, efficiency, customer service, public safety and the like (see Collins 1981; Wilensky 1964). Extended further, one could say that the solidarity of classes—that is, of income and occupational groups— is largely composed of the solidarity of teams and groups in enacting frontstage performances and guarding their backstage from intruders.

10. An analysis of the *Daily News* and the *New York Times* by James Chambers showed significant differences between the two papers in the use of syntax and vocabulary. The simplified wording and sentences of the *Daily News* correlated, as would be expected, with the class background of its readership, which tends toward a restricted code, while the more complex vocabulary and syntax of the *New York Times* corresponded to the generally elaborated code of its middle-class readers. Contrary to what some followers of Bernstein would have us expect, however, the *Daily News* tends to break local political stories earlier than the Times, to engage in energetic muckraking, and to present a more accurate picture of political reality from the

working-class perspective. See James Chambers, "The Content Analysis of Two Newspapers to Determine the Existence of Class Specificity," M.A. thesis, Hunter College, 1972. Similar studies have been conducted of German media: for example Ekkehart Mittelberg, *Wortschatz und Syntax der Bildzeitung,* (Marburg: Ewert Verlag, 1967). Also see Kress and Trew (1978) and Kress and Hodges (1981) pp. 15–35, for the latters' analysis of the mystification of power inherent in the syntax of an editorial from the *Manchester Guardian.*

    11. I had a similar experience some years later at the bilingual Université d'Ottawa in Canada. Teaching sociology to Francophones of working-class background in the morning, and to Anglophones from professional families in the afternoon, I was struck by the sociological acuity of the French Canadians as compared to the denseness of the dominant English-speaking group, especially when dealing with theories and issues of power. From a conventional sociolinguistic viewpoint this was all the more remarkable in that my "standard French" and the "nonstandard Canadian French" of the Quebecois were probably as different from each other as standard English is from nonstandard black English. Again, the theories of language deficit and learning deficiency didn't fit my personal experience.

    These examples suggest limitations in theories of linguistic backwardness, but they do not indicate that the poor are not otherwise deprived. There is such a thing as functional illiteracy. And there are obvious differences by class in terms of money, status, and power. Moreover, access to certain types of organizational experience and information, and time, encouragement, and training in critical reflection are limited resources for all elements of society, including the college-educated strata, but they are probably scarcer for the lower than the upper orders. Whether members of different classes take advantage of such differentially distributed opportunities for greater cognitive development and political awareness, however, is another matter.

    We also should remember that, despite the disappointment of both radicals and conservatives, many liberal reform programs have achieved some success. Food stamps have greatly reduced malnutrition and Medicare and Medicaid have greatly extended the availability of health services. In terms of political mobilization or non-distorted communication, however, the results of liberal programs have been limited. A new cadre of politicians and professionals has been created in the black community, and many other formerly quiescent groups (such as gays, women, the elderly, or Hispanics) are now active and vocal. But the political causes and consequences of these developments are far from obvious. Liberal governmental programs have been directed more toward counterinsurgency, pacification, and co-optation than toward fundamental structural change, as the worsening of income inequalities suggests. There is a new black bourgeoisie, for example, created in part through civil rights, antipoverty, and affirmative action programs. But the overall income share for blacks as a whole has remained stable or declined in relation to that of whites. Cloward and Piven (1972, 1979) noted that the War on Poverty and the Great Society programs helped integrate blacks into existing political systems. The same point could be made with respect to the Community Action Program. Eisinger's study of "The Community Action Program and the Development of Black Political Leadership" (Institute for Research of Poverty, 1978) provided evidence of the importance of experience in the civil rights movement as well as community action programs for black elected officials. Figures of the Joint Center for Political Studies show that the number of black elected officials in the United States rose from about 70 in 1964 to 4,311 in 1977.

Erlanger's data also support such a relationship, and findings of his study (*Social Science Quarterly*), suggest strongly that "the Movement" was important in bringing gang boys together in Los Angeles barrios and thereby lessening internecine gang conflict. And Short found that the black detached workers he studied more often moved from street work to careers in business and politics than did the white workers, suggesting that youth work of this type provided an avenue for social mobility and political leadership to a greater extent for blacks than for whites. These and other studies suggest that conventional programs to give power to the poor have been successful in creating political leadership, but that these programs and this leadership have not significantly affected the basic political and economic inequalities of our society. Moreover, at the level of street gangs, efforts at co-optive politicization have been less successful, as Miller (1957), Keiser (1979), Suttles (1968), Spergel (1969), and Jacobs (1981) have noted.

12. See also Abner Cohen, *The Politics of Elite Culture: Explorations in the Dramaturgy of Power in a Modern African Society* (Berkeley: University of California Press, 1981). A similar analysis has been made of modern social and political theories as elite mystification in Anthony Skillen *Ruling Illusions: Philosophy and the Social Order* (Atlantic Highlands: Humanities Press, 1978). According to Skillen, much of social science can be seen as an elaborate justification for things as they are, and for accepting the status quo as inevitable. Likewise, much of applied sociology—even when it functions as neither an excuse for inaction nor a cover for politically motivated decisions—can be seen as a search for techniques to get people to do things that they don't want to do. Thus Mayo, for example, presented workers' "attributing ills to a hostile world" *(Social Problems)* as a symptom of their pathological obsessions, and then recommended a therapeutic style of management to help them overcome these "disorders." Social control through the manipulation of language operates not only in established organizations and in the polity as a whole. It is also found in movements and groups challenging the status quo. As Weinstein and Weinstein noted, "Lacking financial and political resources, the protest and liberation movements of the 1960s resorted to control through the linguistic manipulations of self-concept in order to mobilize support and break up spontaneous factions based in primary groups" (1976:12).

Chapter 2

1. In this essay I employ the concept of identity described by Roger Wescott: "The English word 'identity,' though of Latin origin, was unknown to the Romans of Cicero's time. It first appeared in the Late Latin writings of such early Christian apologists as Sts. Jerome and Augustine but was not widely used until the time of the early Medieval Scholastic philosophers, like Anselm of Canterbury and Abelard of Taris. Its form, *identitas,* is anomalous. As a derivative of Classical Latin *idem,* the same, it would be expected to take the form *identas.* My own guess as to the reason for its attested form is that *identitas* is a blend . . . of *identas* with post-Classical Latin term *entitas,* 'being' . . . Contemporary lexicographers distinguish three definitions of the identity—sameness, distinctness, and reality or existence. The first and third of these definitions probably can be accounted for by the etmological contamination described above. The contradiction between sameness and distinctness as definitions of the same term, however, probably is due to a shift in the focus of reference: identity denotes sameness when it refers to the interior homogeneity of an

entity but distinctness when it refers to the external heterogeneity among entities" (Wescott 1981:1; see Onions 1971; and Morris 1969). Similarly, Vytautas Kavolis wrote: "The notion of identity, attached to an empirically concrete human being, seems to imply (1) the perception of an overall *coherence*—either 'substantive' or 'methodological'—within the experiences and expressions of an individual; (2) the memory in this individual and, normally, in at least some others, of the *continuity* of the 'story'—or 'tale'—of his life; and (3) a conscious, but not wholly conscious, *commitment* to a particular manner of both comprehending and managing one's own self" (Kavolis 1980:41). Also see Barbu, 1960.

2. Machiavelli's and Goffman's statements, like the other descriptions here, are best taken as ideal types and not as literal descriptions of conduct. Power does make cynics, of course, but so does powerlessness. And though power corrupts, it also ennobles through responsibility. Low persons sometimes "grow" in their high offices. The mask of legitimacy may eventually co-opt the amoral self. Thus the power reductionists must be matched by the moral transcendentalists. As Emerson said, "You cannot wield great agencies without lending yourself to them. . . . Power of any kind readily appears in the manners, [giving them] a majesty which cannot be concealed or resisted" (Emerson 1946).

3. Any critique of a normative social order must idealize some modal type as its object. This essay is no exception. Thus what I have to say about modernity applies to Northern European and Anglo-American societies more than the Third World, to larger states more than smaller, to urbanites more than ruralites, to 'WASPs' more than 'ethnics,' to whites more than blacks, and to men more than women. Indeed, much of the literature of women's studies can be understood as a search for ways of reconciling "female" values of nurturance, bondedness, fidelity, patience and the like, with opportunities for roles that seem to require such "male" attributes as competitiveness, assertive autonomy, and possessive individualism (see Elshtain 1981). To the extent that the women's movement seeks to remake society so that such choices are unnecessary, its project parallels that of humanistic socialism. Such gender images, like my own ideal types, are logically necessary to apprehend and critique social-psychological essences, but they always are in danger of becoming caricatures. See Berger, Berger and Kellner (1973) for a phenomenological ideal typification of the structures of consciousness prerequisite to a modern social order. See Goffman (1963) on the modal normal personality in one advanced capitalist society.

4. When morality is subordinated to instrumentality, we are but a short step from Hitler's dictum that "Morality is what serves the fatherland," or Lenin's saying that "Morality is that which serves to destroy the old exploiting society and to unite all the toilers around the proletariat which is creating a new Communist society" (Lenin 1923:18:322).

5. These are the structural conditions of what is usually called "alienation." This term has endured a long history and much abuse. For an account of these travails see Richard Schacht, *Alienation* (Garden City, NY: Doubleday, 1970). Also see R. Felix Geyer and David R. Schweitzer, eds., *Theories of Alienation* (New York: Methuen, 1981). Studies on work and alienation by empirically oriented American sociologists include Robert Blauner's *Alienation and Freedom: The Factory Worker and his Industry*, Chicago: University of Chicago Press, 1964; and for contrary views, William H. Form, "Auto Workers and Their Machines: A Study of Work, Factory and Job Satisfaction in Four Countries," *Social Forces*, 1973, and Melvin Seeman,

"The Urban Alienation: Some Dubious Theses from Marx to Marcuse," *Journal of Personality and Social Psychology* 35 (1969).

Note also that in the United States, for example, a country often cited as a land of individual initiative and peaceful progress, virtually every major extension of personal liberty—from the Revolution itself to the abolition of slavery, the enfranchisement of women, the labor movement, and contemporary struggles for civil equality and economic justice—all were the product not of Lone Ranger or Horatio Alger individualism, but of collective and often violent political activism.

6. Of course even forced literacy has a liberating potential. Moreover, one great positive result of the growth of state intervention was the protection of daughters from neglect and wives from abuse, as well as the enhancement of the status of mothers as agents of socialization. For further discussion of these themes, particularly with references to the American experience, see Barbara Finkelstein, "Tolerating Ambiguity in Family History: A Guide to Some New Materials," *Journal of Psychohistory* 11, 1 (Summer 1983); Mel Albin and Dominick Cavallo, eds., *Family Life in America, 1620–2000* (New York: Revisionary Press, 1981); Vivian C. Fox and Martin H. Quitt, eds., *Loving, Parenting and Dying: The Family Cycle in England and America, Past and Present* (New York: Psychohistory Press, 1980); Donald M. Scott and Bernard Wishy, eds., *America's Families: A Documentary History* (New York: Harper and Row, 1982); Raymond A. Mohl, *Poverty in New York, 1983–1825* (New York: Oxford University Press, 1971); Joseph M. Hawes, *Children in Urban Society: Juvenile Delinquency in Nineteenth-Century America* (New York: Oxford University Press, 1971); Michael B. Katz, *The Irony of Early School Reform: Educational Innovation in Mid-Nineteenth Century Massachusetts* (Cambridge: Harvard University Press, 1968); Elizabeth Badinter, *L'amour en plus: Histoire de l'amour maternel (17e–20e siècle)* (Paris: Flammarion, 1980); David J. Rothman, *The Discovery of the Asylum: Social Order and Disorder in the New Republic* (Boston: Little, Brown, 1971); Barbara Laslett, "The Family as a Public and Private Institution: An Historical Perspective," in Arlene Skolnick and Jerome Skolnick, eds., *Intimacy, Family, and Society* (Boston: Little, Brown, 1974); 94–114; Barbara M. Brenzel, "Domestication as Reform: A Study of the Socialization of Wayward Girls, 1856–1905," *Harvard Educational Review* 50 (May 1980):196–313; and Joseph Kett, *Rites of Passage: Adolescence in America, 1790 to the Present* (New York: Basic Books, 1977).

7. In his critique of Adam Smith's *Inquiry into the Nature and Causes of the Wealth of Nations*, Hegel noted the tendency of capitalist society *(bürgerliche Gesellschaft)* to privatize consciousness: "As citizens of this [bourgeois] state, individuals are private persons who have as their purpose their own interests" (Hegel 1930:118). This truncates the social dimensions of persons' self-conceptions and social roles, while at the same time making society more reified, making it appear to act on the person as a 'natural necessity,' a blind force that gives his public affairs an 'abstract' character.

8. For Marx, the intrinsic value of any product was in the labor invested in it and in its eventual use. In contrast, commodity value (as opposed to use value) was understood as an artificial moment in the object's life that existed between the real human labor that went into its making and the real human use to which it was put. But in advanced capitalism, labor is a relatively small element of production, and the use value of a product to consumers lies not in its intrinsic properties but in its aspect

as a commodity. The commodity value has become the use value. Also see Rousseau's *Emile:* "There is no subjugation so perfect as that which keeps the appearance of freedom, for in that way one captures volition itself."

9. As Kingsley Widmer noted, "By some weird extrapolation, multiplication of the same translates into diversity and freedom. The epitomization of this may be the McLuhanism of a few years ago in which by multiplying all the automobile models times all the optional accessories we arrive at the fantastic consumer options of 25 million transportation possibilities. Since the choices did not include significantly different power plants, or an inexpensively safe and well-crafted car, or comfortable and efficient public transportation, the millions of trivial variations merely confirmed the lack of significant choice which they helped to disguise" (1975b:8).

10. For similar examples drawn from cross-national studies of social change, see Stanley Milgram, "The Experience of Living in Cities," *Science* 167 (1970):1461; M. Fried and P. Gleicher, "Some Sources of Residential Satisfaction in an Urban Slum," in *Environment and the Social Sciences: Perspectives and Applications*, J. F. Wohlwill and D. H. Carson, eds., American Psychological Association, Washington D.C., 1972; T. G. McGee, *The Southeast Asian City* (London: G. Bell and Sons, 1967); D. Stea and E. Soja, "Environment and Spatial Cognition in African Societies," *ITEMS* 29:3, Social Science Research Council, New York, 1975; L. Yap, *Internal Migration in Less Developed Countries*, Report to the World Bank Urban Poverty Task Force, World Bank, Washington, DC, 1975; and George V. Coelho and Jane J. Stein, "Coping with Stresses of an Urban Planet: Impacts of Uprooting and Overcrowding," *Habitat* 2 (1977):1–12.

11. "Indeed Rousseau's critique of alienation is so radical that to avoid sending man off on the impossible return journey to savage life he is forced in the *Contrat Social* to go to the other extreme: he advocates collective, willed alienation and the subjection of all individual lives to public opinion and the common will" (Starobinski 1973:22). This bifurcation of inner freedom and outer subjection provided a basis for modern totalitarianism, much as Rousseau's technique of confessing in order to judge provided a basis for the modern practice of brainwashing.

12. Helmuth Plessner made a similar point in criticizing both Marxism and existentialism for asserting that man's social being is an alienation of his true self. "In order to be genuinely human, Plessner asserted, man needs the duplication of his self in the form of social roles which are originally not part of this self. Man is only man if he duplicates himself in 'alien' roles and tries to identify himself with these roles. His 'true self' or 'true identity' is not 'something' that is left after his social roles have been stripped off, but can be established only through the individual's act of identification with his roles. It is romanticism (going back as far as Luther's *homo internus*) to defend the individual and his inner or private experiences against the alleged alienation of an 'irritating fact, called society' (Dahrendorf), just as it is romanticism to search for reality, meaning and freedom within man's inner subjective life" (Zijderveld 1970:33).

13. For examples of pseudoparticipation in industry see Bendix (1956:301–18); Buraway (1979), and Baritz (1961); in education, Friedenberg (1963), and Clark (1960); in politics, Levin (1960). Rates of mental and psychosomatic illness tend to be higher for groups—American Negroes for example—who are officially invited to participate in the American Dream but are practically excluded from it Seeman (1956:142–153); Broyard (1950:56–64); Sartre (1960);

and Watzlawick, Beaven, and Jackson (1967). Etzioni (1968:882), citing Kornhauser, Sheppard and Mayer (1956:194), noted that "large segments of the citizens of contemporary industrial societies feel powerless and excluded, and are uninformed about societal and political processes which govern their lives." See also Almond and Verba (1963:226) and Archibald (1976).

A number of other researchers have found that for a wide range of work settings, autonomy at the work place is the major influence on people's overall self-directedness and autonomy (House 1980; Kohn 1969; Kohn and Schooler 1973, 1978; Miller et al. 1977). In contrast to psychologically oriented thinkers who see adult identity mainly in terms of childhood socialization, these investigators conclude that character (and child-rearing values and practices as well) is derived mainly from the job and expresses the larger political economy. "Our findings," concluded Kohn and Schooler, "support the argument of the structuralists. A man's job affects his perceptions, values, and thinking processes primarily because it confronts him with demands he must try to meet. These demands, in turn, are to a great extent determined by the job's location in the larger structure of the economy and the society" (1973:117). Though the evidence is incomplete, it tends to be even more depressing for third world countries that are experiencing the atomization caused by industrial social processes but may lack modern institutions of democratic participation.

14. For examples of failures to deal with such parallelisms between individual and institutional phenomena, see House's summary of current literatures: "Psychologically, we have a tendency to attribute the causes of behavior to the internal dispositions or personalities of actors. Similarly, we tend to see group differences in behavior (between nations, races, social classes, and so forth) as rooted in the different beliefs and values shared within each group, which are in turn generally seen to rise from the different ways people in these groups have been socialized from early in life" (1981:542).

Compare this conception of identity and the notion of the self-concept in contemporary sociology as described by Morris Rosenberg: "Broadly speaking, two rather different emphases have characterized the sociological approach to the self-concept (Hewitt, 1976). One, focusing on the 'biographical' self-concept, views the self-concept as a stable, enduring feature of personality or, to be more precise, as 'a stable set of meanings attached to self as object' (Stryker, 1981). The other, described as the 'situated' self-concept, focuses on the self-concept as a shifting, adjustive process of self-presentation in social interaction" (Rosenberg 1981:593–94; see Blumer 1969). The first of these definitions overlaps my term "identity," especially as it appears in traditional societies. The latter (the "situated self-concept"), is close to our "causal-encounter self," which I deem characteristic mainly of the late modern West.

15. Gerth and Mills (1964:vii) proposed a parallel project: a historically oriented psychology of social institutions. Some critiques of mass culture can be used as elements of such a project. For example, Lasch (1981:10) recommends Max Horkheimer, "Art and Mass Culture," *Studies in Philosophy and Social Science* 9 (1941):290–304; Dwight Macdonald, "A Theory of Popular Culture," *Politics* 1 (February 1944):20–23; Max Horkheimer and Theodor W. Adorno, "The Culture Industry: Enlightenment as Mass Deception," in their *Dialectic of Enlightenment*, originally published in 1947 (New York: Herder and Herder, 1972):120–67; Irving Howe, "Notes on Mass Culture," *Politics* 5 (Spring 1948):120–23; Leo Lowenthal,

"Historical Perspectives of Popular Culture," *American Journal of Sociology* 55 (1950):323–32; Dwight Macdonald, "A Theory of Mass Culture," *Diogenes* 3 (Summer 1953):1–17; Dwight Macdonald, "Masscult and Midcult," *Partisan Review* 27 (1960):203–33, reprinted in his *Against the American Grain* (New York: Random House, 1962):3–75. Some of these essays are collected, together with many others on both sides of the debate, in Bernard Rosenberg and David Manning White, eds., *Mass Culture: The Popular Arts in America* (New York: Free Press, 1975).

"Though these attacks come from the Left, mass culture also has been attacked from the Right. The conservative critique is less interesting, however, partly because it is ideologically predictable, partly because it assumes that the masses have actually overthrown established elites and gained political power for themselves. For example, see Jose Ortega y Gasset, *The Revolt of the Masses* (New York: W. W. Norton, 1932)" (Lasch 1981:10).

Chapter 4

1. The analysis implied by these terms is akin to "sociology of knowledge," but with two provisos. First, sociology of knowledge has often respected the claims that science is independent of ideology. Hence, we have a sociology of knowledge for lay beliefs and intellectual practices, and a sociology of science for what scientists think and do. In the latter, a distinction is often made between the social processes through which knowledge is sought and the logical justifications of the "knowledge itself." In our politics of language we permit no such distinctions. Second, traditional sociology of knowledge has made relatively little use of hermeneutic phenomenology, semiotics, and the critical theory of rhetoric. By contrast, concepts and tools from these approaches are basic to the present analysis. The sociology of knowledge examines how speech affects political action. With two small provisos, however, these apparently disparate pursuits can be shown to investigate the same phenomena from opposite, but complementary, starting points. Belief, knowledge, and speech all take their shapes through discourse—through intersubjective communication. Whether one focuses on the text of this discourse, as in much theory of rhetoric, or on its context, as in most sociology of knowledge, is mainly a matter of emphasis. The methodological resources of rhetoric, however, emerge from a two-thousand-year tradition, whereas those of the sociology of knowledge are essentially modern.

2. These approaches advance under such banners as humanistic sociology, ethnomethodology, phenomenological sociology, the sociology of the absurd, cognitive sociology, reality constructionism, existential sociology, essential interactionism, and reflexive sociology. The importance of such schools lies not only in their substantive findings, but also in their methodological self-reflection; for these investigators have discovered that the process of constructing sociological knowledge—from whatever theoretical perspective—has much in common with the processes by which ordinary people patch together reality and meaning in their everyday lives. This awareness has helped to limit methodological dogmatism and to initiate the search for a broader epistemological justification for the human studies. Recent developments in the history of science are also of interest. As Mauskopf and McVaught pointed out, "By 1960 . . . these historians were coming to focus their research on the

204 Notes to Pages 80–84

social, institutional, and cultural life of science and scientists. . . . One group of historians, for example, had taken a renewed interest in those sciences of the Renaissance (particularly alchemy) that grew marginal in the seventeenth century and had argued convincingly that these must be taken into account in developing a complete picture of scientific activity during the Scientific Revolution. And in order to take these enterprises into account, they had pointed out, it was necessary to begin by trying to comprehend them—and the interest in them of intelligent and even brilliant minds—in terms of their own milieu in the sixteenth and seventeenth centuries. While not forgetting that they were already becoming superseded in this period, it was essential to study them without letting a presentist judgment intrude" (1980:xi–xii).

3. There are exceptions to the neglect of the theory of rhetoric among scholars concerned with the social sciences. Among these are Richard Harvey Brown, *A Poetic for Sociology: Toward a Logic of Discovery for the Human Sciences* (London and New York: Cambridge University Press, 1977); Hugh D. Duncan, *Communication and the Social Order;* (New York: Bedinster Press, 1962); Murray Edelman, *The Symbolic Uses of Politics* (Urbana, IL: University of Illinois Press, 1967); Aaron D. Gresson, "Minority Epistemology and the Rhetoric of Creation," *Philosophy and Rhetoric* 10:4 (Fall 1977):224–62; Joseph Gusfield, "The Literary Rhetoric of Science: Comedy and Pathos in Drinking Research," *American Sociological Review* 41 (1976):16–34; Donald N. McCloskey, *The Rhetoric of Economics* (Madison: University of Wisconsin Press, 1985); John Nelson, Allan Megills, and Donald McCloskey, eds., *The Rhetoric of the Human Sciences: Language and Argument in Scholarship and Public Affairs* (Madison: University of Wisconsin Press, 1987); Michael A. Overington, "A Critical Celebration of Gusfield's 'The Literary Rhetoric of Science,'" *American Sociological Review* 62(1977):171–73; Chaim Perelman and Lucie Olbrechts-Tyteca, *The New Rhetoric: A Treatise on Argumentation* (Notre Dame, IN: University of Notre Dame Press, 1969); Manfred Standley, *The Technological Conscience: Survival and Dignity in an Age of Expertise* (New York: Free Press, 1978); Hayden White, *Topics of Discourse: Essays in Cultural Criticism* (Baltimore: Johns Hopkins University Press, 1978); John M. Ziman, *Public Knowledge: The Social Dimension of Science* (London and New York: Cambridge University Press, 1966); Ricca Edmondson, *Rhetoric in Sociology* (New York: Cambridge University Press, 1985); and the fall 1979 issue of the *Journal of the American Forensic Association*, devoted to the rhetorical implications of the work of Jurgen Habermas.

4. "As early as 1770, Herder and Goethe had insisted that a new art should not be judged by rules derived from antiquity; each civilization, each folk, each nation created its own standards. For Schlegel and Novalis this had become true for each work of art. It is only from within a work that one could derive the principles by which it was to be judged. Criticism was, therefore, immanent in the work itself" (Rosen 1977:32). This turned criticism from an act of judgment into an act of understanding.

5. Fragments of Gorgias' work are in Hermann Diels and Walther Kranz, eds., *Die Fragmente der Vorsokratiker*, 10th ed., vol. 2 (Berlin: Weidmann, 1961); text and commentary of *On Melissus, Xenophanes*, and *Gorgias* are found in Mario Untersteiner, ed., *Sofisti, testimonianze a frammenti*, vol. 2 (Florence:"La Nuova Italia," 1949–1962). See also Untersteiner's *The Sophists* (Oxford: Blackwell, 1954), chaps. 4–9; Guido Calogero, *Studi sull'eleatismo* (Rome: Tipografia del Senato, 1932); G. B. Kerferd, "Gorgias on Nature or That Which is Not," *Phronesis:*1

(1955–1956):3–25; and "Gorgias of Leontini," in Paul Edwards, ed., *Encyclopedia of Philosophy*, vol. 3 (New York: Macmillan, 1967); Plato, *Gorgias*, E. R. Dobbs, ed., (Oxford: University Press, 1959); Richard Leo Enos, "The Epistemology of Gorgias's Rhetoric: A Re-Examination," *Southern Speech Communication Journal* 38 (Fall 1972):27–38; and Richard A. Engnell, "Implications for Communication of the Rhetorical Gorgias of Leontine," *Western Journal of Speech Communication* (Summer 1973):175–184; and W. K. C. Guthrie, *The Sophists* (Cambridge: Cambridge University Press, 1971). The dearth of actual texts of Gorgias invites quite speculative reconstructions of his thought.

Of course Plato and Aristotle were not entirely wrong. Plato did appreciate the mimetic power of art (*Republic*, 10), but in his ontology of forms all mimesis is distortion. Aristotle also had a negative view (see *Rhetoric*, 3:404a), although he did allow that "Words express ideas, and therefore those words are most agreeable that enable us to get hold of new ideas. . . . Midway between the unintelligible and the commonplace, it is a metaphor that most produces knowledge" (*Rhetoric*, 3:404b). Moreover Aristotle linked oral presentation with logic in asserting that "rhetoric is the counterpart of dialectic." See Corcoran (1979:35–51) for a defense of Aristotle on these points.

6. The whole universe is "perfused with signs, if not composed entirely of signs," said Charles Sanders Peirce (1965–1966:5:448, n.1). "Language is the house of Being" (Heidegger 1962:145); it contains the world. Hence the world cannot be an object of language. Rather the object and the statements about it are already enclosed within a horizon of language. "The linguistic nature of the human experience of the world does not include making the world into an object" that we could describe from outside the world (Gadamer 1967:426, 408). We can only make objects within the world (of language). The inevitably symbolic character of reality for humans, even the reality of "things," has long been noted by literary writers. "Things are *already as close to words* as they are to things, and reciprocally, words are *already as close to things* as they are to words" (Ponge 1971:23). Though unrelated to Kenneth Burke in his immediate intellectual lineage, Michael Foucault interprets the human studies in a similar fashion. In *The Order of Things*, Foucault defined a history of modern man's consciousness of himself as existing through language, and discusses the possibilities of constructing a language that would be able to fully represent the world, "as if the world were made to be read by man." Foucault's title is ironic, in that what he described is the disorder of the failure of various theoretical schemata (1970:17–45). In a similar spirit, Pocock warned that the student of paradigmatic thinking has altogether to repudiate "the practice of referring to the extralinguistic as reality, and to the intellectual or linguistic equipment, at least by implication, as nonreality." We must remember "that the paradigms which order 'reality' are part of the reality they order, that language is part of the social structure and not epiphenomenal to it, and that we are studying an aspect of reality when we study the ways in which it appeared real to the persons to whom it was more real than to anyone else" (Pocock 1973:38).

7. See Turbayne (1962) for a comparison of two conflicting metaphors of sight: as a camera taking pictures, and as a person learning a language. Each theoretical metaphor may or may not be accompanied by an appropriate observational metaphor. Certainly, if the theoretical metaphor of vision as the acquisition of language were "tested" with an observational metaphor based on the camera, it would continue to be "falsified." As Feyerabend pointed out, "A correct general theory may

thus be rejected, not because it is itself deficient, but solely because the wrong 'observational' theories are providing the evidence which is used against it" (quoted in Ferguson 1973:132).

8. C. Wright Mills made a similar point: "The function of words is the mediation of social behaviors, and their meanings are dependent upon this social and behavioral function. Semantical changes are surrogates and foci of cultural conflicts and groupal behaviors. Because language functions in the organization and control of behavior patterns, these patterns are determinants of the meanings in a language. Words carry meanings by virtue of dominant interpretations placed upon them by social behaviors. Interpretations or meanings spring from the habitual modes of behavior which pivot upon symbols. Such social patterns of behavior constitute the meanings of the symbols. [Therefore] we can view language functionally as a system of social control" (1974b:432–33).

9. This distinction between the content and the commitment of communication has been expressed as one between report and command (Ruesch and Bateson 1951:179–181), between digital and analogic communication (Watzlawick, et. al. 1967:51–52), between rational discourse and body rhetoric (Haiman 1969:155–56), and between communication and subcommunication. We might also distinguish a third dimension of discourse—metacommunication, or discourse about the nature of discourse. Moreover, as one reviewer noted, I have omitted from this discussion "the Anglo-American tradition in philosophy, . . . with John Stuart Mill and his distinctions between the denotative and connotative aspects of language, continuing through Bertrand Russell, and up through Wittgenstein, among others. They, each and all, were deeply interested in language as a form of symbolism and its relation to the world—the late Wittgenstein spoke of 'language games' which, it is claimed, may have laid the basis for the modern (Kuhnian) conception of 'paradigms.' Nor is there any reference at all to Gottlob Frege, his distinction among *sense* and *reference*, and his importance to the work of the twentieth-century logicical positivists. Finally, and most importantly, there is no attention given to the conceptual distinction between *language* and *rhetoric*. . . . The distinction [originates] in the work of Ferdinand de Saussure, and has ramifications later in the work of Noam Chomsky's distinction between deep and surface linguistic grammars, and also [in the works of] Claude Lévi-Strauss."

10. The ethnomethodologists are used here as a convenient but by no means exclusive illustration. Much the same point has been made, for example, by Erving Goffman writing within a symbolic interactionist tradition, by Michael Polanyi drawing on the heritage of critical rationalism, or by Levi-Strauss in his conception of the myth-making *bricolage* of primitive peoples that draws on both Durkheimian sociology and Saussurean linguistics. My point, of course, is not that Durkheim was well received despite his bad science and because of his good rhetoric. Instead, he was effective as a scientist because he was a master rhetorician. Moreover, although there are important structural parallels between the radio talk show and Durkheim's text, they do not exhaust the intellectual and rhetorical richness of Durkheim's work.

11. I have taken the liberty of citing texts other than *Suicide* to support this contention, because *Suicide* itself was received and interpreted in the context of Durkheim's larger opus.

12. For an interpretation of the interest in Durkheimian sociology in the Soviet Union, see Gouldner (1970).

Chapter 5

1. This logical difficulty also can be understood as a stylistic one. Marx mixed his root metaphors by seeking to combine an organismic procedure in his text with a mechanistic justification of what he was doing. Had he been more consistent in elaborating his organismic root metaphor, he would have been able to declare, as did Spencer, that "until you have got a true theory of humanity, you cannot interpret history; and when you have got a true theory, you do not want history."

Chapter 6

1. The metaphor of the world as text is at least as old as the later Middle Ages. Alain de Lille said: "Omnis mundi creatures/ quasi liber et pictura/ nobis est et speculum." In the same spirit, St. Bonaventura wrote in the thirteenth century: "A creature of the world is as it were a book in which is manifest the creating Trinity." This metaphor continued into the early modern period. In the sixteenth century Luis de Granada asked: "What then are all the creatures of this world, so beautiful and so excellent, if not well shaped and illuminated letters which declare the beauty and the wisdom of their author? You have placed us before the marvelous book of the universe so that we may read the excellence of the creator in the created beings just as we would in living letters." Yet in Sir Thomas Browne's *Religio Medici* the imagery begins to shift: "There are two books from whence I collect my divinity. Besides that one written of God, another of his servant, Nature, that universal and public manuscript." Similarly, Voltaire, in *Zadig* (chap. 3): "Nothing is more beautiful than a philosopher who reads in the great book that God has put before our eyes."

In the Middle Ages the book of nature was taken as evidence for the existence and intent of its author. With Thomas Browne the book and its author are separated, until by the twentieth century the authorship of nature or the social world was almost forgotten. Nature had its own subdivisions—physics, biology, and chemistry—and the image of nature's book became sentimentalized into "sermons in streams" and "laughter in the running brook." I thank Lawrence Eldridge for these observations. For sources of quotations see Ernst Robert Curtius, *Europäische Literatur und lateinisches Mittelalter*, 2d ed. (1954). In more recent times thinkers such as Ricoeur, Gadamer, Geertz, Leach, and Lévi-Strauss have revived this metaphor and envisioned all of culture and society as a text. Of these the Moscow-Tartu exponents of cultural semiotics have submitted the concept of society as text to the most rigorous and extensive analysis (see Winner 1978).

2. These observations invite a sociological redefinition of immorality and of normatively sanctioned social control. Immoral conduct is no longer immoral in and of itself. Instead, it becomes conduct that is considered immoral and that cannot be otherwise accounted for. For example, as Milgram's (1963) own experiments show, inflicting pain on others is considered immoral only to the extent that it cannot be rhetorically justified. Once it is constructed as part of a scientific experiment, for example, it is thereby normalized. Similarly, torturing persons—say by tying them in icy sheets, giving them electric shocks, or cutting out parts of their brains—can be normalized if it is credibly accounted for as therapy.

3. My examples from Solzhenitsyn's texts are taken from K. Pomorska (1980).

4. The weak view of society as having codes is expressed by Basil Bernstein, who assumes that "symbolic systems are both realizations and regulators of the

structure of social relationships" ("Social Class, Language, and Socialization," pp. 157–78 in *Language and Social Context*, P. P. Giglioli, ed. [Harmondsworth: Penguin, 1972]). By contrast, the strong view of society as a code is exemplified by Rom Harre, who holds that "social relationships are themselves a symbolic system, a representation in a form of life of structures, the conceptions of which are prior to their realization. . . . Learning the social system is learning a symbolic system, both in the sense that the social system is auto-referential, in and of itself symbolic, and also in the sense that it may be a kind of iconic representation of that society's theory of the nature of people and their world, a theory in terms of which they can explain to themselves and to each other the situation in which they find themselves" ("Architectonic Man: On the Structuring of Lived Experience," pp. 139–172 in Richard Harvey Brown and Stanford M. Lyman, eds., *Structure, Consciousness, and History* [New York and London: Cambridge University Press, 1978], pp. 141–142).

5. My use of Petrine Russia as an example of polity as text is borrowed and paraphrased from B. A. Uspenskij (1977).

6. For a summary of the linguistic aspects of Pierce and pragmatism in relation to American social science, see Brown (1977), pp. 27–30, 146–147. For a treatment of Pierce's pragmatism and rhetoric, see Lyne (1980).

7. Representative structuralist or semiotic analyses of these topics are provided respectively in Roland Barthes, *Système de la mode* (Paris: Seuil, 1967); Lévi-Strauss, *Le Cru et le cuit* (Paris: Plon, 1968); Mary Douglas, "Deciphering a Meal," in her *Implicit Meanings* (London: Routledge and Kegan Paul, 1975), pp. 249–275; Barthes' essay on the semiotics of Greta Garbo's face in *Mythologies* (New York: Hilland Wang, 1972); Lévi-Strauss, *Les Structures élémentaires de la parenté* (Paris: Presses universitaires de France, 1949); Robert Scholes, "Uncoding Mama: The Female Body as Text," in his *Semiotics and Interprettion* (New Haven: Yale University Press, 1982), pp. 127–42); and Rom Harre's treatment of the *Umwelt* in his essay "Architectonic Man," in Brown and Lyman's collection, *Structure, Consciousness, and History* (London and New York: Cambridge University Press, 1978), pp. 140–72).

Chapter 7

1. For the fullest critique, reformulation, and application of the paradigm approach to the arts see Remi Clignet's brilliant *The Structure of Artistic Revolutions* (Philadelphia: University of Pennsylvania Press, 1985). Some art critics and historians have proposed the use of "paradigm" for the analysis of artistic styles or schools. See James Ackerman, "The Demise of the Avante Garde: Notes on the Sociology of Recent American Art," *Comparative Studies in Society and History* 11 (1969):371–84; Joseph F. Musser, "The Perils of Relying on Thomas Kuhn," Eighteenth-Century Studies 18:2 (Winter 1984–85):215–26. There are also examples of studies that link genre criticism with the sociology of art. Benjamin's study of German baroque drama, Lukács's of the historical novel, Goldmann's of French classical tragedy, Adorno's writing on the twelve-tone musical system, Duby's study of medieval architecture, or Moretti's work on science fiction are examples of such an approach. Such studies by no means exhaust the possibilities of a sociology of aesthetic forms.

The paradigm view needs to be amended, however, in order to include multigenre situations, the complex interactions between genres, and the conflicting political ideologies that may be revealed within texts of a single genre. Also, different genres place themselves within, and may be examined from, different rhetorical perspectives and traditions. See Ralph Cohen, "Reply to Dominick La Capra and Richard Harvey Brown," *New Literary History* 17:2 (Winter 1986):229–32. A focus on aesthetic form is illustrated in the same number of *New Literary History*, the diffuse contributions of which all pose a single question: What are the social bases for common understanding? Moxey's remarks on iconology, for instance, show how intrinsic meanings of symbolic forms are influenced by, and help to shape, the intellectual and spiritual life of specific socio-historical eras. Similarly, Velimirovic's essay on changes in the reception of music highlights the pivotal role of changing socio-historical contexts of interpretation. In the same spirit, Davidson reveals the historical relativity of modes of literary analysis. Finally, Cohen's work on genre and history underlines the social bases of interpretation by arguing that genre classifications "are historical assumptions constructed by authors, audiences, and critics. . . . Groupings [of works into genres] arise at particular historical moments. . . . Genres have popular and polite functions and statuses. Generic transformation can be a social act."

2. As Pocock put it, "only after we have understood what means he had of saying anything can we understand what he meant to say, what he succeeded in saying, what he was taken to have said, or what effects his utterance had in modifying or transforming the existing paradigm structures. Authors—individuals thinking and articulating—remain the actors in any story we may have to tell, but the units of the processes we trace are the paradigms of political speech" (Pocock 1973:25). On authorial intention, see E. D. Hirsch, *Validity in Interpretation* (New Haven, CT: Yale University Press, 1967,); Roy Lawrence, *Motive and Intention* (Evanston: Northwestern University Press, 1972); G. E. M. Anscombe, *Intention* (Ithaca: Cornell University Press, 1957); and Max Black, "Meaning and Intention: An Examination of Grice's Views," *New Literary History* 4 (Winter 1973).

3. "The value of 'dead' metaphors in argument is above all prominent because of the great force of persuasion they possess. . . . This force results from the fact that they draw their effects from an analogic material which is easily admitted because it is not only known, but integrated, by means of language, into the cultural tradition" (Perelman and Olbrechts-Tyteca 1969:543).

4. Whereas tales formerly sought only to convey "the moral of the story," by the nineteenth century, novels tried to express "the meaning of life." Each possible meaning of life involved a different choice of self and career, a choice, for example, between the red and the black. The very possibility of choosing one's identity, however, soon came to mean the impossibility of ever being fully integrated into any chosen self, or of ever forming any integral identity at all. And with the advent of consumer choice of identities through the marketing of "life styles," identity itself became a commodity. For example, a critique of the modern Western view of personality and relationships as commodities appears in E. M. Forster's *A Passage to India*, (1949) as when Fielding says:

> "Your emotions never seem in proportion to their objects, Aziz."
> "Is emotion a sack of potatoes, so much to the pound to be measured out? Am I a machine? I shall be told I shall use up my emotions by using them next."
> "I should have thought you would. It sounds common sense. You can't eat your cake and have it, even in the world of the spirit."

"If you are right, there is no point in any friendship; it all comes down to give and take, or give and return, which is disgusting, and we had all better leap over this parapet and kill ourselves".

5. In *Erewhon* a judge speaks to a boy who has just been convicted of pulmonary consumption:

It is all very well for you to say that you came of unhealthy parents, and had a severe accident in your childhood which permanently undermined your constitution; excuses such as these are the ordinary refuge of the criminal; but they cannot for one moment be listened to by the ear of justice. I am not here to enter upon curious metaphysical questions as to the origin of this or that—questions to which there would be no end were their introduction once tolerated, and which would result in the throwing the only guilt on the tissues of the primordial cell, or on the elementary gases. There is no question of how you came to be wicked, but only this—namely, are you wicked or not. (Butler 1927:88–89)

6. See Hans Gerth and C. Wright Mills:

The distributed product, whether it is seen on the screen or heard from a disk, is a performance that has been carefully selected from a series of less flawless trials. The mass availability of such performances by star actors, orchestras under star conductors, and so on require the communication and amusement industries to establish and market their products as "brands," to command attention by the excellence of performance and reproduction standards. In fact, these items often gain ascendancy over the content or message of the work of art itself. Interest in mass marketing also promotes the selection of what is "safe"—the accepted and proved work. The established work of art—that is, the non-contemporary or the "classical"—stands in the center, and enjoyment of art is not enjoyment of the unheard of and hitherto unseen, of the experimental thrust and the eye opener, but of the acoustically stereotyped and soothing brand, in terms of which the recognition of the composer, opus number, and star performer become conversationally prestigeful, and accordingly train for regressive listening. The reduction of a Beethoven symphony or a Verdi opera to the acoustic dimension of a living room, the photographic reduction of life size to pocket-book size, immerse twentieth-century man in a great stream of mechanically reproduced visual and acoustic images which tend to treat the cultural legacy of the ages as raw material for industrial processing. The original work, torn from its context and aura, tends to be swept away by the flood of its varied reproductions. (1964:304)

7. Further illustrations are provided in a recent number of *New Literary History*, "On Narrative and Narratives" (Spring 1980). Here Alain Robbe-Grillet says he wants his "story" to be "illustrated," but he is unhappy if the visual apparatus has any necessary connection with his textual equipment. In another contribution, Claude Bremond invents a Newtonian physics of the narrative in which any experience of people engaged in actions is reduced to a manifestation of synchronic for-

malist "laws which govern the narrated matter." Narrative disappears, and what remains are principles of textual motion. In a like-minded pursuit, Felix Martinez-Bonati discusses "the act of writing fiction." He is concerned with the paradoxes "implicit in our notions of fiction and reality," the resolution of which "is an ontological and linguistic-analytical task." Fine. But where is the narrative in this? Not at the locus of concern.

The sight of Peter Brooks' article on *Great Expectations* raises our hopes for a story. But the oasis turns out to be a mirage, for this essay is not really about Dickens' work so much as about "repetition, repression, and return." The solid ground of plots turns out to be quicksand, and we become dogpaddlers in a muddy sea of words. The reward of our efforts is not enlightenment or pleasure, but only the avoidance of pain, of being "caught perpetually in the 'blind and thankless' existence, in the illusory middle. Like Oedipus, like Pip, we are condemned to reinterpretation of our names." Our life itself is an endless palindrome, endlessly repeated, forward and back, a negation of identity in the knowledge that "what we discover will always be that there was nothing to be discovered."

One came for an explanation of stories, only to be told that there are no such things. Have we been wrong about this? Are the literary scholars confused? Or is the appearance of error and confusion a symptom of something else—the death of narrative itself? Cadavers invite autopsies, but the very dissection renders the parts unlike the living whole we longingly remember. Similarly, the dissections of narrative undertaken in contemporary literary criticism imply the demise of that form. Following the death-of-God school to its conclusion, the *Tel Quel* school have announced the death of the author and of narrative as well.

For general discussions of narrative structure, see Robert Scholes and Robert Kellogg, *The Nature of Narrative* (New York: Oxford University Press, 1966); Harold Toliver, *Animal Illusions: Explanations of Narrative Structure* (Lincoln: University of Nebraska Press, 1974); Warner Berthoff, *Fictions and Events* (New York: Dutton, 1971); Frank Kermode, *The Sense of an Ending* (Oxford: Oxford University Press, 1967); Ronald Barthes, "An Introduction to the Structural Analysis of Narrative," trans. Lionel Dusuit, *New Literary History* 6 (1975):237–72; Seymour Chatman, "New Ways of Analyzing Narrative Structure," *Language and Style* 2 (1969):1–36; and "Towards a Theory of Narrative," *New Literary History* 6 (1975):295–318; essays collected in Roger Fowler, ed., *Style and Structure in Literature* (Ithaca: Cornell University Press, 1975); A. J. Greimas and J. Courtes, "The Cognitive Dimension of Narrative Discourse," trans. Michael Rengstorf, *New Literary History* 7 (1976):433–47; Paul Ricoeur, "The Model of the Text: Meaningful Action Considered as a Text," *New Literary History* 5 (1973):91–117; and John R. Searle, "The Logical Status of Fictional Discourse," *New Literary History* 6 (1975):319–32. Particularly relevant are two recent essays by Paul Hernadi: "Clio's Cousins: Historiography Considered as Translation, Fiction, and Criticism," *New Literary History* 7 (1976):247–57, and "Re-Presenting the Past: A Note on Narrative Historiography and Historical Drama," *History and Theory* 15 (1976):45–51. There is much that is relevant to historical writing in general in Georg Lukács, *The Historical Novel*, trans. Hannah and Stanley Mitchell (Boston: Beacon, 1963). Erich Auerbach, *Mimesis*, trans. Willard Trask (Princeton: Princeton University Press, 1953) is often suggestive. Among the many relevant works of Kenneth Burke are *Permanence and Change* (Indianapolis, IN: Bobbs-Merrill) and

Attitudes toward History (New York: The New Republic, 1937). There are some materials of interest in two collections of English Institute essays: Phillip Damon, ed., *Literary Criticism and Historical Understanding* (New York: Columbia University Press, 1967); and Angus Fletcher, ed., *The Literature of Fact* (New York: Columbia University Press, 1976). See also the special issues of *Poetics Today* 1, nos. 3 and 4 (Spring and Summer 1980), on narratology. Besides the journals mentioned above, further examples of such critical discourse can be found in *Tel Quel, New German Criticism, Critical Inquiry, Glyph,* and *La Nouvelle Critique*.

8. Aesthetic derealization of philistinism in culture and of oppression in politics is often the cry of the weak and the meek, or even an inverted apologia for the status quo. Given the powers of co-option of elites in modern societies, even sincere personal expressions can be inauthentic in their unawareness of the propagandistic uses to which they can be put by the dominant system. "By expressing their own subjectivity, their own personal impressions and purely individual problems of creative expression with conviction and paradoxical bravado," many clearsighted and honorable writers have sought to resist the levelling and depoeticization of culture. What they often achieve instead, however, "is a further undermining of poetic forms, a 'prophetic' anticipation of literary fashions, of another kind of levelling and impoverishment of literature" (Lukács 1971:191).

9. Norman Holland draws a similar parallel between the unity of a life that yields a coherent identity, and the unity of a text that yields a coherent characterization of self: "In short, within our four terms, *identity* quite resembles *unity,* so much so that once having defined *unity, identity, text,* and *self,* we can fill in the white spaces between them as follows: unity/identity = text/self. Now my title reads: '*Unity* is to *identity* as *text* is to *self,*' or, by a familiar algebraic transportation, '*Unity* is to *text* as *identity* is to *self.*' Or you could say, '*Identity* is the *unity* I find in a *self* if I look at it as though it were a *text*'" (Holland 1975:815).

10. See Walter Benjamin: "More and more often there is embarrassment all around when the wish to hear a story is expressed. It is as if something inalienable to us, the securest among our possessions, were taken from us: the ability to exchange experience" (1968:83). See also Georg Lukács:

> Previous realistic literature, however violent its criticism of reality,
> had always assumed the unity of the world it described and seen it
> as a living whole inseparable from man himself. But the major
> realists of our time deliberately introduce elements of disintegration
> into their work—for instance, the subjectivizing of time—and use
> them to portray the contemporary world more exactly. In this way,
> the once natural unity becomes a conscious, constructed unity. . . .
> But in modernist literature the disintegration of the world of man—
> and consequently the disintegration of personality—coincides with
> the ideological intention. Thus angst, this basic modern
> experience, . . . has its emotional origin in the experience of a
> disintegrating society. But it attains its effects by evoking the
> disintegration of the world of man. (1978:300).

11. Similarly, "when Samuel Beckett concludes *Molloy* by telling us: 'It is midnight. The rain is beating on the windows. It was not midnight. It was not raining,' he brazenly reveals the virtuality of his enunciation, exposes the text as a machine for producing pseudostatements. It is in such doubling of the text, such raising

of the parody to the second power, that 'literary' works may perform productive operations upon the ideological. For if an English chauvinist were able to say 'The Irish are inferior to the English. The Irish are not inferior to the English,' it would not merely be a matter of adopting another position: it would be a question of discovering something of the nature of positionality itself, its production of a closure constantly threatened by the heterogeneity of language" (Eagleton 1981:125–26).

12. Like the information society itself, the world in postmodern representations becomes a "network of neutral and purely contingent relationships" (Leed 1980:53). As Baudrillard noted,

> It is not simply a question of the implosion of the message in the medium, but of the medium and the real in a kind of hyper-real nebula where the very definition and distinctive action of the medium is irrecoverably lost. In a word, "The Medium is the Message" does not merely mean the end of the message, but the end of the medium. There are no more media in the literal sense . . . of mediating between one state of reality and another, and that is true for both form and content. (1980:141)

Contemporary society in this representation is characterized by universal law and individualism degenerated into the corporate totalism of the state and the pathological alienation of the person. The modernist and postmodernist responses to this degenerate opposition are illustrated respectively by Lewis Mumford and John Cage. Mumford associates technics with the values of impersonality, regularity, efficiency, and uniformity. But in rejecting these values, Mumford accepts the terms and categories of the discourse of information that he criticizes. By contrast, Cage sees technology as pregnant with the aesthetic values of heterogeneity, randomness, and plenitude. He thereby "reappropriates technology into a modernist aesthetic, and by doing so hopes to undermine the entire metaphysical framework in which the argument between Mumford and the proponents of the information society takes place" (Streeter 1983:12; see Woodward 1980:176).

13. I am especially indebted for this section to the writings of Walter Fisher, Thomas Frentz, and Alysdair MacIntyre. Most of the quotations concerning narrative here are taken from Fisher (1984).

Chapter 8
1. Kierkegaard tells us that Socrates insisted that his Delphic title as "the wisest man in Greece" was based on his admission of ignorance; Socrates married a nagging wife, as he put it, in order to nourish his patience; his innocence was as shrewd as it was saintly; he chided his tormentors, and died for the laws of the state when they were violated to persecute him. Fra Thoma de Celano provides us with another example of irony of conduct from the life of St. Francis:

> It happened one Easter Day that the brothers at the hermitage of Greccio set the table more lavishly than usual with linen and glassware. When the father [St. Francis] comes down from his cell to go to the table, he sees it with its vain decoration. But the pleasing table in no way pleases him. Furtively and quietly he retraces his steps, puts on his head the hat of a pauper who happened to be there, takes his staff in his hand, and leaves the house. Outside he waits until the brothers begin, for they were

accustomed not to wait for him when he did not come at the signal. When they begin their meal, this true pauper calls out at the door: For the love of God, give this poor sick pilgrim an alms. The brothers answer: Come in, man, for the love of Him whom you have invoked. So he quickly enters and appears before the diners. But what surprise do you think seized the household at the sight of this stranger! At his request he is given a bowl, and alone he sits down on the floor and sets his plate in the ashes. "Now," he says, "I am seated like a Minorite . . ." (i.e., one who has taken the vows of poverty). (Quoted by Auerbach 1953:148–49)

2. Jacob Brackman (1967) in his insightful essay, "The Put-on," adopts the view that irony proper must have some truth external to it but towards which it drives. By this definition Brackman excludes put-ons from the category of irony. Brackman's distinction seems arbitrary, however, because put-ons are well understood as ironies of action, and because irony generally need not aim at a pregiven end. I concede that many of Brackman's examples of put-ons are ironic only in a vulgar romantic sense. To use Brackman's example, the magician who comes on stage and muffs his tricks does treat magicianship ironically and open himself up to redefinition as a clown. A more mastered, dialectical irony, however, would be for the clown to then go on to perform extraordinary feats of magic, all the while appearing to be fumbling. He would thus treat ironically both magicianship *and* clowning, thereby suggesting a transcendent fusion that completes yet goes beyond them both.

3. Schlegel's view was revived a century later by Georg Simmel: "The fetishism which Marx assigned to economic commodities represents only a special case of this general fate of contents of culture. With the increase in culture these contents more and more stand under a paradox: they were originally created by subjects and for subjects: but in their intermediate form of objectivity . . . they follow an immanent logic of development. . . . This is the real tragedy of culture (Simmel 1968:42–43). "Life can express itself and realize its freedom only through forms; yet forms must also necessarily suffocate life and obstruct freedom" (Simmel 1968a:24).

4. For discussions of Kierkegaard's distinction between romantic and mastered irony and of his misrepresentation of the former, see Allemann (1956) and Strohschneider-Kohrs (1960). For a summary of this discourse and penetrating remarks on the relationship of irony to politics and humanism, see Muecke (1969:242–47).

5. In this spirit we might see possibilities for developments hidden in the distinction that Hegel draws between Schlegel's perspective and his own. we would sharpen the distinction into a contradiction (which in fact Hegel already has done); and we would then tap Hegel on the shoulder so that, in turning about, his stream of thought would plunge into a maelstrom of self-contradiction. For example, we might argue that Hegel in his rendering of Schlegel suppresses exactly those qualities that they share, that Schlegel is in fact more synthesizing and objective than Hegel himself, that Hegel's case against romantic subjectivism is the best argument yet made against his own philosophy, and so on. For a Stalinized defense of Hegel-Marx against Schlegel-Marcuse, see Franklin (1970).

6. Compare Kierkegaard's ironist with Felix Krull, the character created by Thomas Mann to treat the bourgeois moral order ironically. "In each disguise," says

Felix, "I assumed I looked better and more natural than in the last. I might appear as a Roman flute-player, a wreath of roses twined in my curly locks; as an English page in a snug-fitting satin with lace collar and plumed hat; as a Spanish bullfighter in spangled jacket and broad-brimmed hat; as a youthful abbe at the time of powdered white wigs. . . . Whatever the costume, the mirror assured me that I was born to wear it, and my audience declared that I looked to the life exactly the person the person whom I aimed to represent." It is also interesting to compare *Felix Krull* to Andre Gide's novel, *Les Caves du Vatican*, in which a chameleonlike character is used to treat ironically not bourgeois society but its opposite, antibourgeois existentialism. We identify with Felix Krull (and against bourgeois conventions) because he is so winning. We become sympathetic with ordinary morality by the end of Gide's novel because the existential antihero turns out to be an empty-hearted loser. Yet Mann himself was archetypically bourgeois in his personal life, whereas Gide was an assertive homosexual. As ironists, however, they shared the goal of unmasking pretensions. For a similar analysis focusing on Kierkegaard's leap toward faith and Nietzsche's leap away from it, see Glicksberg (1969:71–73) and Jaspers, who noted that "rejecting faith and forcing oneself to believe belong together. The godless can appear to be a believer, the believer can appear as godless; both stand in the same dialectic" (1955:36).

7. The answer to this question may in truth be that Smith was less than ironic, for in his day the idea that private greed produces public good had already been popularized by Mandeville and others, and the opposite view—that of Christian economic community—had long since been shattered by Protestantism and the market. Yet this only shows the role of the audience in completing a statement by supplying the context of interpretation that makes it ironic. Whereas persons today with a socialist sense of moral community may take Smith's literally intended statement to have an ironic meaning, other cases could be cited in which an ironically intended statement was taken as merely literal or descriptive. Indeed, authors often have fought with their audiences over whether their intended meaning or their audience's taken meaning was to prevail. Swift, for example, tried to limit the interpretation of his attacks to abuses in religion and learning, and to exclude these pursuits as such. Yet his ironic instrument was too volatile, and a radical rather than reformist interpretation was drawn from his work. The "apology" Swift appended with seeming sincerity to his *Tale of the Tub*, for instance, was taken by his contemporaries as ironic. On Swift as an unintending revolutionary, see Elliott (1960:275). A similar analysis could be made of Molière's *Tartuffe* in relation to the writer's apparently devout Christianity and the Church's implacable condemnation of his work. Erasmus had similar difficulty containing the interpretation of his *Moriae Encomium, The Praise of Folly* (1509); at the end of his life he was still defending it as having really been an exhortation of people to be virtuous. See Huizinga (1955:77).

8. In a similar spirit Louis Schneider noted that "the anthropologist of Malinowskian persuasion goes on the hypothesis that the claims of the primitive magician for the effects of his magic (which claims typically refer to the external world) are incorrect and have little to do with the actual effects of the magic (which typically bear on the human psyche and human group). What if the magician should learn that his vaunted ability to avert storms, say, was not an ability to avert storms at all but an 'ability' to avert a measure of desperation? Would the latter result be attained as

effectively as before, or attained at all, once awareness that it, and not some putative influence on the external world, was in fact being brought about" (1962:496)? See also Seger (1957), Woodward (1944), and Moore and Tumin (1949).

9. For example, Bentham advised that: "Every favor, everything which bears the character of benevolence, ought to be represented as the work of the father of his people. All rigour, all acts of severity need to be attributed to no one. The hand which acts must be artfully hidden. They may be thrown upon some creatur of imagination, some animated abstraction—such as justice, the daughter of necessity and the mother of peace whom men ought always to fear, but never to hate, and who always deserve their first homage" (Bentham 1962:1:371).

10. An excellent collection of social and anthropological accounts of ritual irony is Robert C. Elliott's *The Power of Satire: Magic, Ritual, Art* (Princeton: Princeton University Press, 1960). Many of my examples are taken from Elliott's text.

11. The function of the fool was undertaken by university professors in the courts of Germany until the eighteenth century (Gusfield 1963:6). Modern political leaders also employ professional buffoons, but because the jester role of such savants is unintentional, contemporary princes are open to being seen as fools themselves.

12. This safety-valve or ritual function of irony was explicitly noted by a Doctor of Auxerre with reference to the Feast of Fools. "Wine barrels break if their bung-holes are not occasionally opened to let in the air, and the clergy being nothing but old wine-casks badly put together would certainly burst if the wine of wisdom were allowed to boil by continued devotion to the Divine Service" (Welsford 1935:202). "Frazier records a Saturnalia among the Hos of Northeastern India who at harvest time felt they had so much deviltry boiling within them that they had to 'let off steam' in the interests of safety. The result was an orgiastic period during which they insulted their masters with the utmost freedom, etc. For this and comparable festivals see *The Golden Bough*, IX: The Scapegoat, Part VI, 136–7 and 306–411" (Elliott 1960:80; n. 27).

Bakhtin (1968:10) also noted that "Carnival celebrated temporary liberation from the prevailing truth and from the established order; it marked the suspension of all hierarchical rank, privileges, norms, and prohibitions. Carnival was the true feast of time, the feast of becoming, change, and renewal. It was hostile to all that was immortalized and completed." The Reformation and Counter-Reformation dampened this popular joy in irreverence by taking it too seriously. But as late as 1444 the School of Theology in Paris circulated a letter describing such feasts as gay diversions, necessary "so that foolishness, which is our second nature and seems to be inherent in man might freely spend itself at least once a year. Wine barrels burst if from time to time we do not open them and let in some air. All of us men are barrels poorly put together, which would burst from the wine of wisdom, if this wine remains in a state of constant fermentation of piousness and fear of God. We must give it air in order not to let it spoil. This is why we permit folly on certain days so that we may later return with greater zeal to the service of God" (Bakhtin 1968:75).

Feast or King of Fools in the Middle Ages was subsidized by the aristocracy and featured an inversion of the class structure. The annual village festivals of Japan appear to have the same purpose and consist of extremely unorthodox behavior as well as an inversion of the class structure and other releases from everyday constriction. Ossenberg points out that "similar ceremonies in urbanized societies have not

received . . . as much attention. As a result, we lack adequate studies of the Oktober-
fest of Germany, the Mardi Gras of New Orleans, the Winter Carnival of Quebec, and
the Calgary Stampede of Alberta, not to mention thousands of other community
festivals" (Ossenberg 1969:29–34). Other examples of ritual irony in modern urban
settings would include the annual office parties where the boss is expected to act
foolishly and the staff boldly, as well as roasts such as that given to American presi-
dents by the National Press Club, where journalists can mock the person to whom
normally they pay homage.

References

Abrams, Meyer Howard. 1953. *The Mirror and the Lamp: Romantic Theory and the Critical Tradition*. New York: Oxford University Press.

Adorno, Theodor W. 1958. "Standort des Erzählers im zeitgenossischen Roman" [The Position of the Narrator in the Contemporary Novel]. In Adorno's *Noten zur Literatur*, 1:62–72. Frankfort a. Main: Suhrkamp Verlag. Reprinted in *Prisms*.

———. 1973. *The Jargon of Authenticity*. Evanston: Northwestern University Press.

Aires, Philippe. 1970. *Centuries of Childhood: A Social History of Family Life*. New York: Knopf.

Alleman, Beda. 1956. *Ironie und Dichtung*. Unterjesingen-Tübingen: Gunther Neske, Pfullingen.

Almond, Gabriel A., and Sidney Verba. 1963. *The Civic Culture*. Princeton: Princeton University Press.

Altieri, Charles. 1983. "Surrealist 'Materialism.' " Paper presented to the Conference on Dali, Surrealism, and the Twentieth Century Mind. St. Petersburg, FL., February.

American Heritage Dictionary. See W. Morris 1969.

Anderson, Perry. 1974. *Lineages of the Absolutist State*. London: New Left Books.

Apel, Karl-Otto. 1963. *Die Idee der Sprache in der Tradition des Humanismus von Dante*. Archiv für Begriffsgeschichte, vol. 8. Bonn: Bouriver Verlag.

Archibald, W. Peter. 1976. "Face to Face: The Alienating Effects of Class, Status, and Power Divisions." *American Sociological Review* 41:819–37.

Arendt, Hannah. 1951. *The Origins of Totalitarianism*. New York: Macmillan.

———. 1963a. *Eichmann in Jerusalem: A Report on the Banality of Evil*. New York: Viking.

———. 1963b. *On Revolution*. New York: Viking.

———. 1968. "Introduction: Walter Benjamin, 1892–1940." In Walter Benjamin, *Illuminations*. New York: Harcourt, Brace.

Argyris, Chris. 1968. "Some Unintended Consequences of Rigorous Research." *Psychological Bulletin* 70:185–97.

Aristotle. 1943. *On Man and the Universe*. Louise Loomis, ed. Roslyn, NY: Walter J. Black.

———. 1960. *Aristotle's Physics*. Oxford: Clarendon Press.

Atlas, James. 1984. "Beyond Demographics: How Madison Avenue Knows Who You Are and What You Want." *Atlantic Monthly*, October, 49–58.

Auerbach, Erich. 1953. *Mimesis: The Representation of Reality in Western Literature*. Welland R. Trask, trans. Princeton: Princeton University Press.

Bacon, Sir Francis. 1864. "De augmentis scientiarum." *The Works of Francis Bacon*, ed. Spedding, Ellis, and Heath, vol. 9, p. 62.

Bakhtin, M. M. 1968. *Rabelais and his World*. Cambridge: MIT Press.

Barbu, Zevedi. 1960. *Problems in Historical Psychology*. New York: Grove.

Baritz, Loren. 1961. *Servants of Power*. Middletown, CT: Wesleyan University Press.

Barnett, Steve, and Martin G. Silverman. 1979. *Ideology and Everyday Life.* Ann Arbor: University of Michigan Press.

Bartels, S. 1975. "Der matrifokale Haushalt als gesellschaftliches Massenphaenomen." Ph.D. dissertation, Universität Freiburg, Freiburg/Brsg.

Barthes, Roland. 1966.*Critique et vérité.* Paris: Editions du Seuil.

———. 1967a. "Science versus Literature." *Times Literary Supplement* September 28, 897–98.

———. 1967b. *Système de la mode.* Paris: Seuil.

———. 1972. *Mythologies.* Annette Lavers, trans. New York: Hill and Wang.

Bataille, Georges. 1953. *L'Experience intérieure.* Paris: Gallimard.

Baudrillard, Jean. 1972. *Pour une critique de l'économie politique des signes.* Paris: Gallimard.

———. 1975. *The Mirror of Production.* St. Louis: Telos.

———. 1980. "The Implosion of Meaning in the Media and the Implosion of the Social in the Masses." In Kathleen Woodward, ed., *The Myths of Information: Technology and Postindustrial Culture.* Madison, WI: Coda.

Bays, Gwendolyn. 1964. *The Orphic Vision: Seer Poets from Novalis to Rimbaud.* Lincoln: University of Nebraska Press.

Behrman, Samuel Nathaniel. 1952. *Duveen.* New York: Vintage Books.

Bellah, Robert N., Richard Madsen, William M. Sullivan, Ann Swidler, and Steven M. Tipton. 1985. *Habits of the Heart.* Berkeley: University of California Press.

Belohradsky, Vaclav. 1981. "Bureaucracy and the Banalization of Culture in Modern Society." In Richard H. Brown, ed., *American Society: Essays on the Political Economy and Cultural Psychology of an Advanced Industrial System.* Washington, D.C.: Washington Institute for Social Research Press.

Bendix, Reinhard. 1956. *Work and Authority in Industry.* New York: Wiley.

Benjamin, Walter. 1968. "The Storyteller. Reflections on the Works of Nikolai Leskov." Pp. 83–109 in Benjamin's *Illuminations.* New York: Harcourt, Brace.

Benn, S. I., and G. F. Gaus, eds. 1983. *Public and Private in Social Life.* London: Croom Helm.

Bennett, Charles A. 1931. *The Dilemma of Religious Knowledge.* New Haven: Yale University Press.

Bennett, W. Lance. 1977. "The Ritual and Pragmatic Bases of Political Campaign Literature," *Quarterly Journal of Speech* 63, 3 (October): 219–38.

Bensman, Joseph, and Israel Gerver. 1963. "Crime and Punishment in the Factory: The Functions of Deviancy in Maintaining the Social System," *American Sociological Review* 28 (August): 588–98.

Bentham, Jeremy. 1962. "Principles of Penal Law." In *Works of Jeremy Bentham,* ed. Sir John Bowring, vol. 1, chap. 5. New York: Russell and Russell.

Bereiter, C., and S. Engelmann. 1966. *Teaching Disadvantaged Children in the Preschool.* Englewood Cliffs, NJ: Prentice-Hall.

Berger, Peter. 1975. *Pyramids of Sacrifice: Political Ethics and Social Change.* New York: Basic Books.

Berger, Peter, Brigitte Berger, and Hansfried Kellner. 1974. *The Homeless Mind: Modernization and Consciousness.* New York: Random House.

Bernstein, Basil. 1964. "Elaborated and Restricted Codes: Their Origins and Some

Consequences," Pp. 55–69 in J. J. Gumperz and D. Hymes, eds., *The Ethnography of Communication*. American Anthropologist, Special Publication 66, No. 6, Part 2.

———. 1971. *Class, Codes, and Control*. 3 vols. London: Routledge and Kegan Paul.

———. 1972a. "A Critique of the Concept of Compensatory Education." Pp. 135–51 in C. B. Cazden, V. P. John, and D. Hymes, eds., *Functions of Language in the Classroom*. New York: Teachers College Press.

———. 1972b. "Social Class, Language, and Socialization." Pp. 157–78 in P. P. Giglioli, ed., *Language and Social Context*. Harmondsworth: Penguin.

———. 1973. "A Sociolinguistic Approach to Socialization: With Some Reference to Educability." Pp. 25–61 in Frederick Williams, ed., *Language and Poverty: Perspectives on a Theme*. Chicago: Rand McNally.

Betti, Emilio. 1955. *Teoria generale dells interpretazione*. A. Giuffre, ed. Milan: Instituto di Teoria della Interpretazione, 2 vols. Translated and abridged to one volume as *Allgemeine Auslegungslehre als Methodik der Geisteswissenschaften*. Tübingen: J. C. B. Mohr, 1967.

Black, Max. 1962. *Models and Metaphors: Studies in Language and Philosophy*. Ithaca: Cornell University Press.

Blankenburg, E. 1969. "Die Selektivität rechtlicher Sanktionen. Eine Empirische Untersuchung von Landendiebstählen." *Kölner Zeitschrift für Sociologie und Sozialpsychologie* 21:805–29.

———. 1970. "Das Recht als Kategorie Sozialer Verhaltensregelmässigkeiten." Pp. 227–34 in R. Lautmann, W. Maihofer, H. Schelsky, eds., *Die Funktion des Rechts in der Modernen Gesellschaft*. Jahrbuch für Rechts-Soziologie and Rechtstheorie, vol. 1, Bielefeld: Bertelsmann Universitätsverlag.

Bleicher, Joseph. 1980. *Contemporary Hermeneutics: Hermeneutics as Method, Philosophy, and Critique*. London: Routledge and Kegan Paul.

Blum, Alan, and Peter McHugh. 1971. "The Social Ascription of Motives." *American Sociological Review* 36 (February): 98–109.

Blumer, Herbert. 1969. *Symbolic Interactionism: Perspective and Method*. Englewood Cliffs, NJ: Prentice-Hall.

Boas, Franz. 1896. "The Limitations of the Comparative Method of Anthropology." *Science* 4:901–8.

Boder, David P. 1949. *I Did Not Interview the Dead*. Urbana: University of Illinois Press.

Bohannan, L. 1952. "A Genealogical Charter." *Africa* 22:301–15.

Booth, Wayne C. 1974. *A Rhetoric of Irony*. Chicago: University of Chicago Press.

Bosman, Willem. [1705] 1967. *A New and Accurate Description of the Coast of Guinea*. London: Cass.

Bougle, Celestin. 1935. *Bilan de la sociologie française contemporaine*. Paris: Alcan.

Boulding, Kenneth. 1964. *The Meaning of the 20th Century*. New York: Harper Colophon.

Bourdieu, Pierre. 1977. *Toward a Theory of Practice*. New York: Cambridge University Press.

Bourdieu, Pierre, and Jean C. Passeron. 1964. *Les heritiers*. Paris: Editions de Minuit.

Brackman, Jacob A. 1967. "The Put-On." *New Yorker* (June):37–73.

Braverman, Harry. 1974. *Labor and Monopoly Capital: The Degradation of Work in the Twentieth Century.* New York: Monthly Review Press.

Brecht, Bertolt. 1967. *Gesammelte Werke.* Frankfurt a. Main: Suhrkamp Verlag.

———. 1980. *A Man's a Man.* In John Willett and Ralph Mannheim, eds., *Collected Plays.* New York: Methuen.

Brenkman, John. 1979. "Mass Media: From Collective Experience to the Culture of Privatization." *Social Text* 1 (Winter): 94–100.

Breton, André. 1967. *Manifestes surréalistes.* Paris: Idees/NRF.

Brombert, Victor. 1980. "Opening Signals in Narrative." *New Literary History* 11:3:489–502.

Brown, Richard Harvey. 1977. *A Poetic for Sociology: Toward a Logic of Discovery for the Human Sciences.* New York: Cambridge University Press.

———. 1978a. "Identity, Politics, Planning: On Some Uses of Theoretical Knowledge in Coping with Social Change." In George Coelho, ed., *Uprooting and Development.* New York: Plenum.

———. 1978b. "Symbolic Realism and Sociological Thought: Beyond the Positivist-Romantic Debate." Pp. 13–37 in Richard Harvey Brown and Stanford M. Lyman, eds., *Structure, Consciousness, and History.* New York: Cambridge University Press.

Brown, Richard Harvey, and Stanford M. Lyman, eds. 1978. *Structure, Consciousness, and History.* New York: Cambridge University Press.

Broyard, Anatole. 1950. "A Portrait of the Inauthentic Negro." *Commentary* 10 (July): 56–64. Social Research Press.

Brummett, Barry. 1976. "Some Implications of 'Process' on 'Intersubjectivity': Postmodern Rhetoric." *Philosophy and Rhetoric* 9 (Winter): 21–51.

Buraway, Michael. 1979. *Manufacturing Consent: Changes in the Labor Process Under Capitalism.* Chicago: University of Chicago Press.

Burian, Richard M. 1977. "More than a Marriage of Convenience: On the Inextricability of History and Philosophy of Science." *Philosophy of Science* 44:1–42.

Burke, Kenneth. 1945. *A Grammar of Motives.* New York: Prentice-Hall.

———. 1954. *Permanence and Change: An Anatomy of Purpose.* Indianapolis, IN: Bobbs-Merrill.

———. 1957. *The Philosophy of Literary Form.* New York: Vintage.

———. 1965. *Permanence and Change.* Indianapolis: Bobbs-Merrill.

———. 1966. *Language as Symbolic Action: Essays on Life, Literature, and Method.* Berkeley: University of California Press.

———. 1969. *A Grammar of Motives.* Berkeley: University of California Press.

———. 1976. "The Party Line." *Quarterly Journal of Speech* 62 (February): 62–68.

Bush, Douglas. 1950. *Science and English Poetry.* New York: Oxford University Press.

Butler, Samuel. 1927. *Erewhon.* New York: Modern Library.

Cage, John. 1981. *Empty Words.* Middletown, CT: Wesleyan University Press.

Campbell, John Angus. 1984. "A Rhetorical Interpretation of History." *Rhetorica,* 2:227–66.

Camus, Albert. 1946. *The Stranger.* New York: Random House.

Carlyle, Thomas. 1896. *Works of Thomas Carlyle.* 30 vols. vol. 2. H. D. Trail, ed. New York: Kelmscott Society.

Céline, Louis-Ferdinand. 1953. *Voyage au bout de la nuit.* 2 volumes, including *Mort a credit.* Paris: Pleiade.

Cellini, Benvenuto. 1946. *The Autobiography of Benvenuto Cellini.* John A. Symonds, trans. Garden City, NJ: Doubleday.

Cervantes Saavedra, Miguel de. 1985. *The Adventures of Don Quizote.* 2 volumes. J. W. Clark, ed. Philadelphia: Ridgeway.

Chagnon, Napoleon A. 1968. *Yanomano: The Fierce People.* New York: Holt, Rinehart and Winston.

Cherwitz, Richard. 1977. "Rhetoric as a 'Way of Knowing': An Attenuation of the Epistemological Claims of 'New Rhetoric'." *Southern Speech Communication Journal* 42 (Spring): 219.

Christie, Robert M. 1977. "The Conflict Over Conflict Methodology and the Political Economy of Sociology." Paper presented at the annual meetings of the American Sociological Association, Chicago, September, mimeo. Department of Sociology, California State University, Dominguez Hills.

Cicero. 1947. *De Officiis.* W. Miller, trans. London: Cambridge University Press.

Cicourel, Aaron V. 1974. "The Acquisition of Social Structure: Toward a Developmental Sociology of Language and Meaning." *Cognitive Sociology: Language and Meaning in Social Interaction.* New York: Free Press.

Civ'jan, T. V. 1977. "Etiquette as a Semiotic System." Pp. 103–6 in Daniel P. Lucid, trans. and ed., *Soviet Semiotics: An Anthology.* Baltimore: Johns Hopkins University Press.

Clanton, G., and L. G. Smith. 1977. *Jealousy.* Englewood Cliffs, NJ: Prentice-Hall.

Clark, Burton. 1960. "The Cooling-Out Functions in Higher Education." *American Journal of Sociology* 65 (May): 569–76.

Clark, Terry N. 1972. "Emile Durkheim and the French University." Pp. 152–86 in Anthony Oberschall, ed., *The Establishment of Empirical Sociology.* New York: Harper and Row.

Clausen, John A., and Melvin L. Kohn. 1960. "Social Relations and Schizophrenia: A Research Report and A Perspective." In Don D. Jackson, ed., *The Etiology of Schizophrenia.* New York: Basic Books.

Clignet, Remi, and Nancy DiTomaso. 1981. "Toward a Sociology of Narcissism." Department of Family and Community Development, University of Maryland, College Park, mimeo.

Cloward, Richard A., and Frances F. Piven. 1972. *Regulating the Poor: The Functions of Public Relief.* New York: Random House.

———. 1979. *Poor People's Movements: Why They Succeed, How They Fail.* New York: Random House.

Cohen, A. K. 1955. *Delinquent Boys.* Glencoe, IL: Free Press.

Collingwood, R. G. 1969. "Spengler's Theory of Historical Cycles." Pp. 157–74 in Ronald N. Nash, ed., *Ideas of History,* Vol. 1. New York: Dutton.

Collins, Randall. 1975. *Conflict Sociology.* New York: Academic Press.

———. 1979. *The Credential Society.* New York: Academic Press.

———. 1981. *Sociology Since Midcentury: Essays in Theory Cumulation.* New York: Academic Press.

Cooper, W. 1971. *Hair.* London: Alden Books.

Corcoran, Paul E. 1979. *Political Language and Rhetoric.* Austin: University of Texas Press.

Craig, Albert M., and Donald H. Shively, eds. 1970. *Personality in Japanese History.* Berkeley: University of California Press.

Culler, Jonathan. 1977. *Structuralist Poetics: Structuralism, Linguistics, and the Study of Literature.* Ithaca: Cornell University Press.

———. 1981. *The Pursuit of Signs. Semiotics, Literature, Deconstruction.* Ithaca, NY: Cornell University Press.

Curtiss, Susan. 1977. *Genie: A Psycholinguistic Study of a Modern Day "Wild Child."* New York: Academic Press.

Dallmayr, Paul. 1981. *Beyond Dogma and Despair: Toward a Critical Phenomenology of Politics.* Notre Dame: University of Notre Dame Press.

Davis, Fred. 1979. *Yearning for Yesterday: A Sociology of Nostalgia.* New York: Free Press.

Davis, Kingsley. 1937. "The Sociology of Prostitution." *American Sociological Review* 2 (October): 744–55.

Dawson, Christopher. 1957. *The Dynamics of World History.* New York: Sheed and Ward.

de Bary, William Theodore, ed. 1970. *Self and Society in Ming Thought.* New York: Columbia University Press.

Debus, A. 1970. *Science and Education in the Seventeenth Century: The Webster-Ward Debate.* London: MacDonnald.

De George, Fernande M., and Richard T. De George. 1972. *The Structuralists: From Marx to Levi-Strauss.* Garden City, NJ: Anchor Books.

de Man, Paul. 1973. "Semiology and Rhetoric." *Diacritics* 3:3:27–33.

———. 1974. "Nietzsche's Theory of Rhetoric." *Symposium* 28:1:33–51.

Derrida, Jacques. 1974. "White Mythology: Metaphor in the Text of Philosophy." *New Literary History* 6:5–74.

———. 1977. "Signature, Event, Context." *Glyph* 1:172–97. Johns Hopkins Textual Studies. Baltimore: Johns Hopkins University Press.

Descartes, Rene. 1952. *Rules for the Direction of the Mind.* Chicago: Encyclopedia Britannica.

Deutsch, Martin, and Associates. 1967. *The Disadvantaged Child.* New York: Vintage.

De Vos, George. 1960. "The Relation of Guilt Toward Parents to Achievement and Arranged Marriage Among the Japanese." *Psychiatry* 23:287–301.

Diesing, Paul. 1962. *Reason in Society: Five Types of Decisions and their Social Conditions.* Westport, CT: Greenwood Press.

———. 1982. *Science and Ideology in the Policy Sciences.* New York: Aldine.

Dilthey, Wilhelm. 1957. *Gesammelte Schriften.* Stuttgart: B. G. Teubner.

DiRenzo, Gordon. 1977. "Socialization, Personality, and Social Systems." *Annual Review of Sociology* 3:261–95.

Donzelot, Jacques. 1979. *The Policing of Families.* New York: Random House.

Dostoevski, Fyodor. 1950. *The Brothers Karamazov.* New York: Modern Library.

———. 1982. *Notes from Underground.* Serge Shishkoff, trans. Lanham, MD: University Press of America.

Douglas, Jack D. 1967. *The Social Meanings of Suicide*. Princeton: Princeton University Press.

———. 1970. "The Relevance of Sociology." Pp. 185–233 in Jack D. Douglas, ed., *The Relevance of Sociology*. New York: Appleton.

Douglas, Mary. 1980. "Introduction: Maurice Halbwachs (1877–1945)." In Maurice Halbwachs, *The Collective Memory*. New York: Harper and Row.

Drake, St. C., and H. R. Cayton. 1962. *Black Metropolis*. New York: Harper and Row.

Dreyfus, Herbert. 1980. "Holism and Hermeneutics." *Review of Metaphysics* 34:1.

Drouard, Alain. 1982. "Réflexions sur une chronologie: Le développement des sciences sociales en France de 1945 à la fin des années soixante." *Revue française de sociologie* 23:55–85 janvier-mars.

Dudley, Edward, and Maximilian E. Novak, eds. 1972. *The Wild Man Within: An Image in Western Thought from the Renaissance to Romanticism*. Pittsburgh: University of Pittsburgh Press.

Dumont, Louis. 1965. "The Modern Conception of the Individual." *Contributions to Indian Sociology* 5:20–43.

d'Unrug, Marie-Christine, and Louis Moreau de Bellaing. 1982. *D'une sociologie de la méconnaissance*. Paris: Anthropos.

Durkheim, Emile. 1888. "Cours de science social." *Revue Internationale de l'Ensiegnement* 14.

———. 1909. "Sociologie religieuse et théorie de la connaissance." *Revue de Metaphysique et de Morale* 17:755–56.

———. 1960. *The Division of Labor in Society*. George Simpson, trans. New York: Free Press.

———. 1963. *L'éduction morale*. Paris: Presses Universitaires de France.

———. 1965a. *The Elementary Forms of Religious Life*. Joseph W. Swain, trans. New York: Free Press.

———. 1965b. *The Rules of the Sociological Method*. Sarah A. Solvoay and John H. Mueller, trans. New York: Free Press.

Eagleton, Terry. 1981. *Walter Benjamin: Or Towards a Revolutionary Criticism*. London: Verso Editions and NLB.

Eliade, Mircea. 1959. *The Sacred and the Profane: The Nature of Religion*. New York: Harcourt, Brace.

Elias, Norbert. 1978. *The Civilizing Process*. Edmund Jephcott, trans. New York: Urizen Books.

Elliott, Robert C. 1960. *The Power of Satire: Magic, Ritual, Art*. Princeton: Princeton University Press.

Elshtain, Jean Bethke. 1981. *Public Man, Private Woman*. Princeton: Princeton University Press.

Emerson, Ralph Waldo. 1946. *The Portable Emerson*. Mark van Doren, ed. New York: Viking.

Engels, Frederich. [1884] 1970. "The Origins of The Family, Private Property, and The State." In *Selected Works* by Karl Marx and Frederich Engels. Moscow: Progress Publishers.

Erasmus. [1509] 1983. *Moriae Encomium, The Praise of Folly*. Leonard Dean, ed. Putney, VT: Hendricks House.

Ermarth, Elizabeth Deeds. 1984. *Realism and Consensus in the English Novel.* Princeton: Princeton University Press.

Etzioni, Amitai. 1968. "Basic Human Needs, Alienation and Inauthenticity." *American Sociological Review* 33:6:870–85.

Ewen, Stuart. 1976. *Captains of Consciousness.* New York: McGraw-Hill.

Farrell, Thomas B., and T. Thomas Goodnight. 1981. "Accidental Rhetoric: The Root Metaphor of Three Mile Island." *Communication Monographs* 48:271–300.

Feigl, Herbert. 1970. "The Orthodox View of Theories." In Michael Radner and Stephen Winokur, eds., *Analyses of Theories and Methods of Physics and Psychology.* Minneapolis: University of Minnesota Press.

Ferguson, Thomas. 1973. "The Political Economy of Knowledge and the Changing Politics of the Philosophy of Science." *Telos* 15 (Spring): 124–37.

Feyerabend, Paul. 1978. *Against Method: Outline of an Anarchistic Theory of Knowledge.* London: Verso.

Fingarette, Herbert. 1963. *The Self in Transformation.* New York: Basic Books.

Finkelstein, Barbara, and Kathy Vandell. 1984. "The Schooling of American Childhood." In *A Century of Childhood, 1820–1920.* Rochester, NY: Margaret Woodbury Museum.

Firth, Raymond. 1956. *Two Studies of Kinship in London.* London: Athlone Press.

Fisher, Walter R. 1970. "The Motive View of Communication." *Quarterly Journal of Speech* 56 (April): 131–39.

———. 1978. "Logic of Good Reasons." *Quarterly Journal of Speech* 64 (December): 376–84.

———. 1984. "Narration as a Human Communication Paradigm: The Case of Public Moral Argument." *Communication Monographs* 511:1–22.

Foot, Phillippa. 1973. "Sincerely Yours." *New York Review of Books* 20 (March 8): 22–24.

Forster, E. M. 1949. *A Passage to India.* New York: Harcourt Brace.

Foucault, Michel. 1970. *The Order of Things: An Archeology of the Human Sciences.* New York: Pantheon.

———. 1978. *The History of Sexuality.* Vol. 1, *An Introduction.* Robert Hurley, trans. New York: Random House.

———. 1980. *Power/Knowledge: Selected Interviews and Other Writings, 1972–1977.* Colin Gordon, ed. New York: Pantheon.

Franklin, Mitchell. 1970. "The Irony of the Beautiful Soul of Herbert Marcuse." *Telos* 6 (Fall): 3–35.

Freire, Paulo. 1970. *Pedagogy of the Oppressed.* New York: Herder and Herder.

Frentz, Thomas S. 1985. "Rhetorical Conversation, Time, and Moral Action." *Quarterly Journal of Speech* 71:1(February): 1–18.

Freud, Sigmund. 1954. "Project for a Scientific Psychology." *Complete Works.* London: Hogarth.

Friedenberg, Edgar Z. 1963. *Coming of Age in America.* New York: Random House.

Gabel, Joseph. 1951. "La réification: Essai d'une psychopathologie de la pensée dialectique." *Esprit* 10:459–82.

———. 1962. *La fausse conscience.* Paris: Minuit.

Gadamer, Hans-Georg. 1967. *Kleine Schriften.* 3 vols. Tübingen: J. C. B. Mohr.

————. 1975. *Truth and Method.* New York: Seabury Press.

Gans, Herbert J. 1967. *The Levittowners: Ways of Life and Politics in A New Suburban Community.* New York: Vintage.

————. 1979. *Deciding What's News.* New York: Pantheon.

Garfinkel, Harold. 1963. "A Conception of and Experiments with 'Trust' as a Condition of Stable Concerted Actions." In O. J. Harvey, ed., *Motivation and Social Interaction.* New York: Ronald Press.

————. 1967. *Studies in Ethnomethodology.* Englewood Cliffs, NJ: Prentice-Hall.

Gavronsky, Serge. 1979. "Reality and Literary Languages." Department of French, Barnard College, Columbia University, New York, mimeo.

Gay, Peter. 1974. *Style in History.* London: Jonathan Cape.

Geiger, Theodor. 1964. *Vorstudien zu einer Soziologie des Rechts.* Neuwied: Luchterhand.

————. 1969a. "The Mass Society of the Present." Pp. 169–84 in Renate Mayntz, ed., *Theodor Geiger on Social Order and Mass Society.* Chicago: University of Chicago Press.

————. 1969b. "The Obligatory Character of Legal Norms." Pp. 92–112 in Renate Mayntz, ed., *Theodor Geiger on Social Order and Mass Society.* Chicago: University of Chicago Press.

Gellner, Ernst. 1965. *Thought and Change.* Chicago: University of Chicago Press.

Gerth, Hans, and C. Wright Mills. 1964. *Character and Social Structure: The Psychology of Social Institutions.* New York: Harcourt, Brace.

Geyer, R. Felix, and David R. Schweitzer, eds. 1981. *Theories of Alienation: Problems of Meaning, Theory, and Method.* New York: Methuen.

Glicksberg, Charles I. 1969. *The Ironic Vision in Modern Literature.* The Hague: Martinus Nijhoff.

Goffman, Erving. 1959. *The Presentation of Self in Everyday Life.* Garden City, NY: Doubleday.

————. 1961a. *Asylums: Essays on the Social Situation of Mental Patients and Other Inmates.* Garden City, NY: Doubleday.

————. 1961b. *Encounters. Two Studies in the Sociology of Interaction.* Indianapolis: Bobbs-Merrill.

————. 1963. *Stigma: Notes on the Management of Spoiled Identity.* Englewood Cliffs, NJ: Prentice-Hall.

————. 1967. *Interaction Ritual: Essays on Face to Face Behavior.* Glencoe, IL: Free Press.

Goode, Eric. 1969. "Marijuana and the Politics of Reality." *Journal of Health and Social Behavior* 10:2:83–94.

Goodman, Nelson. 1951. *The Structure of Appearance.* Cambridge: Harvard University Press.

————. 1978. *Way of Worldmaking.* Indianapolis: Hackett.

Gordon, Steve L. 1981. "The Sociology of Sentiments and Emotions." Pp. 562–92 in Morris Rosenberg and Ralph H. Turner, eds., *Social Psychology: Sociological Perspectives.* New York: Basic Books.

Gouldner, Alvin. 1970. *The Coming Crisis in Western Sociology.* New York: Basic Books.

Graff, Gerald. 1982. "Textual Leftism." *Partisan Review* 49:4:558–76.

Gramsci, Antonio. 1975. *History, Philosophy and Culture in the Young Gramsci.* St. Louis: Telos.

Grassi, Ernesto. 1980. *Rhetoric as Philosophy: The Humanist Tradition.* University Park: Pennsylvania State University Press.

Gregory, Stanford. 1977. "The Grammar of Motives as Elicited by Breaching Experiments." Paper presented at the Annual Meeting of the American Sociological Association, Chicago.

Greisman, Harvey, and Sharon Mayes. 1977. "The Social Construction of Unreality." *Dialectical Anthropology* 2:1 (February): 57–67.

Gross, Bertrand. 1980. *Friendly Fascism: The New Face of Power in America.* New York: M. Evans.

Grunbaum, Adolf. 1979. "Epistemological Liabilities of the Clinical Appraisal of Psychoanalytic Theory." *Psychoanalysis and Contemporary Thought,* December.

Gup, Ted. 1985. "The Smithsonian's Secret Contract." *The Washington Post Magazine,* May 12, 8–20.

Gusfield, Joseph. 1963. "The 'Double Plot' in Institutions." *Patna University Journal* 18:1:1–9.

Habermas, Jurgen. 1968. "Dilthey's Theory of Understanding Expression: Ego Identity and Linguistic Communication." Pp. 140–160 in *Knowledge and Human Interests.* Boston: Beacon.

———. 1968. *Knowledge and Human Interests.* Boston: Beacon.

———. 1970. "Toward a Theory of Communicative Competence." In Hans Peter Dreitzel, ed., *Recent Sociology No. 2, Patterns of Communicative Behavior.* New York: MacMillan.

———. 1971. *Theory and Practice.* John Viertel, trans. Boston: Beacon.

———. 1984. *The Theory of Communicative Action.* Vol. 1, *Reason and the Rationalization of Society.* Boston: Beacon.

Haiman, F. S. 1969. "The Rhetoric of 1968: A Farewell to Rational Discourse." In W. A. Linkugel, R. R. Allen, and R. L. Johannesen, eds., *Contemporary American Speeches,* 2d ed. Belmont, CA: Wadsworth.

Halevy, Elie. 1955. *The Growth of Philosophic Radicalism.* Boston: Beacon.

Hanna, Thomas. 1962. *The Lyrical Existentialists.* New York: Athenaeum.

Harre, Rom. 1978. "Architectonic Man: On the Structuring of Lived Experience." Pp. 140–72 in Richard Harvey Brown and Stanford M. Lyman, eds., *Structure, Consciousness, and History.* New York: Cambridge University Press.

Harrington, Alan. 1959. *Life in the Crystal Palace.* New York: Knopf.

Harrington, Michael. 1985. "Norman Thomas, Dignified Democrat: A Socialist's Centennial." *The New Republic* January 7 and 14, 16–18.

Hartman, Geoffrey H. 1979. In Harold Bloom, Paul de Man, Jacques Derrida, Geoffrey H. Hartman and J. Hillis Miller, *Deconstruction and Criticism.* New York: Seabury Press.

Hass, Hans-Egon, and Gustav-Adolf Mohrluder, eds. 1973. *Ironie als Literarisches Phänomen.* Cologne: Kiepenheuer and Witsch.

Hassler, Alfred. 1954. *Diary of a Self-Made Convict.* Chicago: Henry Regnery.

Hawthorne, Geoffrey. 1976. *Enlightenment and Despair: A History of Sociology.* London: Cambridge University Press.

Hays, Douglas. 1970. *Trial by Prejudice*. New York: Capo.
Heckstall-Smith, Anthony. 1954. *Eighteen Months*. London: Allan Wingate.
Hegel, Georg Friedrich W. 1920. *The Philosophy of Fine Art*. F. Osmaston, trans. London.
———. 1930. *Jenenser Realphilosophie*. Johannes Hoffmeister, ed. Hamburg: F. Meister.
———. 1942. *Philosophy of Right*. T. Knox, trans. London: Oxford University Press.
———. 1971. *Encyclopedia of the Philosophical Sciences*. William Wallace, trans. Oxford: Clarendon Press.
Heidegger, Martin. 1962. *Being and Time*. New York: Harper and Row.
———. 1973. "Letter on Humanism." Pp. 141–81 in D. Zaner and D. Ihde, eds., *Phenomenology and Existentialism*. New York: Capricorn Books, G. P. Putnam's Sons.
———. 1982. *On the Way to Language*. New York: Harper and Row.
Heilbroner, Robert. 1974. *An Inquiry into the Human Prospect*. New York: Norton.
Hernadi, Paul. 1981. "Entertaining Commitments: A Reception Theory of Literary Genres." *Poetics* 10 (June): 195–211.
Hesse, Mary B. 1972. "The Explanatory Function of Metaphor." In *Logic, Methodology, and Philosophy of Science*. Y. Bar-Hillel, ed., Amsterdam: North-Holland.
Hessel, Vitia. 1969. *Le temps des parents*. Paris: Mercure de France.
Hewitt, J. P. 1976. *Self and Society*. Boston: Allyn and Bacon.
Hinkle, L. E., and H. G. Wolff. 1956. "Communist Interrogation and Indoctrination of 'Enemies of the State.' " *A.M.A. Archives of Neurology and Psychiatry* 76.
Hirsch, Fred. 1976. *The Aims of Interpretation*. Chicago: University of Chicago Press.
———. 1976. *Social Limits to Growth*. Cambridge: Harvard University Press.
Hirschman, Albert O. 1977. *Passions and Interests: Political Arguments for Capitalism Before Its Triumph*. Princeton: Princeton University Press.
Hobbes, Thomas. [1651] 1957. *Leviathan, or the Matter, Form and Power of a Commonwealth*. Oxford: Basil Blackwell.
Hocking, Ian. 1981. "The Archeology of Foucault." *New York Review of Books* May 14, 32–36.
Holland, Norman N. 1975. "Unity Identity Text Self." *Publications of the Modern Languages Association* 90:5 (October): 813–22.
Holquist, Michael, and Walter Reed. 1980. "Six Theses on the Novel—and Some Metaphors." *New Literary History* 11:3:413–24.
Horkheimer, Max. 1939. "The Relation between Psychology and Philosophy in the Work of Wilhelm Dilthey." *Studies in Philosophy and Social Sciences* 8:3:430–43.
———. 1974a. *The Eclipse of Reason*. New York: Seabury Press.
———. 1974b. "The Revolt of Nature." Pp. 92–127 in *Eclipse of Reason*. Boston: Seabury Press.
Horkheimer, Max, and Theodor W. Adorno. 1973. *Dialectics of Enlightenment*. London: Allen Lane.
House, James S. 1980. *Occupational Stress and the Physical and Mental Health of Factory Workers*. Ann Arbor: Institute for Social Research.

————. 1981. "Social Structure and Personality." Pp. 525–61 in Morris Rosenberg and Ralph H. Turner, eds., *Social Psychology: Sociological Perspectives*. New York: Basic Books.

Hudson, L. 1972. *The Cult of the Fact*. London: Jonathan Cape.

Huizinga, Johan. 1955. *Homo Ludens: A Study of the Play Element in Culture*. Boston: Beacon.

Hume, David. 1941. *Treatise on Human Nature*. L. A. Selby-Bigge, ed. London: Oxford University Press.

Hyers, M. Conrad. 1969. "The Dialectic of the Sacred and the Comic." In M. Conrad Hyers, ed., *Holy Laughter: Essays on Religion in the Comic Perspective*. New York: Seabury Press.

Hymes, Dell. 1980. *Language in Education: Ethnolinguistic Essays*. Washington, DC: Center for Applied Linguistics.

Israel, Joachim. 1978. "From Level of Aspiration to Dissonance, or What the Middle Class Worries About." In A. R. Buss, ed., *The Social Context of Psychological Theory: Toward a Sociology of Psychological Knowledge*.

Issacharoff, Michael. 1976. *L'espace et la nouvelle*. Paris: Jose Corti.

Jacobs, Bruce. 1981. *The Political Economy of Organizational Change: Urban Institutional Response to the War on Poverty*. New York: Academic Press.

Jacobsen, T. 1976. *The Treasures of Darkness: A History of Mesopotamian Religion*. New Haven, CT: Yale University Press.

Jankélévitch, Vladimir. 1950. *L'ironie ou la bonne conscience*. Paris: Presses Universitaires de France.

Jaspers, Karl. 1955. *Reason and Existence*. William Earle, trans. New York: Noonday.

Jeffrey, Kirk. 1972. "The Family as Utopian Retreat from the City: The Nineteenth-Century Contribution." *Soundings* 55:21–41.

Jung, Hwa Yol. 1982. "Language, Politics, and Technology." *Research in Philosophy and Technology* 5:43–63.

Kafka, Franz. 1962. *Amerika*. William Muir and Edwin Muir, trans. New York: Schocken.

Kann, R. 1973. "The Professionals." *Wall Street Journal*, August 6, 1.

Kant, Immanuel. [1784] 1949a. *Fundamental Principles of the Metaphysic of Morals*. T. K. Abbott, trans. Chicago: Regnery.

————. 1949b. *The Philosophy of Kant*. Carl J. Friedrich, ed. New York: Modern Library.

Kaplan, Abraham. 1964. *The Conduct of Inquiry*. San Francisco: Chandler.

Kavolis, Vytautas. n.d. "Histories of Selfhood, Maps of Sociability." Unpublished manuscript.

————. 1980. "Logics of Selfhood and Modes of Order: Civilizational Structures for Individual Identities." In Roland Robertson and Burkart Holzner, eds., *Identity and Authority: Explorations in the Theory of Society*. Oxford: Basil Blackwell.

Keiser, Lincoln. 1979. *The Vicelords: Warriors of the Streets*. Fieldwork edition. New York: H. Holt.

Kerrigan, William. 1980. "The Articulation of the Ego in the English Renaissance." Pp. 261–308 in *Psychiatry and the Humanities: The Literary Freud: Mechanisms of Defense and the Poetic Will*. New Haven: Yale University Press.

Kierkegaard, Søren. 1944a. *Concluding Scientific Postscript.* David F. Swenson, trans. Princeton: Princeton University Press.

———. 1944b. *Either/Or: A Fragment of Life.* David F. Swenson and Lillian M. Swenson, trans. Princeton: Princeton University Press.

———. 1959. *Either/Or.* Vol. 2. Garden City: Doubleday.

———. 1965. *The Concept of Irony, with Constant Reference to Socrates.* Lee M. Capel, trans. New York: Harper and Row.

Kilton, Stewart. 1972. "Dream Exploration Among the Senoi." In Theodore Roszak, ed., *Sources.* New York: Harper and Row.

King, Richard. 1972. *The Party of Eros: Radical Social Thought and the Realm of Freedom.* Chapel Hill: University of North Carolina Press.

Klapp, Orrin E. 1969. "Style Rebellion and Identity Crisis." Department of Sociology, San Diego State University, San Diego. Mimeo.

Knorr-Cetina, Karin D. 1981. "The Micro-Sociological Challenge of Macro-Sociology: Towards a Reconstruction of Social Theory and Methodology." In Karin D. Knorr-Cetina and Aaron V. Cicourel, eds., *Advances in Social Theory and Methodology.* London: Routledge and Kegan Paul.

Knox, Norman. 1961. *The Word Irony and its Context.* Durham, NC: Duke University Press.

Kobrin, S. 1951. "The Conflict of Values in Delinquency Areas." *American Sociological Review* 16:643–61.

———. 1961. "Sociological Aspects of the Development of a Street Corner Group." *American Journal of Orthopsychiatry* 32:685–702.

Kock, S. 1964. "Psychology and Emerging Conceptions of Knowledge as Unitary." Pp. 1–41 in T. W. Wann, ed., *Behaviorism and Phenomenology.* Chicago: Phoenix.

Kogon, Eugen. 1958. *The Theory and Practice of Hell.* New York: Berkeley.

Kohn, Melvin L. 1969. *Class and Conformity: A Study in Values.* Homewood, IL: Dorsey.

Kohn, Melvin L., and C. Schooler. 1973. "Occupational Experience and Psychological Functioning: An Assessment of Reciprocal Effects." *American Sociological Review* 34:659–78.

———. 1978. "The Reciprocal Effects of Substantive Complexity of Work and Intellectual Flexibility: A Longitudinal Assessment." *American Journal of Sociology* 84:24–52.

Kornhauser, Arthur. 1956. *When Labor Votes: A Study of Auto Workers.* New York: University Books.

Kress, Gunther, and Robert Hodges. 1981. *Language as Ideology.* London: Routledge and Kegan Paul.

Kress, Gunther, and T. Trew. 1978. "Ideological Transformations of Discourse; or, How the Sunday Times Got Its Message Across." *Sociological Review* 26:4:755–76.

Krisberg, B. A. 1972. *The Gang and the Community.* School of Criminology, University of California, Berkeley. Mimeo.

Krysinski, Wladimir. 1977. "The Narrator as a Sayer of the Author: Narrative Voices and Symbolic Structures." *Strumenti critici* 32–33 (giugno): 44–89. Editore. Torino: Giulo Einaudi.

Kuhn, Thomas. 1972. *The Structure of Scientific Revolutions*. Chicago: University of Chicago Press.

———. 1979. "Metaphor in Science." Pp. 409–19 in Andrew Ortony, ed., *Metaphor and Thought*. Cambridge: Cambridge University Press.

Kundera, Milton. 1984. "The Novel and Europe." *New York Review of Books*, July 19, 15–20.

Labov, William. 1972a. "The Logic of Nonstandard English." Pp. 179–215 in P. P. Giglioli, ed., *Language and Social Context*. Harmondsworth: Penguin.

———. 1972b. "The Study of Language in its Social Context." Pp. 283–307 in P. P. Giglioli, ed., *Language and Social Context*. Harmondsworth: Penguin.

La Capra, Dominick. 1972. *Emile Durkheim: Sociologist and Philosopher*. Ithaca, NY: Cornell University Press.

Lacombe, Roger. 1926. *La méthode sociologique de Durkheim: Etude critique*. Paris: Alcan.

Laing, Ronald D. 1969. *The Politics of the Family*. Toronto: Canadian Broadcasting Corporation Publications.

Lakatos, Imre. 1970. "Falsification and the Methodology of Scientific Research." Pp. 91–196 in Imre Lakatos and Allan E. Musgrave, eds., *Criticism and the Growth of Knowledge*. London: Cambridge University Press.

———. 1974. "History of Science and Rational Reconstructions." In Roger C. Buck and Robert S. Cohen, eds., *Boston Studies in the Philosophy of Science*, Vol. 8. Dordrecht-Holland: D. Reidel.

La Ramee, Pierre de. 1970. *Scholae in liberales artes*. Walter J. Ong, ed. Hildesheim, NY: G. Olms.

Langman, Lauren, and Leonard Kaplan. 1979. "Terror and Desire: The Social Psychology of Late Capitalism." Paper presented at the American Sociological Association Meetings, August 27, Mimeo.

Lasch, Christopher. 1976. "The Narcissistic Society." *New York Review of Books* 23:5–13.

———. 1981. *The Culture of Narcissism*. New York: Warner Books.

Laslett, Peter. 1960. "The Sovereignty of the Family." *The Listener* 63 (April 7): 607–9.

Latour, Bruno, and Steve Woolgar. 1979. *Laboratory Life: The Social Construction of Scientific Facts*. Beverly Hills, CA: Sage.

Lawton, D. 1972. *Social Class, Language, and Education*. London: Routledge and Kegan Paul.

Leacock, Eleanor B. 1972. "Abstract Versus Concrete Speech: A False Dichotomy." Pp. 111–34 in C. B. Cazden, V. P. John, D. Humes, eds., *Functions of Language in the Classroom*. New York: Teachers College Press.

Leed, Eric. 1980. " 'Voice' and 'Print': Master Symbols in the History of Communication." In Kathleen Woodward, ed., *The Myths of Information: Technology and Postindustrial Culture*. Madison, WI: Coda.

Lefebvre, Henri. 1968. *La vie quotidienne dans le monde moderne*. Paris: Gallimard.

Leff, Michael C. 1978. "In Search of Ariadne's Thread: A Review of the Recent Literature on Rhetorical Theory." *Central States Speech Journal*, 29 (Summer): 73–91.

Liebow, Elliott. 1967. *Talley's Corner*. Boston: Little, Brown.

Lenin, Nikolai. 1923. *Collected Works.* New York: International Publishers.

Lenneberg, Eric H. 1969. "On Explaining Language." *Science* 164:635–43.

Lenski, Gerhard. 1976. "History and Social Change." *American Journal of Sociology* 82:3:548–64.

Lenski, Gerhard, and Jean Lenski. 1978. *Human Societies: An Introduction to Macrosociology.* New York: McGraw-Hill.

Levi-Strauss, Claude. 1963. *Structural Anthropology.* Vol. 1, Jacobson and Schoepf, trans. New York: Basic Books.

———. 1976. *Structural Anthropology*, Vol. 2, Monique Layton, trans. New York: Basic Books.

Levin, Murray B. 1960. *The Alienated Voter.* New York: Holt, Rinehart and Winston.

Lifton, Robert. 1956. "The 'Thought Reform' of Western Civilians in Chinese Communist Prisons." *Psychiatry* 19:2:173–95.

Lotman, Iurii M., and Boris A. Uspenskij. 1985. "Binary Models in the Dynamics of Russian Culture to the End of the Eighteenth Century." Pp. 30–66 in Alexander D. Nakhimovsky and Alice Stone Nakhimovsky, eds., *The Semiotics of Russian Cultural History.* Ithaca: Cornell University Press.

Luckmann, Thomas. 1967. *The Invisible Religion.* New York: Macmillan.

Lukács, Georg. 1971a. *History and Class Consciousness: Studies in Marxist Dialectics.* Cambridge: MIT Press.

———. 1971b. *The Theory of the Novel.* Cambridge: MIT Press.

———. 1971c. *Writer and Critic.* New York: Grosset and Dunlap.

———. 1978. *Marxism and Human Liberation.* New York: Dell.

Lyman, Stanford M. 1978. *The Seven Deadly Sins: Society and Evil.* New York: St. Martin's.

Lyman, Stanford M., and Marvin B. Scott. 1967. "Territoriality: A Neglected Sociological Dimension." *Social Problems* 15:2:236–48.

———. 1970a. "Accounts." In Lyman and Scott, *A Sociology of the Absurd.* New York: Appleton-Century-Crofts.

———. 1970b. *A Sociology of the Absurd.* New York: Appleton-Century-Crofts.

Lyne, John. 1980. "Rhetoric and Semiotic in C. S. Pierce." *Quarterly Journal of Speech,* 66,2(April): 155–68.

———. 1985. "Rhetorics of Inquiry." *Quarterly Journal of Speech* 71:1(February): 65–73.

MacCannell, Juliet Flower. 1976. "Reading Social Life: Literary vs. Sociological Approaches." Paper delivered to the annual meetings of the American Sociological Association, September.

MacCormac, Earl. 1976. *Metaphor and Myth in Science and Religion.* Durham, NC: Duke University Press.

Machiavelli, Niccolò. 1965. *Machiavelli. The Chief Works and Others.* Trans. Allan Gilbert. 3 vols. Durham, NC: Duke University Press.

MacIntyre, Alasdair. 1980. "Epistemological Crises, Dramatic Narrative, and the Philosophy of Science." Pp. 54–74 in Gary Gutting, ed., *Paradigms and Revolutions: Applications and Appraisals of Thomas Kuhn's Philosophy of Science.* Notre Dame, IN: University of Notre Dame Press.

———. 1981. *After Virtue: A Study in Moral Theory.* Notre Dame, IN: University of Notre Dame Press.

Macpherson, C. B. n.d. *The Political Theory of Possessive Individualism.* London: Oxford University Press.

Makkreel, Rudolf A. 1985. "Husserl, Dilthey, and the Relation of the Life-World to History." *Research in Phenomenology* 12:39–58.

Malinowski, Bronislaw. 1948. *"Magic, Science, and Religion, and Other Essays."* Glencoe, IL: Free Press.

Mandelstam, Nadezhda. 1970. *Hope Against Hope: A Memoir.* New York: Atheneum.

Mann, Thomas. 1950. "Irony and Radicalism." In Joseph W. Angell, ed., *The Thomas Mann Reader.* New York: Knopf.

Marcel, Gabriel. 1962. *Man Against Mass Society.* Chicago: Regnery.

Marcuse, Herbert. 1969. *An Essay on Liberation.* Boston: Beacon.

———. 1978. *The Aesthetic Dimension: Toward a Critique of Marxist Aesthetics.* Boston: Beacon.

Marx, Karl. 1946. *Capital.* New York: Everyman's Library.

Marx, Karl, and Friedrich Engels. 1967. *The Communist Manifesto.* Harmondsworth: Penguin.

Mauskopf, Seymour H., and Michael R. McVaught. 1980. *The Elusive Science: Origins of Experimental Psychical Research.* Baltimore: Johns Hopkins University Press.

McCanles, Michael. 1976. "The Literal and the Metaphorical: Dialectic or Interchange." *Publications of the Modern Language Association* 91:2(March): 279–90.

McCormick-Piestrup, A. 1973. *Black Dialect Interference and Accomodation of Reading Instruction.* Monographs of the Language Behavior Research Laboratory, University of California at Berkeley, No. 4, Berkeley.

McGee, Michael. 1977. "The Fall of Wellington: A Case Study of the Relationship Between Theory, Practice and Rhetoric in History." *Quarterly Journal of Speech* 63(February): 28–42.

Mead, George Herbert. 1934. *Mind, Self, and Society.* Chicago: University of Chicago Press.

———. 1956. "The Problem of Society." Pp. 17–42 in Anselm Strauss, ed., *The Social Psychology of George Herbert Mead.* Chicago: University of Chicago Press.

Mehan, Hugh, and Houston Wood. 1975. *The Reality of Ethnomethodology.* New York: John Wiley.

Melville, Herman. n.d. *White Jacket.* New York: Grove Press.

Merleau-Ponty, Maurice, 1964. *Signs.* Evanston, IL: Northwestern University Press.

Merton, Robert K. 1957a. *Social Theory and Social Structure.* New York: Free Press.

———. 1957b. "The Sociology of Knowledge." Pp. 456–88 in *Social Theory and Social Structure.* New York: Free Press.

Michels, Robert. 1966. *Political Parties: A Sociological Study of the Oligarchical Tendencies of Modern Democracy.* New York: Free Press.

Milgram, Stanley. 1963. "Behavioral Study of Obedience." *Journal of Abnormal and Social Psychology* 67:371–78.

———. 1974. "The Frozen World of the Familiar Stranger: We are All Fragile Creatures Entwined in a Cobweb of Social Constraints." An interview with Carol Tavris in *Psychology Today* (June): 71–80.

Mill, James. 1878. *Analysis of the Phenomena of the Human Mind.* London: Longmens, Green, Reader, and Dyer.

Miller, J., C. Schooler, M. L. Kohn, and K. A. Miller. 1977. "Women and Work: The Psychological Effects of Occupational Conditions." *American Journal of Sociology* 85:66–94.

Miller, W. B. 1957. "The Impact of a Community Group Work Program on Delinquent Corner Groups." *Social Service Review* 31:390–406.

———. 1958. "Lower Class Culture as a Generating Milieu of Gang Delinquency." *Journal of Social Issues* 3:5–19.

Mills, C. Wright. 1940a. "Methodological Consequences of the Sociology of Knowledge," *American Journal of Sociology* 46:3 (November): 316–30.

———. 1940b. "Situated Actions and Vocabularies of Motive." *American Sociological Review* 5 (December): 904–13.

———. 1961. *The Sociological Imagination.* New York: Oxford University Press.

———. 1974a. "Mass Media and Public Opinion." Pp. 577–98 in *Power Politics and People: The Collected Essays of C. Wright Mills.* New York: Oxford University Press.

———. 1974b. *Power, Politics and People: The Collected Essays of C. Wright Mills.* Irving Louis Horowitz, ed. New York: Oxford University Press.

Mink, Louis O. 1978. "Narrative Form as a Cognitive Instrument." Pp. 129–50 in Robert H. Canary and Henry Kozicki, eds., *The Writing of History: Literary Form and Historical Understanding.* Madison: University of Wisconsin Press.

Mitchell, W. C. 1918. "Bentham's Felicific Calculus." *Political Science Quarterly* 33:161.

Mittenthal, B. 1979. "Preorgasmic Women: A Pattern Emerges." *New York Times* (October 4) 3:1:1.

Moore, Wilbert. 1966. "Global Sociology: The World as a Singular System." *American Journal of Sociology* 71 (March): 475–82.

Moore, Wilbert E., and Melvin M. Tumin. 1949. "Some Social Functions of Ignorance." *American Sociological Review* 14:6(December).

More, Thomas. 1965. *Utopia.* E. Surtz, ed. New Haven, CT: Yale University Press.

Moretti, Franco. 1983. *Signs Taken for Wonders: Essays in the Sociology of Literary Forms.* London: New Left Books.

Morris, Colin. 1972. *The Discovery of the Individual 1050–1200.* New York: Harper and Row.

Morris, William, ed. 1969. *The American Heritage Dictionary.* Boston: Houghton Mifflin.

Muecke, Douglas Colin. 1969. *The Compass of Irony.* London: Methuen.

Mueller, Claus. 1973. *The Politics of Communication: A Study in the Political Sociology of Language, Socialization, and Legitimation.* New York: Oxford University Press.

Mulkay, Michael. 1985. *The Word and the World: Explorations in the Forms of Sociological Analysis.* London: George Allen and Unwin.

Musil, Robert. 1052. *Der Mann ohne Eigenschaften.* Hamburg: Rowohlt.

Nakamura, Hajime. 1964. *Ways of Thinking of Eastern Peoples: India/China/Tibet/Japan.* Honolulu: East-West Center Press.

Nelson, Benjamin. 1969. *The Idea of Usury: From Tribal Brotherhood to Universal Otherhood.* Chicago: University of Chicago Press.

———. 1970. "The Omnipresence of the Grotesque." *Psychoanalytic Review* 57:3:505–18.

Nelson, John S. 1977. "Meaning and Measurement Across Paradigms: Metaphor and Irony in Political Inquiry." Paper delivered a the meeting of the American Political Science Association, Washington, D.C.

———. 1983. "Political Theory as Political Rhetoric." Pp. 169–240 in John Nelson, ed., *What Should Political Theory Be Now?* Albany: State University of New York Press.

Newsweek. 1979. "Helping Women to Have Orgasms." October 22, 77.

———. 1982. "The Hard Times Summit." June 7, 31–41.

Nichols, Elizabeth. 1985. "Skocpol on Revolution: Comparative Analysis vs. Historical Conjuncture." Paper presented to the meetings of the American Sociological Association, August, Washington, D.C.

Nietzsche, Friedrich. 1960. "Über Wahrheit und Lüge im aussermoralischen Sinn" (On Truth and Lie in an Extra-Moral Sense). In *Werke in Drei Bänen.* Karl Schlechta, ed. Vol. 3. Munchen: Hanser.

Norbeck, E., and George De Vos. 1972. "Culture and Personality: The Japanese." In Francis L. Hsu, ed., *Psychological Anthropology.* Cambridge, MA: Schenkman.

Oakeshott, Michael. 1962. "The Voice of Poetry in the Conversation of Mankind." In Michael Oakeshott, *Rationalism in Politics and Other Essays.* London: Methuen.

Ognibene, Elaine. 1976. "Review of Wayne Booth, *Modern Dogma and the Rhetoric of Assent* and *A Rhetoric of Irony*," *Southern Speech Communication Journal* 42 (Fall): 81–84.

O'Neill, John. 1970. *Perception, Expression, and History: The Social Phenomenology of Maurice Merleau-Ponty.* Evanston, IL: Northwestern University Press.

O'Neill, N., and G. O'Neill. 1972. *Open Marriage: A New Life Style for Couples.* New York: Avon.

Ong, Walter J. 1971. *Rhetoric, Romance, and Technology: Studies in the Interaction of Expression and Culture.* Ithaca, NY: Cornell University Press.

———. 1975. "The Writer's Audience is Always a Fiction." *Publications of the Modern Languages Association* 90:1 (January): 9–21.

———. 1977. *Interfaces of the Word: Studies in the Evolution of Consciousness and Culture.* Ithaca, NY: Cornell University Press.

———. 1982. *Orality and Literacy: The Technologizing of the Word.* London: Methuen.

———. 1983. *Ramus, Method, and the Decay of Dialogue: From the Art of Discourse to the Art of Reason.* Cambridge: Harvard University Press.

Onions, C. T. 1971. *The Compact Edition of the Oxford English Dictionary.* London: Oxford University Press.

Organ, Troy Wilson. 1964. *The Self in Indian Philosophy.* The Hague: Mouton.

Ortony, Andrew. 1979. *Metaphor and Thought.* Cambridge: Cambridge University Press.

Ossenberg, Richard J. 1969. "Social Class and Bar Behavior During the Calgary Stampede." *Human Organization* 28:1 (Spring): 29–34.

Overington, Michael A. 1978a. "Doing the What Comes Rationally: Some Developments in Metatheory." *American Sociologist* 14:1 (March): 2–12.

———. 1978b. "Situated Discourse: A Rhetorical Investigation of Durkheim's Suicide." Typed manuscript, Department of Sociology, Saint Mary's University, Halifax, Nova Scotia.

———. 1982. "Responsibility and Sociological Discourse." *Qualitative Sociology* 5:2 (Summer): 106–20.

Oxford English Dictionary. See Onions 1971.

Padioleau, Jean G., and Michel Eymeriat. 1982. "Etude des styles cognitifs dans la pensée sociale ou politique," *L'Année Sociologique* 32:39–61.

Parfit, Derek. 1984. *Reasons and Persons*. London: Oxford University Press.

Parker, H. J. 1974. *Views from the Boys*. North Pomfret, VT: David and Charles.

Parsons, Talcott. 1937. *The Structure of Social Action*. New York: Free Press.

Pavese, Cesare. 1961. *The Burning Bed: Diaries 1935–1950*. A. E. Murch, trans. New York: Walker.

Peel, J. D. Y. 1974. "Spencer and the Neo-Evolutionists." Pp. 188–209 in R. Serge Denisoff, Orel Callahan, and Mark H. Levine, eds. *Theories and Paradigms in Contemporary Sociology*. Itasca, IL: F. E. Peacock.

Peirce, Charles Sanders. 1960. *Collected Papers*. Charles Hartshorne and Paul Weiss, eds. Cambridge: Harvard University Press.

———. 1966. "Values in a Universe of Chance." *Selected Writings*. New York: Dover.

Pennock, J. Roland, and John W. Chapman, eds. 1971. *Nomos XIII: Privacy*. New York: Atherton Press.

Perelman, Chaim. 1982. *The Realm of Rhetoric*. William Kluback, trans. Notre Dame, IN: University of Notre Dame Press.

Perelman, Chaim, and Lucie Olbrechts-Tyteca. 1969. *The New Rhetoric: A Treatise on Argumentation*. Notre Dame, IN: University of Notre Dame Press.

Peters, E. L. 1960. "The Proliferation of Segments in the Lineage of the Bedouin of Cyrenaica." *Journal of the Royal Anthropological Institute*, 90:29–53.

———. 1967. "Some Structural Aspects of the Feud among the Camel-Herding Bedouin of Cyrenaica," *Africa*, 37:261–81.

Pico della Mirandola, Giovanni. 1956. *Oration on the Dignity of Man*. A. Robert Caponigri, trans. New York: Oxford University Press.

Pjatigorskij, A. M., and Boris A. Uspenskij. 1977. "The Classification of Personality as a Semiotic Problem." Pp. 137–56 in Daniel P. Lucid, ed., *Soviet Semiotics*. Baltimore: Johns Hopkins University Press.

Pocock, J. G. A. 1973. *Politics, Language and Time: Essays on Political Thought and History*. New York: Atheneum.

Polanyi, Michael. 1958. *Personal Knowledge: Toward a Post-Critical Philosophy*. Chicago: University of Chicago Press.

Pomorska, Krystyna. 1980. "The Overcoded World of Solzhenicyn." *Poetics Today* 1:3 (Spring): 163–70.

Ponge, Francis. 1965. *Pour un Malherbe*. Paris: Gallimard.

———. 1971. *La fabrique du pré*. Geneva: Skira.

Pope, Whitney. 1976. *Durkheim's Suicide: A Classic Analysed*. Chicago: University of Chicago Press.

Popitz, H. 1961. "Soziale Normen." *European Journal of Sociology* 11:185–98.

————. 1967. *Der Begriff der sozialen Rolle als Element der soziologischen Theorie.* Tübingen: J. C. B. Mohr.

————. 1968. *Über die Präventivwirkung des Nichtwissens.* Tübingen: J. C. B. Mohr.

Popper, Karl. 1969. *Conjectures and Refutations.* London: Routledge and Kegan Paul.

Proust, Marcel. 1948. *Maxims of Marcel Proust.* Justin O'Brien, ed. and trans. New York: Random House.

Quine, Willard van Orman. 1960. *Word and Object.* Cambridge: MIT Press.

Rattray, R. S. 1923. *Ashanti.* Oxford: Oxford University Press.

Reichenbach, Hans. 1961. *Experience and Prediction.* Chicago: University of Chicago Press.

Ricoeur, Paul. 1978. "Explanation and Understanding: On Some Remarkable Connections Among the Theory of the Text, Theory of Action, and Theory of History." Pp. 149–66 of *The Philosophy of Paul Ricoeur: An Anthology of His Work.* Charles E. Reagan and David Stewart, trans. Boston: Beacon.

Robertson, D. W. 1968. *Chaucer's London.* New York: Wiley.

Rorty, Richard. 1972. "The World Well Lost." *Journal of Philosophy* 69:649–65.

————. 1979. *Philosophy and the Mirror of Nature.* Princeton: Princeton University Press.

Rosen, Charles. 1977. "The Ruins of Walter Benjamin." *New York Review of Books* 24 (October 24): 31–40.

Rosenberg, Morris. 1984. "A Symbolic Interactionist View of Psychosis." *Journal of Health and Social Behavior* 25 (September): 289–302.

Rosenberg, Morris, and Ralph H. Turner, eds. 1953. "Perceptual Obstacles to Class Consciousness." *Social Forces* 32 (October): 22–27.

————. 1981. *Social Psychology: Sociological Perspectives.* New York: Basic Books.

Ross, L. 1977. "The Intuitive Psychologist and His Shortcomings." *Advances in Experimental Social Psychology* 10:173–220.

Rossi, Paolo. 1970. *Philosophy, Technology, and the Arts in the Early Modern Era.* S. Attanasio, trans. New York: Harper and Row.

Rothschild, Matthew. 1984. "Central Employment Agency. Students respond to the CIA rush." *The Progressive:* 18–21.

Rothstein, Edward. 1980. "The Scar of Sigmund Freud." *New York Review of Books,* October 9, 14–20.

Rousseau, Jean-Jacques. 1967. *Essay on the Origin of Language.* John H. Moran, trans. New York: F. Unger.

Roy, Donald. 1952. "Quota Restrictions and Gold Bricking in a Machine Shop." *American Journal of Sociology* 57 (March): 427–42.

Rubin, Shelly J. 1985. "Self, Culture, and Self-Culture in Modern America: The Early History of the Book-of-the-Month Club." *Journal of American History* 71 (March): 782–806.

Ruesch, Jurgen, and Gregory Bateson. 1951. *Communication: The Social Matrix of Psychiatry.* New York: W. W. Norton.

Ruitenbeek, Hendrik M. 1964. *The Individual and the Crowd: a Study of Identity in America.* New York: New American Library.

Sahlins, Marshall. 1977. "The State of the Art in Social/Cultural Anthropology:

Search for an Object." In Anthony F. C. Wallace, ed., *Perspectives in Anthropology*. American Anthropological Association.

Sahlins, Marshall, and Elman R. Service. 1960. *Evolution and Culture*. Ann Arbor: University of Michigan Press.

Sandel, Michael J. 1982. *Liberalism and the Limits of Justice*. New York: Cambridge University Press.

Sartre, Jean-Paul. 1943. *L'être et le néant: Essai d'ontologie phenomenologique*. Paris: Gallimard. Trans. by Hazel E. Barnes as *Being and Nothingness*. New York: Philosophical Library, 1956.

————. 1960. *Anti-Semite and Jew*. New York: Grove Press.

Schachtel, Ernest G. 1961. "On Alienated Concepts of Identity," *American Journal of Psychoanalysis*, 21.

Scheeman, Naomi. 1979. "Anger and the Politics of Naming." Department of Philosophy, Université d'Ottawa, Ottawa, Canada. Mimeo.

Scheffler, I. 1967. *Science and Subjectivity*. Indianapolis: Bobbs-Merrill.

Schelting, Alexander von. 1953. "Review of Karl Mannheim's *Ideologie und Utopie*." *American Sociological Review* 1:4:634.

Schlegel, Friedrich von. [1797–1799] 1938. Fragmente die Periods des Athenäums, *Kritische Schriften*. München: Hauser.

Schneider, Louis. 1962. "The Role of the Category of Ignorance in Sociological Theory: An Exploratory Statement." *American Sociological Review* 27:4 (August):492–508.

Scholes, Robert. 1982. *Semiotics and Interpretation*. New Haven, CT: Yale University Press.

Schott, Susan. 1984. "Emotions and Social Life: A Symbolic Interactionist Analysis." *American Journal of Sociology* 6:1317–34.

Schrag, Calvin. 1961. *Existence and Freedom*. Evanston, IL: Northwestern University Press.

Schuman, H. 1969. "Free Will and Determinism in Public Beliefs about Race." *Transaction* 7:44–48.

Schwartz, Howard. 1980. "Phenomenology and Ethnomethodology." Unpublished manuscript.

Scott, Robert L. 1967. "On Viewing Rhetoric as Epistemic," *Central States Speech Journal* 18 (February): 9–16.

Searle, John R. 1977. "Reiterating the Differences: A Reply to Derrida." *Glyph* 1:198–208. Johns Hopkins Textual Studies. Baltimore: Johns Hopkins University Press.

————. 1983. "The Word Turned Upside Down." *New York Review of Books*, October 27, 74–79.

Searle, Leroy. 1976. "Epistemological Mediation: A Proposal for Criticism between Science and the Humanities." Paper presented at the Conference on The Origin of Knowledge: The Relationships between the Sciences and the Humanities. Miami University, April 8–10.

Sears, R., E. Maccoby, and H. Levin. 1957. *Patterns of Childrearing*. Indianapolis: Bobbs-Merrill.

Sedgewick, Garnett G. 1948. *Of Irony, Especially in the Drama*. Toronto: University of Toronto Press.

Seeman, Melvin. 1956. "Intellectual Perspective and Adjustment to Minority Status." *Social Problems* 3 (January): 142–53.

———. 1967. "Powerlessness and Knowledge: A Comparative Study of Alienation and Learning." *Sociometry* 30:2:105–23.

Seger, Imogen. 1957. "Durkheim and his Critics on the Sociology of Religion." Columbia University Bureau of Applied Social Research, New York.

Seneca, Lucius Annaeus. 1910. *Questiones naturales*, trans. John Clark, sec. 29. London: Macmillan.

Sennett, Richard. 1978. *The Fall of Public Man: On the Social Psychology of Capitalism*. New York: Vintage.

Shattuck, Robert. 1980. "How to Rescue Literature." *New York Review of Books*, April 17, 29–35.

Shimanoff, S. 1980. *Communication Rules*. Beverly Hills, CA: Sage.

Short, James F., Jr. 1976. "Gangs, Politics, and the Social Order." Pp. 129–63 in J. F. Short, Jr., ed., *Delinquency, Crime, and Society*. Chicago: University of Chicago Press.

Silberstein, P. 1969. "Favela Living: Personal Solutions to Larger Problems." *America Latina* 12:183–200.

Silvers, Anita. 1981. "The Secrets of Style." *Journal of Aesthetics and Art Criticism* 39:3 (Spring): 268–271.

Simmel, Georg. 1965. "How is Society Possible?" In Georg Simmel et al., *Essays on Sociology, Philosophy, and Aesthetics*. Kurt H. Wolff, ed. New York: Harper and Row.

———. 1968a. "On the Concept and the Tragedy of Culture." In *The Conflict in Modern Culture*. New York: Teachers College Press.

———. 1968b. *Soziologie*. Berlin: Duncker and Humblot.

———. 1977. *The Problems of the Philosophy of History: An Epistemological Essay*. Guy Oakes, trans. New York: Free Press.

———. 1978. *The Philosophy of Money*. Tom Bottomore and David Frisby, trans. London: Routledge and Kegan Paul.

Simons, Herbert W. 1981. "The Management of Metaphor." Pp. 127–48 in C. Wilder-Mott and J. Weakland, eds., *Rigor and Imagination: Essays from the Legacy of Gregory Bateson*. New York: Praeger.

Skillen, Anthony. 1978. *Ruling Illusions: Philosophy and the Social Order*. Atlantic Highlands, NJ: Humanities Press.

Skocpol, Theodora. 1979. *States and Social Revolutions*. Cambridge: Cambridge University Press.

Solomon, Robert C. 1976. *The Passions*. Garden City, NY: Anchor.

Solzhenitzyn, Alexander. 1963. *One Day in the Life of Ivan Denisovitch*. New York: Dutton.

———. 1973, 1975. *The Gulag Archipelago*. Thomas P. Whitney, trans. New York: Harper and Row.

Speier, Hans. 1953. "Review of Ernst Grunwald's *Das Problem einer Soziologie des Wissens.*" *American Sociological Review* 1:4:682.

Spencer, Herbert. 1886. *Social Statics*. New York: Appleton.

Spergel, I. 1969. *Politics, Policies, and the Youth Gang*. University of Chicago, School of Social Service Administration. Mimeo.

Spinley, B. M. 1953. *The Deprived and the Privileged*. London: Routledge and Kegan Paul.

Spittler, G. 1967. *Norm und Sanktion*. Olten: Walter Verlag.

———. 1970. "Probleme bei der Durschsetzung szialer Normen." Pp. 205–25 in R. Lautmann, W. Maihofer, and H. Schelsky, eds., *Die Funktion des Rechts in der modernen Gesellschaft*. Jahrbuch für Rechtssoziologie und Rechtstheorie, vol. 1. Bielefeld: Bertelsmann Universitätsverlag.

Sprat, Thomas. [1667] 1959. *The History of the Royal Society*. J. I. Cope and N. W. Jones, eds. St. Louis: Washington University Press.

Stack, Carol B. 1975. *All Our Kin: Strategies for Survival in a Black Community*. New York: Harper and Row.

Stanley, Manfred. 1978. *The Technological Conscience: Survival and Dignity in an Age of Expertise*. New York: Free Press.

Starobinski, Jean. 1973. "Rousseau and Modern Tyranny." *New York Review of Books*, November 29, 20–25.

States, Bert O. 1971. *Irony and Drama: A Poetics*. Ithaca, NY: Cornell University Press.

Streeter, Thomas. 1983. "Some Thoughts on Criticizing the Information Society." Paper presented to the Fifth International Conference on Culture and Communication, Philadelphia.

Strohschneider-Kohrs, Ingrid. 1960. *Die romantische Ironie in Theorie und Gestaltung*. Tübingen.

Strong, Tracy B. 1978. "Dramaturgical Discourse and Political Enactments: Toward an Artistic Foundation for Political Space." Pp. 237–60 in Richard Harvey Brown and Stanford M. Lyman, eds., *Structure, Consciousness, and History*. New York: Cambridge University Press.

Stryker, Sheldon. 1981. "Symbolic Interactionism: Themes and Variations." In Morris Rosenberg and Ralph H. Turner, eds., *Social Psychology: Sociological Perspectives*. New York: Basic Books.

Suttles, G. D. 1968. *The Social Order of the Slum*. Chicago. University of Chicago Press.

Tavis, Irene. 1969. "Changes in the Form of Alienation: the 1900s vs. the 1950s." *American Sociological Review* 34 (February): 46–57.

Tertz, Abram. 1960. *On Socialist Realism*. New York: Pantheon.

Thibaudet, Albert. 1927. *La république de professeurs*. Paris: Grasset.

Thomas, William I. 1966. *On Social Organization and Social Personality: Selected Papers*. Chicago: University of Chicago Press.

Thrasher, P. M. 1963. *The Gang*. Chicago: University of Chicago Press.

Tocqueville, Alexis de. 1957. *Democracy in America*. 2 vols. New York: Knopf.

Todorov, Tsvetan. 1977. *The Poetics of Prose*. Richard Howard, trans. Ithaca, NY: Cornell University Press.

Toynbee, Arnold. 1961. *Reconsiderations*. Vol. 12 of *A Study of History*. London: Oxford University Press.

Treiber, H. 1973. "Entlastungseffekte des Dukelfeldes. Anmerkungen zu einer Dunkelzifferbefragung." *Kriminologisches Journal* 2:97–115.

Trilling, Lionel. 1971. *Sincerity and Authenticity*. Cambridge: Harvard University Press.

Trotha, Trutz von. 1974. *Jugendliche Bandendeliquenz*. Stuttgart: Ferdinand Enke.

Turbayne, Colin M. 1962. *The Myth of Metaphor*. New Haven: Yale University Press.

Turnbull, Colin M. 1983. *The Human Cycle*. New York: Simon and Schuster.

Turner, Victor W. 1969. *The Ritual Process*. Chicago: Aldine.

Twain, Mark [Samuel Clemens]. 1904. *Extracts from Adam's Diary*. New York: Harper and Brothers.

Tyler, Edward Burnett. 1878. *Researches into the Early History of Mankind and the Development of Civilization*. New York.

Uspenskij, Boris A. 1977. "Historia sub specie semioticae." Pp. 107–15 in Daniel P. Lucid, ed. and trans., *Soviet Semiotics: An Anthology*. Baltimore: Johns Hopkins University Press.

van Gunsteren, Herman. 1979. "Public and Private." *Social Research* 46:2 (Summer): 255–71.

Veblen, Thorsten. 1899. *The Theory of the Leisure Class*.

Vico, Giambattista. 1965. *On the Study Methods of Our Time*. Elio Gianturco, trans. Indianapolis: Bobbs-Merrill.

———. [1744] 1972. *The New Science of Giambattista Vico*. Thomas Goddard Bergin and Max Harold Frisch, trans. Ithaca, NY: Cornell University Press.

Voegelin, Eric. 1952. *The New Science of Politics*. Chicago: University of Chicago Press.

von Mises, Ludwig. 1960. *Epistemological Problems of Economics*. Princeton, NJ: Van Nostrand.

Vygotsky, Lew Semenovich. 1972. *Thought and Language*. Eugenia Hanfmann and Gertrude Vakar, trans. Cambridge: MIT Press.

Waller, W. 1930. *The Old Love and the New Divorce and Readjustment*. New York: Liveright.

Wallerstein, Immanuel. 1974. *The Modern World-System: Capitalist Agriculture and the Origins of the European World Economy in the Sixteenth Century*. New York: Academic Press.

Wallwork, E. 1972. *Durkheim: Morality and Milieu*. Cambridge: Harvard University Press.

Walzer, Michael. 1965. *The Revolution of the Saints*. Cambridge: Harvard University Press.

———. 1967. "On the Role of Symbolism in Political Thought." *Political Science Quarterly* 82:2:191–204.

Wander, Philip C. 1976. "The Rhetoric of Science." *Western Speech Communication* 40: (Fall): 226–35.

Warren, Carol A. B. 1982. "Adolescent Psychiatric Hospitalization and Social Control." Department of Sociology, University of Southern California, Los Angeles. Mimeo.

Watzlawick, Paul, J. H. Beaven, and Don Jackson. 1967. *Pragmatics of Human Communication: A Study of Interactional Patterns, Pathologies, and Paradoxes*. New York: Norton.

Weber, Max. 1949. *Methodology of the Social Sciences*. Edward Shils and Henry Finch, eds. Glencoe: Free Press.

Webster, C. 1976. *The Great Instauration: Science, Medicine, and Reform 1626–1660*. New York: Holmes and Meier.

Weick, Karl E. 1969. *The Social Psychology of Organizing.* Reading, MA: Addison-Wesley.

Weigert, Andrew J. 1970. "The Immoral Rhetoric of Scientific Sociology." *The American Sociologist* 5:2 (May): 111–19.

Weimer, Walter. 1977. "Science as a Rhetorical Transaction: Toward a Nonjustificational Conception of Rhetoric." *Philosophy and Rhetoric* 10, Winter.

Weinstein, Deena, and Michael A. Weinstein. 1976. "An Extential Analysis of Social Control: A Neglected Dimension." Paper presented to the meeting of the American Sociological Association, New York.

Wellmer, Albrecht. 1971. *Critical Theory of Society.* New York: Herder and Herder.

Welsford, Enid. 1935. *The Fool: His Social and Literary History.* New York.

Wescott, Roger W. 1981. "The Identities of Civilizations." Paper presented to the Annual Meeting of the International Society for the Comparative Study of Civilizations, Bloomington, Indiana (May 31). Mimeo.

West, Nathaniel. 1962. *Miss Lonely Hearts and the Day of the Locusts.* Norfolk, CT: J. Laughlin.

White, Hayden. 1973. *Metahistory: The Historical Imagination in the Nineteenth Century.* Baltimore: Johns Hopkins University Press.

———. 1978a. "The Historical Text as Literary Artifact." Pp. 81–100 in *The Tropics of Discourse: Essays in Cultural Criticism.* Baltimore: John Hopkins University Press.

———. 1978b. "History of Literature." Pp. 3–40 in Robert H. Canary and Henry Kozicki, eds., *The Writing of History: Literary Form and Historical Understanding.* Madison: University of Wisconsin Press.

———. 1980. "The Value of Narrativity in the Representation of Reality." *Critical Inquiry* 7:5–27.

Whyte, William F. 1955. *Street Corner Society.* Chicago: University of Chicago Press.

Widmer, Kingsley. 1975a. "On the Inadequacy of Culture: Some Rebellious Memoirs: Paul Goodman *et al.*" Pp. 99–130 in *The End of Culture: Essays on Sensibility in Contemporary Society.* San Diego: San Diego State University Press.

———. 1975b. "On Processed Culture: In Praise of Waste." In *The End of Culture: Essays on Sensibility in Contemporary Society.* San Diego: San Diego State University Press.

———. 1980. *Edges of Extremity: Some Problems of Literary Modernism.* University of Tulsa Monograph Series, no. 17. Tulsa, OK.

Wilber, Ken. 1981. *Up from Eden: A Transpersonal View of Human Evolution.* Boulder, CO: Sambhala.

Wilensky, Harold L. 1964. "The Professionalization of Everyone?" *American Journal of Sociology* 70:137–158.

Willey, Basil. 1934. *The Seventeenth Century Background: Studies in the Thought of the Age in Relation to Poetry and Religion.* Garden City: Doubleday.

Winner, Irene Portis. 1978. "Cultural Semiotics and Anthropology." Pp. 335–63 in R. W. Bailey, L. Matejka, and P. Steiner, eds., *The Sign: Semiotics Around the World.* Ann Arbor: Michigan Slavic Publications.

Wolin, Sheldon. 1960. *Politics and Vision: Continuity and Innovation in Western Political Thought.* Boston: Little, Brown.

Woodward, James W. 1944. "The Role of Fiction in Cultural Organization." *Transactions of the New York Academy of Sciences* Series 2:6 (June 8).

Woodward, Kathleen, ed. 1980. *The Myths of Information: Technology and Postindustrial Culture.* Madison, WI: Coda.

Worcester, David. 1960. *The Art of Satire.* New York: Russell and Russell.

Worsley, P. 1956. "Emile Durkheim's Theory of Knowledge." *Sociological Review* 4:1:47–61.

Wright, Edmond. 1978. "Sociology and the Irony Model." *Sociology* 12:3 (September): 523–43.

———. 1985a. "A Defense of Sellars." *Philosophy and Phenomenological Research* 46, 1 (September): 73–90.

———. 1985b. "A Design for a Human Mind." *Conceptus, Zeitschrift fur Philosophie* 19: 47:21–37.

Yablonsky, L. 1967. *The Violent Gang.* Harmondsworth: Penguin.

Yates, Francis. 1966. *The Art of Memory.* London: Routledge and Kegan Paul.

———. 1972. *The Rosicrucian Enlightenment.* London: Routledge and Kegan Paul.

Zaretsky, E. 1976. *Capitalism, the Family and Personal Life.* New York: Harper and Row.

Zeitz, Gerald. 1984. "Interorganizational Dialectics." *Administrative Science Quarterly* 25:72–88.

Zijderveld, Anton C. 1970. *The Abstract Society: A Cultural Analysis of Our Time.* Garden City, NY: Doubleday.

Zorza, Richard. 1970. *The Right to Say We.* New York: Praeger.

INDEX